To recent studies of Renaissance subjectivity, *Anxious masculinity in early modern England* contributes the argument that masculinity is unavoidably anxious and volatile in cultures that distribute power and authority according to patriarchal prerogatives. Drawing from current arguments in feminism, cultural studies, historicism, psychoanalysis, and gay studies, Mark Breitenberg explores the dialectic of desire and anxiety in masculine subjectivity in the work of a wide range of writers, including Shakespeare, Bacon, Burton, and the women writers of the "querelles des femmes" debate, especially Jane Anger. Breitenberg discusses jealousy and cuckoldry anxiety, hetero- and homoerotic desire, humoural psychology, anatomical difference, cross-dressing and the idea of honor and reputation. He traces masculine anxiety both as a sign of ideological contradiction and, paradoxically, as a productive force in the perpetuation of western patriarchal systems.

Cambridge Studies in Renaissance Literature and Culture 10

Anxious masculinity in early modern England

Anxious masculinity in early modern England

Mark Breitenberg

CAMBRIDGE
UNIVERSITY PRESS

Published by the Press Syndicate of the University of Cambridge
The Pitt Building, Trumpington Street, Cambridge CB2 1RP
40 West 20th Street, New York, NY 10011–4211, USA
10 Stamford Road, Oakleigh, Melbourne 3166, Australia

© Cambridge University Press 1996

First published 1996

Printed in Great Britain at the University Press, Cambridge

A catalogue record for this book is available from the British Library

Library of Congress cataloguing in publication data
Breitenberg, Mark.
Anxious masculinity in early modern England/Mark Breitenberg.
      p.   cm. – (Cambridge studies in Renaissance literature and culture : 10)
ISBN 0 521 48141 4 (hardback). – ISBN 0 521 48588 6 (paperback)
1. English literature – Early modern and Elizabethan,1500–1600 – History
and criticism.   2. Masculinity (Psychology) in literature.   3. Man-woman
relationships in literature.   4. Patriachy in literature.   5. Anxiety in
literature.   6. Sex in literature.   7. Burton, Robert, 1577–1640. Anatomy of
melancholy.   8. Bacon, Francis, 1561–1626 – Criticism and interpretation.
9. Shakespeare, William, 1564–1616. Rape of Lucrece.   10. Shakespeare,
William, 1564–1616. Love's labour's lost.   I. Title.   II. Series.
PR428.M37B74   1996
820.9'353–dc20   95–12793   CIP

ISBN 0 521 48141 4 hardback
ISBN 0 521 48588 6 paperback

CE

For my mother,
Brita Mae Almquist Breitenberg

Contents

Acknowledgments

Earlier versions of material in this book have appeared in print: "Reading Elizabethan Iconicity: *Gorboduc* and the Semiotics of Reform," *English Literary Renaissance* 18, no. 2 (Spring, 1988): 194–217; "Anxious Masculinity: Sexual Jealousy in Early Modern England," originally published in *Feminist Studies* 19, no. 2 (Summer, 1993): 377–398, reprinted here in a revised version by permission of the publisher, *Feminist Studies*, Inc., c/o Women's Studies Program, University of Maryland, College Park, MD 20742; "The Anatomy of Masculine Desire in *Love's Labor's Lost*," *Shakespeare Quarterly*, 43, no. 4 (Winter, 1992): 430–449.

Despite the singular authority designated on the title page, this book is profoundly marked by the voices of other scholars, friends, colleagues teachers and students. I'm grateful to the research staffs at the Furness Library of the University of Pennsylvania, the Huntington Library and the Folger Shakespeare Library, as well as to my superb copy-editor at Cambridge University Press, Deborah McLauchlan. I would also like to thank the remarkably insightful and provocative students I had the pleasure to teach in my Shakespeare seminars at Swarthmore College over the years. Many friends and colleagues have contributed valuable suggestions and encouragement during the process of writing this book, notably: Alex Juhasz, Roxanne Lin, Don Wayne, Adam Haslett, Tom Heacox, Nick Jackiw, Arthur F. Kinney, Peter Erickson, Stephen Orgel, Philip Weinstein and Gail Kern Paster. I am especially grateful to Louis Montrose for his discerning critiques of early drafts and for his advocacy of the project every step of the way.

Eve Oishi endured and elucidated many of the ideas in *Anxious Masculinity* as no one else could. Her voice resonates deeply through the following pages.

Introduction

The central proposition of this book is that the phrase "anxious masculinity" is redundant. Masculine subjectivity constructed and sustained by a patriarchal culture – infused with patriarchal assumptions about power, privilege, sexual desire, the body – inevitably engenders varying degrees of anxiety in its male members. In early modern England, despite a broad and powerful discourse that assumed a natural, divinely ordained basis for authority based on gender and status, signs of anxiety among those whose privilege might have seemed inviolable are widespread; once identified and brought to the surface, masculine anxiety appears as ubiquitous as E. M. W. Tillyard's discoveries of "order" in every facet of Elizabethan life.[1] If Tillyard and the tradition of scholarship he represents could see that earlier historical moment as a static and orderly "picture," my own portrait would be better drawn by the witches in *Macbeth*: a cauldron of bubbling anxieties, a language of unresolvable contradictions and paradoxes, a world gray and ambivalent rather than clear and categorizable. To the extent that we may say "order" prevailed, it did so not because "God hath created everything in its proper place," as Elizabeth's "Homily on Obedience" asserts, but because anxiety, paradox and contradiction could be assimilated, assuaged, contained, or put to some productive use. The same homily also offers a dire vision of its own underside – a kind of cultural unconscious that lurks beneath the theoretically placid surface: "For where there is no ryght ordre, there reigneth all abuse, carnal libertie, enormitie, synne, and Babilonical confusyon."[2] Against the tranquil model of order, in which hierarchical relationships and circumscribed, individual identities are securely in place, the homily conversely imagines chaos and disorder largely in terms of erotic indulgence riotously out of control: sexuality is by definition an anarchic force constantly besieging the gates of collective order and individual self-control. Most generally, this book dwells at the contradictions that necessarily result from the confrontation between these two depictions: the largely abstract discourse that identifies a natural, God-given social order in which every individual's place is safely and securely

1

designated over and against a discourse that reveals the volatile lives and practices that such a vision constantly contends with and represses. Specifically, it pursues the confrontation between the "natural" superiority of men and the profound costs of maintaining that superiority.

It must be said at the outset that the images I develop to portray early modern England are as rooted in the cultural moment from which they are drawn as Tillyard's; they are descriptions and analyses of another culture that in part reflect and derive from our own. I do not see this admission as in any way compromising the value of this book; for me, at least, such an interaction is what makes literary history compelling. Although I have tried to present my sense of the early modern period as persuasively as possible, my own understanding of masculinity in the late twentieth century and my hopes for its radical transformation inform this study every step of the way. Neither an objective, dispassionate account of another culture, nor a political polemic about our own, this book is admittedly a dialogue between the two, an attempt to think about another historical period (one of our many antecedents) from the perspective of the present. It is also, just as importantly, an attempt to interrogate our own culture – to imagine it different and better – by holding up a contemporary critical lens to early modern England.

Masculinity is inherently anxious: according to this argument, anxiety is not a secondary effect of masculinity, nor simply an unpleasant aberration from what we might hypothetically understand as normative. Instead, I argue that masculine anxiety is a necessary and inevitable condition that operates on at least two significant levels: it reveals the fissures and contradictions of patriarchal systems and, at the same time, it paradoxically enables and drives patriarchy's reproduction and continuation of itself. Thus we may say that anxiety is not only a constituent element of masculinity but also that it is deployed in positive ways; more than merely an unpleasant symptom, anxiety is so endemic to patriarchy that the issue becomes not so much its identification but rather an analysis of the discourses that respond to it – the compensatory or transferential strategies operating behind its representations and projections. Thus anxiety is both a negative effect that leads us to patriarchy's own internal discord, but it is also an instrument (once properly contained, appropriated or returned) of its perpetuation. If anxiety were *only* a critical lens showing us the contradictions of the system that produced it, we would not see the function, the cultural work, that this physiological and psychological condition accomplishes – it would merely be an effect. And if only an effect, an indicator of cultural or individual turmoil, we might additionally expect (given the considerable, often excessive display of masculine anxiety in this period) that early modern patriarchy was on the brink of collapse – by all accounts, it was obviously not. Taken on both these levels, anxiety is an inevitable product of patriarchy at the same time as it contributes to the reproduction of patriarchy. In the following pages I thus employ the term as a means of critique and as a way of understanding the considerable resilience – the strategies of containment, re-circulation, appropriation – of a social system whose most fundamental assumption, at least in theory, was the natural inequality of its members.

Anxiety and masculinity: the terms must be wed if only for the obvious reason that any social system whose premise is the unequal distribution of power and authority always and only sustains itself in constant defense of the privileges of some of its members and by the constraint of others; even though historically and culturally specific patriarchal models function with considerable variety, they are by definition forms of social organization that produce distress and disequilibrium. From this premise, it follows that those individuals whose identities are formed by the assumption of their own privilege must also have incorporated varying degrees of anxiety about the preservation or potential loss of that privilege. Once again: the critical task of this book is thus to read masculine anxiety in these two inseparable ways: as a signifier of cultural tensions and contradictions, but also as an enabling condition of male subjectivity in early modern patriarchal culture. Such an analysis draws from Althusser's definition of ideology as simultaneously illusory *and* constitutive of subjectivity: just as we might seize upon the fissures that lie beneath the interpellation of the subject, masculine anxiety reveals both the contradictions inherent in patriarchal culture and the ways that culture smoothes over those contradictions.[3]

What exactly do I mean by anxiety? How is it possible to employ a term apparently indebted to psychoanalysis in a study of early modern culture? To begin to answer this question, the meaning and context of the term has remained fairly stable since the seventeenth century, although the frequency with which we now employ it is not seen until the first stirrings of psychoanalysis in the late nineteenth century. (Shakespeare, for example, never uses the word but often describes the sense.) In *The Anatomy of Melancholy*, Robert Burton writes that "Love Melancholy" is "full of fear, anxiety, doubt, care, peevishness, it turns a man into a woman . . ."[4] A few sentences later, he adds, "doubts, anxieties [and] suspicions" appear as more or less synonymous symptoms of the love-melancholic; and finally, "a Lover's life is full of agony, anxiety, fear, and grief, complaints, sighs, suspicions, and cares" (729: III,2). If we understand anxiety as synonymous with doubt and suspicion, as Burton does, the term is consistent with its postmodern currency – a kind of fear without knowable referent or cause. In usages from 1603 and 1636, for example, the *Oxford English Dictionary* offers a similar definition: "troubled or uneasy in mind about some uncertain event; being in painful or disturbing suspense."[5] Anxiety thus describes a state of suspicion without trust, doubt that is incapable of faith, perpetual uncertainty instead of what Othello demands as "ocular proof" (III.iii.365). Indeed, it is possible to say that anxiety is the negative condition against which an age of faith defines itself: in both cases, one responds to an origin or cause that cannot be fully apprehended, and in both cases the response is a copious discourse seeking to discover and affirm the elusive source. The term feels postmodern in Burton's usage and in the *OED* definition because it exists entirely on the level of the signifier: anxiety is a restless, agitated, never-consummated search for something that may not exist, a state in which certainty is always suspended. Additionally, as Burton suggests in his discussions of the melancholic's mental fantasies and delusions, anxiety is self-referential without admitting it – something like a benign or less developed version of paranoia, which Paul Smith usefully defines (for many of the arguments that follow) as the wish "to maintain its rights on a reality which it will yet not recognize as its own offspring or construction."[6] Following Smith, anxiety may be seen as the result of projecting one's own mental constructions onto the world or onto another person and then mistaking them as objectively true.

Nonetheless, although Burton uses the term in a way similar to our contemporary usage, the material and ideological foundations for his understanding of the subjectivities that might suffer from anxiety are considerably different from our own. A larger problem than the historical transportability of the term "anxiety," then, is how we can look back at the early modern male subject through critical lenses that derive from ways of thinking which were at best inchoate in that period. Perhaps at the outset we might admit that our own critical models of subjectivity are best understood as allegories, in the way James Clifford employs the term to describe the ethnographer's complicated negotiation between his own culture and the one he writes about. "A recognition of allegory," Clifford writes, "emphasizes that realistic portraits, to the extent that they are 'convincing' or 'rich,' are extended metaphors, patterns of associations that point to coherent . . . additional meanings."[7] This understanding recognizes that any portrait of another culture we might employ is not just (in part) the creation of the ethnographer, but also that the "truth" of that portrait owes itself to a set of predispositions already in place – "additional meanings" revealed by the model itself. It also implies that the critical models we utilize exist in the same dialogue between the culture under study and the culture from which we speak. They are heuristic devices that might reveal as much about ourselves as the subjects under study. This is not, of course, to advocate simply collapsing historical or cultural difference in the face of re-writing ourselves in another period; it is instead to recognize that stories we tell about others are additionally stories about our own culture. To employ psychoanalytic tools in theorizing early modern subjectivity, for example, would thus not require the claim that Freud's family drama was formative in that period, rather that our analysis would function as an allegorical story derived in part from our inheritance of Freud's own narratives, a way of opening up early modern culture with the tools available to us.

We might begin such a process by locating the term in the psychoanalytic discourse we have inherited. In *Beyond the Pleasure Principle*, Freud defines anxiety as "a particular state of expecting the danger or preparing for it, even though it may be an unknown one." In a subsequent elaboration, he adds, "anxiety . . . protects its subject against fright and so against fright-neuroses."[8] In these definitions Freud, not unlike Burton, suggests that anxiety in the minds of its sufferers precedes any identifiable cause; indeed, it is the condition of preparation for an anticipated threat whose origin "may be an unknown one." One important objective of this book is to identify the ideological sources of these expectations of fear and danger in early modern patriarchy, to name the systemic origins of masculine anxiety in a way that those who live within that ideology could not.

Anxiety is thus both cause and effect: it is the effect of dangers the subject may not be aware of, but it also anticipates those dangers in advance, whether they are real or not. If we take these definitions as psychological metaphor, we can begin to open up a characteristically early modern instance of male subjectivity at work, even though the material and ideological conditions of the late nineteenth century do not entirely obtain in the early seventeenth century. To take an example that will preoccupy a good deal of this book, Freud's understanding of anxiety leads us to a useful way of thinking about the pervasive masculine anxiety toward female chastity and women's sexuality in general that is so common in early modern texts. The anticipation of being cuckolded, for example, exists prior to any definitive signs of its prospect: cuckoldry anxiety rehearses a play that may never be performed since it is largely a projection of the husband's own fears translated into a story about his wife's inevitable infidelity or concupiscence. It thus becomes important to look at the function of the rehearsal, the importance of representing masculine anxiety independent of any actual source or cause. Of course there are *only* representations and traces of anxiety left to us by another historical period, but the point is that representations of anxiety exceed any knowable referents; they function as signifiers within a discourse of masculinity, neither independent of actual events, on the one hand, nor transparently indicative of them, on the other. Once this largely psychoanalytical model is in place, the critical task of historicism is to think differently about the specific conditions in the early modern period that may have produced, in this case, cuckoldry anxiety. This critical process informs the central arguments that follow.

As I have suggested, understanding anxiety as an inevitable part of a discourse of masculinity allows us to see more clearly its positive or enabling function in the construction and maintenance (however tumultuous or contradictory) of masculine subjectivity. Freud suggests as much in his claim that anxiety "protects its subject," as if it were a kind of psychic armor intended to safeguard the vulnerable ego within. Freud is once again useful if we imagine his discussion of the child's "fort/da" game as if it were a collective ritual played out among men. By pretending to lose and then find a given object, the child enacts a repetition of that most painful possibility – the loss of his mother. He "stages" her departure not just for the sake of the pleasure of experiencing her return, but especially to exhibit his own control over the game itself. Again imagining this process as an allegory rather than as a literal description, we can view the discourse of anxiety as staging masculine loss and vulnerability for the purpose of maintaining control of the performance of one's gendered identity. Or, more specifically, and indeed ironically, in the repetition or staging of anxiety men compensate for an anticipated danger that derives from the very patriarchal system in which they are engendered as subjects in the first place. This foundational contradiction lies at the heart of the readings that follow and it explicates my earlier conviction that the coupling of "anxious" and "masculinity" is indeed redundant.

But this danger may not literally spring from the potential loss of the mother in a culture where the nuclear family drama was not pre-eminent in the formation of subjectivity, as Freud's reading would have it; masculine vulnerability and the threat of loss exists for both Freud and Shakespeare, but not necessarily for the same reasons. Men need to "make themselves master of the situation," Freud writes, but the perilous "situation" to which they are responding derives ineluctably from an historically specific sex-gender system that anxiously figures masculinity in relation to specific constructions of woman – the very system that is intended to sustain the privileges of its male subjects. I believe that this deep paradox can be found in any patriarchal distribution of power and authority, but in importantly different ways and according to different economies. Without this recognition, without assiduously looking for what is unique about the early modern sex-gender system at the same time as we employ the critical tools of our own period, we are left with an eternal recurrence of the same – a vision as historically inaccurate as it is politically impotent. This perception drives Gayle Rubin's vital observation that the use of the term "patriarchy" risks eliding over distinctions among the considerable variety of male-dominated political economies: "But it is important – even in the face of a depressing history – to maintain a distinction between the human capacity and necessity to create a sexual world, and the empirically oppressive ways in which sexual worlds have been organized. Patriarchy subsumes both meanings into the same term."[9] In the following pages I often follow Rubin's lead by opting for her term, "sex-gender system," which better "indicates that oppression is not inevitable in that domain, but is the product of the specific social relations which organize it."[10] Or, I have avoided the universalizing tendency of the term by specifying *early modern* patriarchy as my object of study. Rubin's observation is absolutely necessary if we are to free gender oppression from the realm of historical inevitability, but historicist thinking of this kind should not allow us – especially male critics engaged in feminist critique – to imagine ourselves completely removed from the history of gender oppression that has shaped who we are. We can only speak from a complicated position of complicity and critique: an acknowledgment that we are still at least partly embedded in the history we seek to transform. As a male critic working in the field of gender studies, I understand my most productive contribution to be the interrogation of the masculine subject as historically rather than essentially constituted and thus free of the necessity to re-enact itself in the same ways.

Older accounts of the emergence of a distinctly modern identity in the Renaissance have been decidedly masculine without saying so, as if to ask questions about identity were by definition to ask them about men. It is not surprising to find such an assumption in Jacob Burckhardt's celebration of the "perfecting of the individual" in Renaissance Italy, nor in Tillyard's pronouncement that in Elizabethan England "not only did Man, as man, live with uncommon intensity at that time, but he was never removed from his cosmic setting."[11] In these narratives, only men have subjectivities, and only men play a part on the political and cosmic stage. As this book is in some ways yet another study of "Renaissance Man," it is important at the outset to clarify the nature of my project in relation to this tradition. I have attempted here to read the early modern masculine subject *as male* based on the assumption that both "masculine" and "feminine" are historically specific deployments of gender differences sensible only in relation to one another. Since the subject of this study is masculinity, one of my central tasks involves uncovering and deconstructing – in the most general sense – the ways in which the "feminine" functions in the early modern period to legitimate and sustain many of the privileges and prerogatives of men. This is obviously (but not simply) to say that this book is more concerned with how ideas of "woman" function in this period rather than with the actual lives of women, and it is more interested in how those ideas reveal the anxieties and contradictions of masculinity in early modern patriarchy rather than in its oppressive and pernicious effects on women. As to the danger of reproducing in my own criticism the erasure or illegitimacy of women's subjectivities that is such a part of early modern patriarchy, let me say that this book's focuses are also its limitations – limitations that have already been answered by a considerable body of early modern social and literary history that has recovered and studied the lives and writings of early modern women. By delineating my project as such, this book succeeds to the extent that it contributes to the following critical project as articulated by Luce Irigaray: "For what is important is to disconcert the staging of representation according to *exclusively* 'masculine' parameters, that is, according to a phallocratic order."[12] Or, similarly, to deconstruct in the way that Derrida suggests in his re-formulation of Levi-Strauss' notion of *bricolage*: "the necessity of borrowing one's concepts from the text of a heritage which is more or less coherent or ruined."[13] Most generally, this book is an attempt to take up the tools and concepts with which early modern patriarchy is built and to use them to take it apart.

In addition to the two decades of feminist critique of early modern patriarchy from literary and social historians, a further displacing of traditional studies of masculinity has come from a growing body of scholarship applying the theoretical work of gay and lesbian studies to Renaissance texts.[14] The central arguments of *Anxious Masculinity* admittedly depend upon and critique interpretive paradigms that are largely, but not entirely, applicable to heterosexual economies of desire as well as to a dyadic model of identity constructed between men and women. However, if it is true (as Alan Bray and others have pointed out) that it is ahistorical to posit heterosexuality and homosexuality as oppositional practices in the early modern period (indeed, neither term even exists), then it need not be the case that hetero and homoerotic discourses or representations of desire are themselves necessarily discrete. At least in the texts I rely upon in this book, the dialectic between masculine subjectivity and erotic desire applies to a spectrum of erotic practices that vary according to their degree of danger to the preservation of rational, self-controlled masculinity. The inexhaustible body of writing about heterosexual desire from the period (in relation to a comparatively small one about homoerotic desire) of course does not mean that homoeroticism was necessarily rarely practiced or talked about, but it does mean that the cultural codes in which desire is expressed are more often based on heterosexual models even if individual practices are not always consonant with that model. To cite briefly an example I develop in the first chapter, Burton articulates the considerable perils of masculine erotic desire directed at both men and women in the same terms; if anything, homoerotic desire results in a more devastating overthrow of male reason and self-control, but the humoural model of desire functions no differently in relation to either object. In saying this, I by no means wish to suggest that homoerotic desire did not have its own forms of expression, only that those forms were not always exclusive of heterosexuality any more than the reverse. Shakespeare's depiction of Achilles' emasculating desire for Patroclus in *Troilus and Cressida* does not obey a specifically homoerotic sensibility; rather, it shows the debilitating consequences for masculinity of any form of desire in excess.

Francis Bacon, the subject of my second chapter, more than likely preferred sex with boys (as John Aubrey unremarkably reports),[15] but his expression of the new science as the "penetration" of "chaste nature" is clearly embedded in heterosexual discourses of power drawn from the period's concern with marriage, the family and female chastity. Inasmuch as Bacon's version of anxious masculinity derives from his need to preserve status difference as much as to secure gender difference, it appears that gender and gendered desire are very much questions of class, not necessarily one form of sexuality as opposed to another. I doubt Bacon saw any contradiction between his own erotic life and the heterosexist vocabulary in which he thought and expressed himself, nor do I think his work possesses a deeper code that is revealed by his homoerotic practice. Such a way of thinking must wait until the nineteenth century. Indeed, Alan Bray encourages us to think of sexual desire in the early modern period as including a spectrum of practices in which homosociality serves as a more pertinent term for the politically important relations between men, erotic or not. Thus my discussions of homoeroticism in this book arise when the texts under study treat erotic relations between men as part of a generalized discourse of desire and homosociality, not as the silent or repressed Other to "normative" sexuality.

A third aspect of my critical use of the term masculine subjectivity involves the problem of individual agency in relation to the overarching system of early modern patriarchy. In general I have tried to retain a dialectical understanding of subjectivity in which we are actors as much as acted upon, without which any possibility of change would be negated at the outset. This reciprocity is succinctly described in Louis Montrose's definition of "a process of *subjectification* that, on the one hand, shapes individuals as loci of consciousness and initiators of actions; and, on the other, positions, motivates, and constrains them within networks of power beyond their comprehension or control."[16] One of the advantages of this formulation is that it does not erase the possibility of personal agency or volition in the face of a monolithic cultural network. Rather than choosing between the traditional humanistic model in which the subject is the origin of his actions, and a deterministic model in which he is merely an effect, Montrose positions the subject (following Althusser) as enabled and activated by ideology as much as constrained. Perhaps the most compelling analogy for this model is the public theater itself, where the identities of characters are fashioned in the act of performance. Individuals may be said to be "interpellated" as subjects by the roles they play and by the scripts they enact, but the improvisations of any given performance (and no two are the same) provide opportunities – indeed, encourage – limited but nonetheless vital versions of agency within its malleable structure. Of course, the scripts handed down to a given culture's "players" are inevitably going to possess the same contradictions as the culture itself. We are only interpellated by a consistent, harmonious script provided by a single, all-knowing "author" on the most abstract, theoretical level; in our actual practices, we are given a range of often incompatible possibilities, resulting in a kind of cultural dissonance that can be excavated in the textual traces left to us. Furthermore, the process of subjectification in the theater calls attention to the fact that not only is identity performed, but it is performed publicly in front of an audience, always enacted in relation to and dependent upon an Other – a useful reminder of the specifically social basis of subjectivity in the early modern period.

For my purposes in focusing on masculinity, this analogy is particularly appropriate in terms of the early modern theater, since the performance of gendered identities, so frequently the focus of interest in the plays, is enacted exclusively by males. And just as importantly, it is enacted in front of an audience probably half-composed of women – a revealing model for investigating the dependence of men upon women (or more accurately, their constructions of woman) for the confirmation of their own masculinity. As several critics have argued, the public theater and the opposition it provoked call attention to the constructedness of identity, the alarming possibility in a world of at least theoretical absolutes that to be male means only to manifest the outward signs of masculinity. In Judith Butler's contemporary version of this idea, "there is no gender identity behind the expressions of gender . . . identity is performatively constituted by the very 'expressions' that are said to be its results."[17] For Butler, this leads to her belief that parody, theatricality, and cross-dressing, for example, are inherently subversive since they "expose the contingent acts that create the appearance of a naturalistic necessity."[18] In terms of the early modern public theater, we can say that the potential for this kind of subversion is always available but not always carried out; indeed, the theater also functioned in many cases to contain the dangerous prospect of non-essential gendered identities that its very composition inevitably opens up. But if nothing else, it is certainly an arena in which these vital questions were confronted.

The analogy between theatricality and identity is an important aspect of Stephen Greenblatt's now-familiar model in *Renaissance Self-Fashioning*, where "self-fashioning is achieved in relation to something perceived as alien, strange, or hostile. This threatening Other – heretic, savage, witch, adulteress, traitor, Antichrist – must be discovered or invented in order to be attacked and destroyed."[19] The theatricality of this process is especially evident in Greenblatt's chapter on *Othello*, in which Iago fosters and exploits Othello's "submission to narrative self-fashioning." According to this argument, Othello exhibits "unmistakably the conditions of theatrical identity, where existence is conferred upon a character by the playwright's language and the actor's performance."[20]

I have drawn considerably from Greenblatt's version of the self/Other model of identity in the early modern period, particularly his claim that self-fashioning necessarily involves "some effacement or undermining, some loss of self."[21] In applying this model to a gendered dyad (as Greenblatt does in his chapters on Spenser and Shakespeare), one risks reifying the formula in which the subject is always male, the object/Other necessarily female, as if the binarism itself were transhistorical and thus immutable. My objective throughout this study is to employ this model in order to demonstrate the inherent instability and anxiety that results from construing masculinity in this fashion, and to reveal the historical contingencies of the model in order to escape from its apparent essentiality. Thus my attention has been given to the ways in which early modern masculinity relies on a variety of constructions of woman as Other – on the perceived necessity of maintaining a discourse of gendered difference and hierarchy – that reveal in their most excessive moments a deeper suspicion that the model itself may be merely functional rather than descriptive of inherent truth. The extravagant rhetoric of Joseph Swetnam's angry insistence that woman is "nothing else but contrary to man,"[22] or of John Williams' harangue from the pulpit that God "divided male and female, but the devil hath joined them,"[23] belies the very claims each makes and reveals an ideological struggle waged precisely in terms of the binary model itself. My own intervention in this struggle is intended to bring to the surface the historical conditionality of constructing masculinity in these terms and thus to be able to imagine and articulate (as we have certainly begun to do) a series of alternatives.

Following this call for historical specificity, I would now like to build on my earlier remarks about the uses and abuses of psychoanalysis in the hopes of outlining what I see as a largely but not entirely different basis for masculine subjectivity in the early modern period. By now it is almost axiomatic in early modern scholarship to recognize that the seductively descriptive power of psychoanalytic concepts and insights must be weighed against the historically specific construction of terms such as subjectivity, desire, and anxiety. My own premise in this book is that the application of psychoanalysis to early modern subjectivity is a useful (and, to some extent, unavoidable) heuristic device as long as we keep in mind that what Freud and his legacy develop as individual, psychic phenomena exists in the Renaissance as predominately *social* phenomena. While psychoanalysis locates subjectivity in the individual's psychic struggle, the early modern period discovers identity in the more public context we associate with shame cultures, where such factors as property, reputation and status are preeminent. Indeed, quite possibly psychoanalysis articulates what was only beginning to emerge, or perhaps, submerge, in the early modern period. Hamlet is a useful figure for this nascent interiority: his dilemma is surely the result of social factors (loss of place, public title), but his response appears to us as familiar for its interior manifestations.[24]

Consequently, Freud's descriptions of anxiety must be re-read in the early modern period as social, public phenomena. The nuclear family drama becomes the public theater, court trials and descriptions of community practices such as the Skimmington ritual and the use of the cucking-stool, or the securing of property and title through patrilineal inheritance. Thus, whatever we may borrow from Freud's psychic dramas of defense must be re-placed in the context of the public development and display of masculine identity in the decidedly homosocial world of early modern England. For my purposes one of the primary consequences of this recognition is that anxiety is largely a discourse articulated and played out between men, a way for men to confirm their identity through a shared language of suffering and distress. In other words, reading masculine anxiety as a largely social rather than psychic phenomenon requires an analysis of the productive discourse of anxiety in the culture in which it is manifested: the functions of its statements in specific contexts through the ways it includes and excludes, distributes power and confers legitimacy. To take one example elaborated in my final chapter: even though the experience of jealousy is described so often as the worst form of suffering imaginable, it is nonetheless described over and over again, in every imaginable medium. This observation leads us to look at the importance of staging or articulating anxiety as a way to construct identity by naming a common experience and a shared adversary. If anxiety were a private affair, we could not see as well its discursive function in the production of masculinity.

Thus my use of the term "anxious masculinity" is intended to convey the internalization of specifically social tensions that are endemic to the early modern sex-gender system, the very tensions that produce the masculine subject in the first place. And, as I have suggested, if anxiety occupies such a formative position in the development of the masculine subject, it must also be understood as possessing an enabling function. Although writers from the period such as Burton always use the word in its debilitating sense, the very "expression" of anxiety, recalling Freud's definition, contributes in a positive way to the formation and positioning of masculinity if only by upholding the discursive authority of the writer in relation to the supposed source of his anxiety and, in so doing, by linking him to fellow sufferers.

In an essay from 1986 entitled "Psychoanalysis and Renaissance Culture," Stephen Greenblatt argues against using psychoanalytic concepts to discuss early modern subjectivity through a discussion of the exemplary story of Martin Guerre. Here Greenblatt shows that Guerre's subjectivity is the product and not the cause of a broad set of social relations, including status, wealth, property rights and communal and familial relations, all of which secure a "name" in a very social sense. Since identity can only be accomplished in front of others, we are led to the formula that also preoccupied Greenblatt in *Renaissance Self-Fashioning*: "identity is only possible as a mask, something constructed and assumed."[25] This leads to the conclusion that "[p]sychoanalysis is, from this perspective, less the privileged explanatory key than the distant and distorted consequence of this cultural nexus."[26] For my purposes, one of the important consequences of this re-figuring of the bases for early modern identity is that, again following Greenblatt, it is difficult to posit the individual body as the key to subjectivity since it functions as the effect of various contestatory social factors, a way of thinking scientifically supported in the early modern period by humoural psychology.

If we apply this insight to a specifically masculine identity, we find an array of cultural anxieties implanted in the male body – not at all a certainty according to early modern psychology and anatomical science. For example, as my opening chapter contends, humoural psychology comprehends the male body as constantly in need of regulating its dangerous but nonetheless essential fluidity; the ability to do so depends upon the vigilance of male reason, which can be easily overthrown for a number of reasons, as Burton illustrates over hundreds of pages in *The Anatomy of Melancholy*. Thus, on a corporeal level (always at the same time psychological), masculinity is understood scientifically as precarious – the enemy may be named "femininity" but it resides within the very definition of masculinity proffered by humoural science in the first place. To follow another, well-known line of early modern anatomical science, the structural similarity between male and female reproductive organs handed down from Galen meant that, as Stephen Orgel has written, "the line between the sexes was blurred, often frighteningly so."[27] Since the differentiation between men and women is a matter of degree (more or less heat, the descent of the genitals), anatomical science presents an intrinsic contradiction to the belief in essential, God-given sexual difference. "The frightening part of the teleology for the Renaissance mind," Orgel continues, "is precisely the fantasy of its reversal, the conviction that men can turn into – or be turned into – women; or perhaps more exactly, can be turned *back* into woman, losing the strength that enabled the male potential to be realized in the first place."[28] From the perspective of anatomical science, we may thus understand masculine anxiety as a social phenomenon (arising from the contradictions endemic to patriarchy) that is played out reciprocally in the male body, a body that is the site of socially constructed anxieties about sex and gender but is by no means their origin.

Such observations challenge psychoanalytic accounts that rely upon a single key or original experience to explain the formation of the masculine subject. Among the most persuasive of these approaches, critics such as Coppélia Kahn and Janet Adelman have argued in different studies that masculine identity is achieved through the difficult negotiation of separating from the mother, an originary moment that is re-enacted throughout the man's life. Thus, in Kahn's account, men's need for control over women's sexuality "arises from this disparity between men's social dominance and their peculiar emotional vulnerability to women."[29] Similarly, for Adelman, this "primitive infantile terror" leads to a recurring "fantasy of maternal malevolence," and a desire to free [oneself] from "the suffocating maternal matrix."[30] The explanatory power of each of these narratives is considerable, especially when they suspend the originary moment and begin to analyze socio-political phenomena on their own terms, such as Kahn's brilliant discussion of cuckoldry anxiety as "an affair between men."[31] Even if we grant the existence of a powerful mother-son bond in the early modern period, conceding with Adelman that the role of wet-nurses is not categorically different from that of mothers, we are still left with a single explanatory origin for masculine anxiety, one that considers the political only insofar as it reflects or derives from the psychological. Inasmuch as all interpretations are in varying degrees allegories of the interpreters' own personal and cultural situations, to borrow again James Clifford's use of the term, one cannot discount psychoanalytic readings merely on the basis that the period under study precedes the analytical model, or because the affective bonds analyzed by psychoanalysis may not have been as prominent as they have become since. My departure from the models used by Kahn and Adelman is shaped by my belief that the psychological state is better applied as the name given to the interiorization of social (and thus political) factors, a process that is as uneven and contradictory within individuals as it is in the social field itself. Understanding interiority in this way encourages a much more varied account of masculine subjectivity, one that is not harnessed to an originary moment but instead exists as the contestatory site of an array of disequilibriating forces. It thus seems more profitable to see a given moment of masculine anxiety as intersected by a variety of cultural tensions not derived from the psyche so much as implanted there. For example, if we look briefly at the pervasive use of drowning at sea as a symbol of masculine loss, the explanation of maternal engulfment does not take into account the way Gail Kern Paster reads humoural psychology as a model in which an excess of fluids constitutes an anatomically-based threat to the (male) individual.[32] We could, in response, argue that the anxiety toward fluidity in humoural psychology is an effect of the repressed, original scene, but that would fail to recognize how humoural psychology re-writes specifically cultural tensions – in this example those based on humoural science. Nor would the exclusively psychoanalytic reading recognize the simple fact that in a society dependent on ocean travel for its commerce and exploration, drowning is as much a real danger as a symbolic one.

This multiplicity of factors acting in an apparently psychological drama is illustrated by a brief anecdote from *The Anatomy of Melancholy*. At this point in Burton's account, he is discussing male jealousy, or the fear of being cuckolded, as one of the most disabling symptoms of the melancholic. Burton relates quite nonchalantly and without any commentary the story of a baker who became so obsessed by the prospect of his wife's adultery that he "gelded himself to try [her] honesty" (847: III,3). The first definition of "geld" in the *OED* – "to deprive (a male) of generative power or virility, to castrate or emasculate"[33] – might suggest a psychoanalytic reading of the baker's self-mutilation as, perhaps, a masochistic response to his own original fear of castration. According to this approach, he paradoxically castrates himself as a way of taking control of the primal fear that founded his male identity in the psychic drama of his childhood. Or, one could read this anecdote as a version of cuckoldry anxiety, an encoded fear of castration, in which case the baker would be pre-empting his wife's symbolic power to castrate him if she were to commit adultery. The first reading may be understood in Freudian terms, since the baker acts against the threat of losing his penis, while the second reading might draw from Lacan's understanding of the symbolic function of the phallus in the symbolic realm. Both explanations depend on figuring male identity in terms of the presence or absence of the penis/phallus, and thus both see the threat of masculine lack as essentially or symbolically linked to anatomy.

But a different interpretive narrative ensues if we define gelding as removing the testicles, a sense more developed in the second definition from the *OED*: "to deprive of some essential part, to cut down the resources of . . ."[34] Here the "logic" of the baker's act is evident in a different way: he cuts off his testicles in order to know with certainty that if his wife becomes pregnant, she has certainly committed adultery, since he is now unable to impregnate her himself. Although this explanation appears to be the most obvious, it still possesses considerable complexity and paradox, since the baker has deliberately given up the patrilineal basis for his identity in order to be certain of his wife's chastity. But since the regulation of women's sexuality has no meaning outside of a patrilineal system, the baker's solution to his anxiety ignores the social code which produced his anxiety in the first place. In other words, he abides by the cultural imperative that figures his identity in relation to his wife's chastity, but in so doing he destroys another – the patrilineal basis of his identity dependent upon his offspring. Masculine identity in patrilineal cultures largely derives from the "resources" men inherit, including his status, and what he is able to pass on to his children. The baker claims his own power to disseminate property and status by committing an act that at the same time prevents dissemination. How are we to explain this contradiction? Any psychological explanation – and clearly there is some psychological process at work here – must interpret the baker as having internalized the social system in which his identity is shaped and conferred. In his self-castration he enacts upon himself the vulnerability of men in patrilineal cultures since their identities depend to a large extent on the proper dissemination of property and status through women. The baker's desire to maintain *control* over his own dissemination – even if it means castration – overwhelms even the dissemination itself.

One might say that this explanation is really a claim for the importance of representation over actuality, since the baker has represented or enacted his control at the expense of actually losing it. Or, he decides in favor of actively representing himself rather than passively being represented by his wife as a cuckold. And of course, in addition to placing the anecdote in the context of a patrilineal culture, the telling of the story in Burton's book requires another level of analysis, since the anecdote functions in that written context regardless of whether it ever really happened. Thus yet a third level of analysis would consider what it means to articulate the baker's act of self-castration – in *The Anatomy* and in the culture where it presumably had some currency. This brief analysis illustrates the interpretive process I have adopted in *Anxious Masculinity*: select a text or textual moment that displays an excessive response to a specifically masculine anxiety, search for the cultural tensions or contradictions that inform the response, then consider the function of the articulation within a specifically textual (or literary) context as well as in the general context of early modern patriarchy.

The historical narrative which I have found most useful for my explorations of anxious masculinity argues, in general, that the early modern sex/gender system experienced an especially heightened period of agitation and unrest. "Fears of an impending breakdown of the social order have been common in many periods of history," D. E. Underdown writes, but never "were they more widespread, or more intense, than in early modern England: the 'crisis of order' detected by modern historians in the sixty years before the civil war accords with the perceptions of many people in that period."[35] In the years demarcated by Elizabeth's ascension in 1559 and the beginning of the Puritan revolution in 1640, England confronted and negotiated profound changes in virtually all aspects of its economic, political and social fabric. These changes were registered to a large extent in competing, often contradictory, conceptions of the family and, consequently, in the roles of men and women. This is largely due to the fact that the family in the early modern period was an especially politicized institution; it was made to serve as an analogy for virtually all other relations in society – between God and man, the monarch and the people, husbands and wives, masters and servants. Here we might pause to consider William Gouge's often repeated definition from "Of Domesticall Duties" (1620), originally delivered as a series of controversial sermons in London: "A family is

. . . a little Commonwealth . . . a school wherein the first principles of government and subjection are learned . . . So we may say of inferiors that cannot be subject in a family; they will hardly be brought to yield such subjection as they ought in Church or Commonwealth."[36] Gouge's portrait emphasizes the disciplinary and instructive role of the family as the "school" that shapes individual subjectivities within a set of hierarchical social relations; one's "subjection" to religious and political authority is analogous to and derived from authority in the family. However "natural" and God-given the proper relations of authority and obedience might have been in theory, they were increasingly perceived as disruptive in practice, hence the motivation to articulate models of social order such as Gouge does in "Of Domesticall Duties," or in the typically dire vision of the puritan Philip Stubbes: "Was there ever seen less obedience in youth of all sorts, both menkind and womenkind, towards their superiors, parents, masters and governors?"[37]

Gouge's vision of social order assumes a set of analogies between the three most central social institutions of the early modern period – the family, the state and the church – but it also extends to the proper governance of the self, especially men. This view is corroborated in John Dod and Robert Clever's "A Godly Forme of Household Government" (1612): "It is impossible for a man to understand how to govern the common-wealth, that doth not know to rule his own house, *or order his own person*; so that he that knoweth not to govern, deserveth not to reign."[38] Here masculine identity is portrayed as a potential site of disorder and misrule, a "state" in and of itself whose competing elements must display proper obedience and "subjection" to the internal authorities of reason and self-control. What we might in the twentieth century call individual, psychic anxiety or disorder is thus understood by Gouge as neither a consequence of social disorder nor an origin; it is rather a homologous realm in which similar forms of disorder are reciprocally enacted. Thus the fear of "an impending breakdown" perceived by Underdown in society at large was played out simultaneously (at least in theory) on the level of the individual – an individual who is not only interpellated by competing ideologies but who is also, according to the physiological composition advanced by humoural psychology, constantly at war with himself.

I cannot in this brief overview begin to analyze the multiplicity of factors at work in early modern England's "crisis of order," but a general sketch of its evidence and sources will help to substantiate my claim for the endemic anxiety of its masculine subjects. This historical field is not so much the background for my analysis of individual texts, but rather the cultural field in which a variety of texts and practices –

including those I focus on – are circulated and exchanged. Thus when I refer to a "discourse of masculine anxiety" I mean to situate masculinity as the site of contestations and contradictions that were perceived on a broadly social level as well as in the bodies and psyches of individual men. The perceptual framework of homologies and correspondences described above make it impossible to do otherwise.

The evidence for what Underdown describes as the "crisis in gender relations in the years round 1600,"[39] or for Susan Bordo's more specific understanding of the period as particularly "gynophobic"[40] may be drawn from a wide variety of sources. I wish to focus on those most relevant to the texts discussed in this book. Particularly important for my discussion of adultery and cuckoldry anxiety in several chapters in the records of the ecclesiastical and consistory courts, where sexual crimes were tried with such increasing frequency that by the end of the 1570s they outdistanced all other offenses brought to suit. Lawrence Stone notes the "staggering number of prosecutions in Church courts for sexual offences in the Elizabethan period."[41] Many of these cases were defamation suits involving sexual slander, often brought by women who sought to defend their reputations, which not surprisingly were almost exclusively attached to their sexual behavior. (The reputations of men were conferred or threatened by a wider set of issues.) As Susan Dwyer Amussen notes, sexual insults "became increasingly common for both men and women over the period [1560–1640], but throughout (if the general charge of being a whore is included), they were of greater concern to women."[42] These statistics support the argument for a social basis for identity in what has been described as a shame culture, where public perception confirms or withholds an acceptable identity. Further signs of the growing perception that sexual behavior required greater regulation and attention may also be found in the steady stream of bills initiated by parliament that proposed more severe punishment for adultery, fornication and bastardy, although only in the last case were the bills significantly implemented.[43]

The double standard toward punishing sexual crimes and sexual slander is particularly evident in the prosecution of illegitimate births, which began to increase alarmingly (at least according to the records) in the 1570s, tapering off only in the decade before the revolution.[44] James' statute of 1610 reveals that bastardy was perceived as the exclusive responsibility of women and a sign of their promiscuity: "Every lewd woman which shall have any bastard which may be chargeable to the parish, the justices of the peace shall committ such woman to the house of correction, to be punished and set to work, during the term of one whole year."[45] The severe punishment for giving birth outside of wedlock was largely based on economic concerns, as bastards were the responsibility of local parishes. But the fact that men could not as easily be held accountable encouraged the ideas that social and domestic order depended upon the regulation and scrutiny of women's sexuality – perceived "by nature" to be more prone to transgression. As Lawrence Stone observes, "fornication and adultery were exclusively male prerogatives," but "women were regarded as more lustful in their appetites."[46] The gross injustice of this double standard was surely apparent to the women who suffered from it. In her response to Joseph Swetnam's vitriolic condemnation of women, for example, "Esther Sowernam" (a pseudonym almost certainly adopted by a woman) writes: "Likewise, if a man abuse a maid and get her with child, no matter is made of it – but as a trick of youth; but it is made so heinous an offence in the maid that she is disparaged and utterly undone by it."[47]

A similar preoccupation with the supposed link between the dangers of women's infidelity and social unrest shows up in the increased visibility of accusations against scolds or domineering wives in this period. Before "the middle of the sixteenth century," Underdown points out, "the authorities do not seem to have been particularly concerned with them" [scolds] . . . From the 1560s, however, many places began to show an increasing concern about the problem."[48] At the same time, evidence of a deeper anxiety toward women perceived as insubordinate can be found in a variety of rituals that were intended to ridicule dominated or cuckolded husbands and to punish their "unruly" wives. The cucking-stool was utilized more frequently in this period, and reports of skimmingtons or "rough music" processions – public dramatizations of "the woman on top," in Natalie Davis' phrase – are in England increasingly directed at wives who in some way have abused their husband's authority.[49] Similarly, the accusation of witchcraft was often made against women perceived as scolds or as sexually incontinent; it thus provided a convenient outlet for a variety of social and sexual tensions by scapegoating especially widows and poor women for any one of a number of supposed inversions of the normative order. Although Keith Thomas downplays the specifically sexual aspect of witchcraft, he nonetheless observes that "the mythology of witchcraft was at its height at a time when women were generally believed to be more sexually voracious than men."[50]

Many of these same anxieties fueled the controversy about women that was waged in a series of pamphlets printed in the late sixteenth and early seventeenth centuries – the well-known "querelles des femmes" debates in which women for the first time responded in print to misogynistic charges directed against them. I shall discuss some of these treatises in chapter five; for the moment they serve as yet another indication of the period's impassioned preoccupation with the status of women, the proper behavior for husbands and wives and the disruptive potential of sexuality – particularly women's. A brief passage from Swetnam's "Arraignment of Lewd, idle, froward, and unconstant women" (1615) illustrates (or perhaps, caricatures) the considerable anxiety and vulnerability generated in men by women who were not, as the litany goes, "chaste, silent and obedient": "For women have a thousand ways to entice thee and ten thousand ways to deceive thee . . . They lay out the folds of their hair to entangle men into their love; betwixt their breasts is the vale of destruction; and in their beds there is hell, sorrow, and repentance."[51] Sowernam responds to this and to other of her adversary's diatribes by locating them as projections of men: "Do not say and rail at women to be the cause of men's overthrow, when the original root is in yourselves."[52] In this claim Sowernam perceptively gives the lie to the tendency among men to scapegoat women as the source of their own anxieties, and in a familiar formula I discuss in several chapters, she more importantly exposes the very construction of woman as an Other who either confirms or disrupts masculine identity. This model is also at stake within the "querelles des femmes" debate about the controversy generated by a few actual women who dressed publicly in masculine attire. The "Hic Mulier" and "Haec Vir" pamphlets that describe this occurrence in 1620, if nothing else, demonstrate that the prevailing anxiety about gender roles and identities could be set off by otherwise insignificant events. The volatility of the practice additionally reveals the tenuousness of masculine identity as constructed according to a particular expression of what it means to be female: if women wear men's clothing, how can men know who *they* are? Many recorded male responses to these women are clearly in excess of any real danger cross-dressing (clearly not a widespread fashion) might have posed. For example, James ordered his clergy "to inveigh vehemently in their sermons against the insolence of our women."[53] The period was decidedly nervous about social disorder in general and, at least from the perspective of men, that threat was all too easily located in misogynistic caricatures of women and in depictions of female sexuality as monstrous or destructive to themselves.

Also during this period, an abundance of marriage manuals, practical handbooks describing the duties and responsibilities of husbands and wives, are printed in response to a growing readership increasingly interested in such matters, such as Gouge's "Of Domesticall Duties" and guides for choosing a spouse such as Alexander Niccholes "A discourse of marriage and wiving" (1615). The vast majority of these treatises are written by men.[54] The prevalence of such texts is undoubtedly due in part to the growth in literacy among men and women, but their emergence in a period that was re-negotiating its understanding of the roles of men and women in the family also suggests a growing anxiety about the potential for disorder, especially among women. Suzanne Hull notes the essentially instructive character of many of these books, adding that the "man as instructor was a deep-seated concept." She adds:

> Male authors gave women directions on how to dress (with decorum befitting their rank), how to talk (as little as possible), how to behave toward their husbands (with subservience, obedience), how to walk (with eyes down), what to read (works by and about good and godly persons, not romances), and how to pray (frequently). Men wrote about how to know if a woman would conceive; then men wrote the midwifery books when they did (presumably after some further action by a man). They were particularly fond of instructing women in how they were to behave toward their husbands.[55]

Hull points out that these wide-ranging instructions were not necessarily followed, adding that the fact that women were reading them at all "perhaps inadvertently opened the door a crack for more independence." But it seems clear that the need to "write" women's behavior in such a panoptical fashion, to instruct women in experiences so completely alien to men's own (such as childbirth, midwifery and cooking), and to maintain by writing the role of authority over women's lives, can only derive from the male perception that women required instruction in order to combat their supposedly transgressive nature. Thus we see the same paradoxical formula for masculine anxiety operating in the guide-books as in the accusations against witches and scolds: men scurry about trying to contain a threat to their authority that they have themselves constructed in the first place. They possess an anxious "need to know" women that is fed by their construction of women as essentially incapable of self-government, a quality which itself functioned as perhaps the most important basis for distinguishing men from women. No better description of this anxiety can be found than Virginia Woolf's observation in the British Museum, 300 years later, when she writes in *A Room of One's Own*: ". . . when the professor insisted a little too emphatically upon the inferiority of women, he was concerned not with their inferiority, but with his own superiority. That was what he was protecting, rather hot-headedly and with too much emphasis, because it was a jewel to him of the rarest price."[56]

Finally, the imaginative literature and public drama of the period offers yet another indication that the general "crisis of order" was played out through issues involving gender and sexuality. As Leonard Tennenhouse has written, the period "seemed bent on figuring out the permissible and forbidden forms of sexual relations."[57] The vast number of plays that attempt to negotiate male jealousy and cuckoldry anxiety, the securing of marriage as a form of delivery from anarchic sexual desire, the portrayal of shrewish or scolding women, the punishment of aristocratic women who transgress status and sexual boundaries, all indicate the very same concerns that fuel the controversies I have delineated thus far. At the same time, the Petrarchan poetry and sonnet sequences, raised to a new height of popularity in the 1590s, often utilize the opposite yet complementary version of the misogynistic portraits in their idealization of women as chaste, unattainable objects of desire. These examples by no means exhaust the considerable evidence for perceiving this period as deeply concerned with and in many cases anxiously troubled by relations between men and women, but they indicate at least some of the cultural forms in which masculine anxiety was negotiated. As I have suggested, that this anxiety should find expression in a variety of symbolic forms is by no means surprising since anxiety is by definition a condition of distress in excess of any particular referent or cause that must be negotiated discursively. We may thus read these texts and practices as collective projections; that is, as attempts to make sense in representation of what is largely confused and illogical in practice. This is not to suggest that the symbolic forms resolve the tensions and contradictions from which they derive; indeed, in the readings that follow I attempt to reveal the residual masculine anxieties that lie beneath the apparent resolutions offered in the texts themselves. In this sense, we may say that the representations by men of women's sexuality, chastity and general behavior attempt to assuage the anxieties which propel them into existence in the first place, but they never fully succeed in this cultural work if only because they find the cause not in themselves but in others. As Jane Anger poignantly remarks in her treatise of 1589, "men's dishonesty is revealed by the fact that they often cloak their lustfulness in railing criticisms of women."[58]

The most obvious projection that occurs in the texts I discuss is the construction of women as either the site or the cause of social dislocations that occur in political, religious and economic institutions. Underdown's observation that "late Elizabethan and Jacobean writers do seem to have been uncommonly preoccupied by themes of female independence and revolt"[59] is persuasively explained by a process in which deep structural and ideological tensions in society are conveniently located and addressed in the figure of the unruly or disobedient woman. Although this practice of scapegoating women is by no means unique to early modern England, it may have been more readily available as a result of the homologous relationship between the family and every other institution: correspondences and homologies provide an easy way of thinking of one thing in terms of another. Indeed, many of the signs of agitation in the early modern sex/gender system (especially the evidence from the courts) appear to have subsided by 1660, after which, according to Amussen, "[g]ender became less tied to other aspects of the social system; the family became less central to political and social order."[60] Thus, in addition to the forms of social discontent particular to the early modern period, the centrality of the family provides an available discourse for linking or assigning those discontents to women. Perhaps we are now witnessing a similar linkage in the contemporary emergence of "family values" as part of a conservative political vocabulary just as women are beginning to occupy greater positions of authority and independence.

Similar to the late twentieth century as well, social historians have located in the early modern period a number of material and ideological transformations that contributed to a general sense of crisis in the efficacy of traditional institutions. This "crisis of order," in Underdown's phrase, occurs in the period's sex/gender system as older concepts of marriage and the roles of men and women undergo reconsideration and debate. But it is also the case that other aspects of social disorder not directly connected to gender and sexuality are nonetheless figured or articulated in that sphere; once again, the functional homology between the family and the state provides this conduit. As I have suggested above, nowhere is this more evident than in the period's obsession with female chastity, which is so often described as the linchpin of every other aspect of the social network. About this issue we may say in general that a wife's chastity functioned to secure and preserve actual economic interests (patrilineal inheritance and the avoidance of bastardy), but that it also functioned symbolically as a more generalized guarantee of social order and cohesion. Thus, in the case of female chastity, we are always dealing with a material history that is informed by the considerable weight of symbolic capital. The frequently expressed anxiety on the part of husbands toward their wives' chastity – indeed, the just as frequently articulated *anticipation* of his own cuckoldry as if it were a fact of marriage – derives not merely from an actual threat but more from the symbolic functions assigned to women's sexuality in the period. Once again, it is revealing that accusations of infidelity and sexual slander in the courts decrease dramatically once the family declines in its expressly political function.

This relationship between material conditions and symbolic capital reveals a significant contradiction in the early modern period between the increased demand for women to contribute to the labor force and the threat this responsibility posed to the supposedly natural gender hierarchy. The combination of growing inflation until about 1620 and a series of poor harvests throughout the 1590s led to an increase in vagrancy, poverty and crime, which in turn stretched the resources of village parishes, additionally contributing to a more generalized fear of disorder.[61] (Since parishes were largely responsible for supporting bastards, the idea of unconstrained female sexuality was perceived as even more threatening.) The contradiction that emerges in this time of hardship is that although women play a greater, more independent role in the family's economic affairs, that same independence also exacerbates fears and anxieties among men – anxieties which are then located in women's sexuality. Women achieved positions of greater responsibility in household economies, contributing to the idea of the family as an economic partnership (albeit a still hierarchical one), but that degree of equality was at the same time perceived as threatening. Once again, the analogue to our own period – now twenty-five years into a profound transformation of its own labor force along gender lines – is readily apparent.

The emergence of a new concept of the family, largely inaugurated by Protestantism, additionally complicated and confused the socially prescribed roles of men and women, resulting in what Amussen calls a "double message"[62]: on the one hand, a husband still (in theory) maintained absolute authority within the family, a position legitimated by his analogous relationship to God and to the king; but on the other hand, the idea of marriage as a companionate partnership characterized by mutual respect appeared to elevate the wife's position from a merely subordinate role. In *Of Domesticall Duties*, Gouge argues that the husband "ought to make her [his wife] a joint governor of the family with himself, and refer the ordering of many things to her discretion." But he also maintains that if the husband "be wise and conscionable in observing [his duties], his wife can have no just cause to complain of her subjection."[63] Although clearly the husband's ultimate authority is never in question, there is nonetheless a good deal of potential ambiguity between the wife's "subjection" and her status as "joint governor." As Amussen points out, "such vague formulations were troubling in a society which valued clear lines of authority."[64] It is worth mentioning that, especially after James' ascension in 1603, an analogous debate was taking place between the king and parliament, in which the latter body was demanding a version of "joint governorship" or consensual rule against James' insistence on absolute authority – indeed, the two spheres could not be imagined separately. In the case of the family, there can be little doubt that husbands received competing instructions as to the roles and behaviours they were supposed to enact – a recipe, one imagines, for inconsistency if not confusion on their part.

The ambivalence resulting from this new conceptualization of the family also contributed to an anxiety among men toward the fidelity of their wives. As Protestantism increasingly valorized the nuclear family as a microcosm of the state, women were more likely to be idealized as chaste and obedient wives rather than as virgins – formerly the paragon of Catholic femininity. The new prescription for wives involved a precarious balance between an earlier veneration of sexual renunciation and a new emphasis on female generativity. Thus the considerable clamor for chastity in marriage so prevalent in the period in part derived from the tension between an insistence on the sexual restraint of wives while still acknowledging the necessary role of women's sexuality in procreation – what Lawrence Stone calls "matrimonial chastity."[65] this tension can only have been exacerbated by the belief that women could not conceive without orgasm – women's sexual pleasure was fundamental but it also potentially threatened (at least in the male imagination, since women were by definition less able to govern themselves) her ability to remain chaste. The husband was expected to give his wife enough satisfaction to avoid her being obliged to go elsewhere, but not to arouse her so much as to provoke extra-marital sex – a recipe for masculine anxiety if ever there was one. Perhaps the strain involved in maintaining these conflicting constructions of female sexuality contributed to the gradual decline of the belief in the mutual orgasm theory of conception during the seventeenth century. In any case, among men the belief contributed to the complementary yet extreme depictions of women's sexuality as either monstrous and excessive or, in the case of the "good" wife, little more than a necessary aspect of procreation.

In this brief account of the social history of early modern England I have addressed only some of the issues and transformations that contribute to the agitations and contradictions in the period's sex/gender system. A more expansive account would need to consider many secondary but nonetheless contributory factors, such as the considerable demographic mobility of the period, especially evident in London, or the profound reconfiguration in its status delineations, which leads Stone to conclude that "families were moving up and down in the social and economic scale at a faster rate than at any time before the nineteenth and twentieth centuries."[66] As I discuss in my chapter on Francis Bacon, the perceived endangerment of the aristocratic body was frequently figured once again in terms of the purity or impurity of the female body – patrilineal privilege was symbolically and actually confirmed by the regulation of female sexuality. Another consideration that especially fuels the dramatic and literary work before 1603 is certainly Elizabeth's anomalous position at the apex of authority in such an otherwise thoroughly patriarchal power structure. And finally, it is worth noting the seemingly paradoxical role taken up by James as the leading "pater familias" who nonetheless openly displays his homoerotic affection, at least within the orbit of his court.

The anthropologist James Clifford analyzes the function of ethnographic allegory as "a practice in which a narrative fiction continuously refers to another pattern of ideas or events. It is a representation that 'interprets' itself."[67] While I would by no means consign the historical narrative I have just sketched to the realm of fiction, it is nonetheless important to recognize that no rendering of another historical period or another culture can ever speak from a position of objectivity, a position outside one's own ideological and conceptual framework. This book is a kind of ethnography of early modern England; my informants are the textual traces I have chosen to listen to, my focus is on the ways that one of our own antecedent cultures constructs and legitimates masculinity and in so doing enables and constrains its male members. Among the broad set of practices known as "new historicism," some recent literary histories have benefited from the ethnographic model if only to encourage a recognition of our own "pattern of ideas or events" that shape what we say about another culture.

As I suggested at the outset of this introduction, such an acknowledgment should not be perceived as undermining the authority of our claims about another period but rather as an opportunity to engage dialectically in a simultaneous interpretation of ourselves. We are thus better served by understanding the production of meaning as, in Michael McCanles' phrase as a "the constitution of [the] text through an intertextuality whereby two texts are brought together and fused: the constituted discourse of the Renaissance and the constitutive discourse of scholar himself."[68] Such an observation opens up the nature of the voice we bring to the dialogue: the personal investments in the truths we advance and the political consequences for the historical moment from which we speak. A "recognition of allegory," Clifford concludes, "requires that as readers and writers of ethnographies, we struggle to confront and take responsibility for our systematic constructions of others and of ourselves through others. This recognition need not ultimately lead to an ironic position – though it must contend with profound ironies. If we are condemned to tell stories we cannot control, may we not, at least, tell stories we believe to be true."[69]

Each of the following chapters is a kind of story in its own right written about a single text or a configuration of texts from the period roughly between the late Elizabethan period and the Puritan revolution. In the chapters where I have sustained a long discussion of a single author, a particular work or, in the case of Bacon, an entire corpus, my objective has been to locate these stories within what Foucault called the "discursive formation" of early modern England. This kind of historicism involves trying to uncover the "traces of social circulation," to borrow Greenblatt's phrase,[70] that are embedded in and between literary and non-literary texts. I have also tried to maintain a dialectical approach between a systematic level of analysis, in which we might identify broadly ideological patterns, and a more focused analysis of unique discernments of those patterns in specific texts and by individual authors. Even though each of the authors whose works I discuss are players in the same cultural script, they also occupy various and perhaps conflicting roles, and they write in different genres for different audiences. Consequently, we cannot overlook the unique perspectives of each author nor the often different interests served by particular texts.

I have mostly suspended traditional ways of ordering the material addressed in this book – by author, chronology, genre or overarching theme – since to do so seemed like an unwieldy attempt to impose unity and wholeness where none really existed. If we are only left with traces of earlier cultures, fragments that even if collected in their entirety would still not transparently provide a unified picture, then it would seem almost disingenuous to offer one's own account of that culture as a smooth and logical narrative. This book may be better read as a collection of interventions, each pursuing the dialectic of desire and anxiety in the discursive construction of masculine subjectivity in early modern England. Nor is it possible to offer an overriding logic for the texts that I have included – so many suggested themselves that I am now aware more of its omissions rather than what I have managed to include. My process of selection has been motivated for the most part by an interest in the way certain issues and problems are negotiated in these texts, in some cases by the prominence of a given author and in others by his or her relative obscurity, still in others by the sheer accident of serendipitously falling upon something during the course of my research. The recurrence of Shakespeare may be explained by my own training and by his cultural predominance, but also by my admission (as in some critical circles it would have to be) that Shakespeare's imaginative examinations of masculinity are usually more complex and more subtle than that of any of his contemporaries, or at least that they more richly manifest his culture's anxieties about gender and sexuality. Indeed, I once imagined that if somehow Iago and Emilia could find it in themselves to co-write a book, little in the following pages would be left to say.

Nonetheless, despite these disclaimers and caveats, it might still be useful to my readers to provide some introduction to the specific discussions that follow. I begin with Robert Burton's *Anatomy of Melancholy*, chronologically the last of my selections but in many ways more characteristic of the generation before its twenty year period of composition. Burton's lengthy tome provides a material basis for many of the ensuing discussions since its preoccupation is with a psychological state understood as inseparable from the corporeal body. *The Anatomy* is thus especially useful at the beginning of a book on masculine subjectivity since it reminds us right off that, under the sway of humoural psychology, the early modern period imagined identity as derived from the often contentious fluids of the body, not as the largely mental condition that displaced this model in the Enlightenment. *The Anatomy* also introduces another fundamental difference between early modern conceptions of the subject and many of those that followed: the assumption that the corporeal body, the body politic and nature itself were homologously similar, even to the point where conditions in one could directly affect the other. Burton's very serious meditations on planetary influences on mental states, or herbal remedies for melancholy, are by no means the superstitious beliefs of a hermetic scholar; they depend upon an understanding of the essential correspondences and homologies that define and give meaning to everything and everyone in the world. Contemporary criticism that insists on the political or social aspect of early modern literature, medicine, biology, psychology, or any other discourse, is certainly involved in current critical fashion, but it is also acknowledging the linkages and connections that made the world comprehensible to that period.

This realization also underscores my discussion of Bacon's "new science" in the second chapter. Here I read Bacon's corpus as a body of writing shaped by – indeed, inseparable from – an aristocratic body whose basis of privilege was being challenged and a construction of the female body that required constant surveillance to secure its chaste purity. Thus Baconian science not only negotiates with the received scientific tradition since Aristotle, it is also in dialogue (less intentionally) with early modern beliefs about domestic relationships, female chastity, the endangered royal prerogative and the increasingly porous status delineations that preoccupy the Jacobean period. Especially in this chapter, I have also discussed the form in which his texts are written – the medium in which knowledge is disseminated for Bacon – as another level that intersects with non-scientific discourses. Here the key word is "disseminate," which I utilize in both the general sense – to pass along, impart – but also in its etymological connection to semen as that which is passed to women to insure procreation and (ideally, he would say) to maintain patrilineal descent. Bacon's version of anxious masculinity derives in part from the potentially hazardous dependence on women required by this dissemination; consequently, the "plain and simple style" he advocates encodes an attempt to avoid the "unfortunate" mediation of women and female sexuality.

The third chapter further develops the function of the figure of female chastity in relation to masculine honor among men through a close reading of Shakespeare's "The Rape of Lucrece." Here my interest is in showing the inescapable circularity between the desire to possess and the possession by one's desire; for Tarquin, the "sundry dangers of his will's obtaining" and his compulsion "to obtain his will resolving." This poem perhaps best exemplifies one of the most pervasive themes of *Anxious Masculinity*: masculine desire – directed at either men or women – is a destabilizing if not self-destructive force, one that requires constant vigilance by reason and self-control. (This is also one of Burton's central preoccupations and anxieties in *The Anatomy*). And yet, the very economy of desire that upholds honor and reason as important constituents of masculinity additionally places men under constant attack: the object of masculine desire must be published – known among other men – for it to accrue honor and value for its possessor, but the very same publication leads to the *loss* of ownership of that object. In the poem, Collatine's honor is achieved only through the publication of Lucrece's celebrated chastity, but it is that publication that impels Tarquin to rape her. This chapter additionally builds upon the idea of publication and masculine authorship to discuss the homology between sexual and textual corruption, as exemplified particularly in the printer John Day's prefatory note to an early Elizabethan play – Sackville and Norton's *Gorboduc*.

The next chapter also takes up an Elizabethan work by Shakespeare – the early comedy *Love's Labor's Lost* – introduced by way of a discussion of Montaigne's fascinating essay, "Upon some verses of Vergil," translated by John Florio in 1603. If my previous discussion of Shakespeare's "Lucrece" depended on "publication" to activate a destructive contradiction in the masculine economy of desire, in *Love's Labor's Lost* the key term is deferral. As in the poem, erotic desire is encouraged and inflamed by the perceived value of the desired object in an economy that fetishizes female chastity. However, similar to the Petrarchan tradition that informs the comedy, consummation must be deferred if the object of desire is to retain its value for the desiring male subject. If masculinity is constituted by the act or process of desiring, then satisfaction becomes something to be feared even though it is what impels this erotic economy in the first place. This inherent contradiction leaves men hovering anxiously between the desire for conquest and possession, on the one hand, and the fear (sometimes horror) of the cessation of desiring, on the other. As Shakespeare writes in sonnet 129, "Th' expense of spirit in a waste of shame . . . [is] Enjoy'd no sooner but despised straight."

The principal focus of chapter five is to develop the idea that erotic desire is threatening to men in part because it is perceived as effeminizing. This is an especially anxiety-producing prospect in a period where a biological basis for sex differentiation (as Thomas Laqueur has shown) was far less secure than it has become since. If masculine identity is fundamentally unstable, then the assertion of gender difference – especially where it is most adamantly expressed – functions as a way to compensate for the lack of anatomical guarantee of difference. I pursue this proposition by looking at anti-theatrical tracts, the cross-dressing controversy, a number of the polemical defenses and excoriations of women, and at some of the responses to these attacks written by women – especially Jane Anger's *Her Protection for Women*. As Anger suggests, the misogynistic depictions of women in the "querelles des femmes" debate are projections of what men fear most about themselves – the purpose being to construct gender and sex differences in order to maintain the basis of masculine superiority. As in all my arguments throughout the book, this dynamic again exemplifies the perceived need among men to construct "woman" in a way that appears to serve their interests but which, in fact, tortures and agitates them at nearly every turn, undermining the masculinity that this idea of "woman" is intended to legitimate.

Finally, the concluding chapter offers a discussion specifically of male sexual jealousy. Along with the fear of cuckoldry, sexual jealousy will have made many appearances in the book before this final chapter – it is easily the most pervasive masculine anxiety of the early modern period and it is either an overt or disguised anxiety in all the texts I discuss. In this chapter, Shakespeare's extraordinary anatomy of masculinity in *Othello* is threaded through a variety of non-literary texts – treatises, popular pamphlets, religious tracts – in order to demonstrate once again that masculine anxiety (in this chapter from male sexual jealousy) is endemic to early modern patriarchy – symptomatic of its "normal" operations rather than an aberration or unfortunate disease. This chapter also plays considerably with the double sense of the word "knowledge" as a critical form of masculine empowerment: on the one hand, carnal knowledge (sexual ownership), and on the other, interpretive knowledge, needing to know women as a means of panoptical control in which woman is figured as a set of signs requiring interpretation. *Othello* is largely about the intermingling – the interdependence, perhaps – of these two definitions. But the ultimate tragedy of this play is that Othello does not realize that his false and insidious constructions of Desdemona are the cause of his jealousy and of the play's final violence. Nor does he realize the inherent self-destructiveness of a model of identity in which "woman" functions as the Other – the guarantee or legitimation – of masculine identity. When Othello cries, "When I love thee not, / Chaos is come again" (III,iii.93–94), he is imagining not so much the end of his own love *for* Desdemona, but rather the dire prospect of not being loved *by* her – in effect, of not being at all. This model of dependence on an Other would be sufficient cause for anxiety alone, but what makes it such a paradigmatic instance of anxious masculinity in general – what makes it so tragically self-fulfilling – is that it operates in relation to a false idea of "woman" rather than to women themselves. And because this model is so fundamental to masculine identity in the first place, because it has already shaped who men imagine themselves to be, the alternative can very well appear as chaos. In the world of *Othello*, this lies behind Iago's observation, "I never found man that knew how to love himself'" (I,ii.316–317) – perhaps the most appropriate introductory epithet to *Anxious Masculinity*. But it is not the most appropriate conclusion: if we can identify the historically specific operations of early modern patriarchy, acknowledge the residual effects of that history as well as confirm our distance from it; if we can bring to the surface the contradictions and anxieties that have shaped masculinity rather than merely acting on its symptoms; indeed, if we can listen to women, or to characters like Emilia in *Othello*, then perhaps Iago's trenchant remark might lose some of its stinging accuracy.

As I have suggested, the historical narrative that I developed above to characterize the early modern England as experiencing a "crisis" in its traditional sex/gender system seems to me both "true" as a compelling description of that period and, at the same time, a pertinent and productive allegory for our own historical moment. This is not meant to suggest an exact parallel between late twentieth-century America and the early modern period in England – such a comparison would obscure the considerable transformations that have occurred during that span. Nor does it claim that no other period in between experienced changes or reconfigurations in its sex/gender system – culture is always, of course, a continual process of retrenchment and modification. In the process of writing this book I have been particularly attentive to contemporary allegories of the issues I discuss, both on a broadly social level but also in my own personal life.

Our own version of a "crisis of order" in terms of sexuality and gender has also developed out of difficult economic times, dramatic re-configurations in the nuclear family, a new code of sexual behavior. And if the early modern period witnesses a burgeoning feminism among the women who take up their pens in the "querelles des femmes" pamphlets, our own has been led by the considerable achievements of the feminist movement in the last twenty-five years. But if there are now innumerable contemporary versions of women such as Jane Anger and Esther Sowernam, we also have our own versions of John Stubbes and Joseph Swetnam – men whose responses to women's social and economic gains and to the changes in gender roles take the form of retrenchment in traditional values, misogynistic scapegoating of women for the supposed failure of the nuclear family, aggression and violence toward women that masks their own insecurity and vulnerability. Anxious masculinity may no longer lead to the cucking stool or to the accusation of witchery, but it has certainly been at work in our legal system, where celebrated cases involving sexual harassment, paternity rights, rape, gay and lesbian parenting, Lorena Bobbitt's infamous castration of her husband and the widely followed trial of O. J. Simpson for allegedly murdering his wife in a jealous rage have become national preoccupations. And in perhaps the most visible display of anxious masculinity, Hollywood has recently released a number of films that may be said to comprise a new genre, one I have not surprisingly termed "anxious masculinity films": the most widely viewed and discussed include "Fatal Attraction," "The Hand That Rocks the Cradle," "Basic Instinct," "Sea of Love" and "Disclosure," films that typically focus on aggressive, independent women who in a variety of ways threaten the men with whom they are involved. Most often, the threat they represent is transformed into an unavoidable yet dangerous female eroticism, as if female independence can only be figured in terms of threatening sexuality; or, in some cases, women are constructed as an interpretive dilemma, a set of unreliable signs, the indecipherability of which becomes another indication of their fearful independence; and just as typically, they are depicted as endangering the nuclear family. More often than not, the female protagonist is punished for her transgression: she functions as the scapegoat whose degradation restores the normative order, still by most people construed as the nuclear family, the man on top, women's sexuality properly under control. Hollywood could find enough of these plots in Jacobean drama to last well into the next century were it not so seemingly determined to portray contemporary life as if it had no history.

The primary focus of this book is, of course, a culture and historical period radically different from the present. But it is not a culture that bears no relevance to our own, if only because it is one of our most influential antecedents. But more than that: we have not left many of the assumptions of early modern patriarchy behind – if Susan Faludi (among others) is right in her book, *Backlash*, we are not even necessarily moving along a progressive path. It thus still seems to me very important for men to look at ourselves and especially at our patriarchal histories with more critical acuteness than we often do, and to build from that awareness less anxious ways of responding to the social and political changes we are witnessing. If anxiety is a symptom of a fear without knowable cause, then a knowledge of the histories we have inherited is the first and most crucial step toward filling in the sources of our fears and thus freeing ourselves from their self-destructive grip. *Anxious Masculinity* is an attempt to insert contemporary, western masculinity back into history in order to allow us to identify part of the cultural legacy we still carry with us, and finally, in my most optimistic moments, to allow us to envision and enact that history differently.

1   Fearful fluidity: Burton's *Anatomy of Melancholy*

> How many strange humours there are in men!
>
> *Democritus to the Reader*, p. 39

There is an unmistakable sense in reading the *Anatomy of Melancholy* that Burton derived a good deal of pleasure and satisfaction not only from his own experience of melancholy but, perhaps even more, from the inscriptive act of dissecting and describing its multifarious forms of self-consuming anxiety and suffering – after all, he wrote and re-wrote the book for over twenty years. This is especially evident in the third partition, where Burton anatomizes "love-melancholy," the most destructive form of the disease, frequently defined elsewhere as "inordinate love." In this lengthiest and most often expanded part of Burton's ever-swelling book, subject matter and textual matters are dialectically poised: either the body of the text valiantly tries to *contain* the over-flowing nature of the disease or, failing that, comes to *resemble* the psycho-physiological body of the melancholic. In the following passage, we could substitute "book" for "love," as many readers of the *Anatomy* would attest: "But this *love* of ours is immoderate, inordinate, and not to be comprehended in any bounds. It will not contain itself ... or apply to one object, but is a wandering, extravagant, a domineering, a boundless, an irrefragable, a destructive passion" (655: III.2, my emphasis). The experience of love-melancholy and the inscriptive act of anatomization are linked by resemblance as well as by opposition.

This dynamic is quite apparent on the level of Burton's authorial relationship to his text. Although Burton claims, in loyal Baconian fashion, "I respect matter, not words" (in part because "[p]rettiness of style is not a manly distinction"), "words" are also the "matter" of the book if only because verbal excess is characteristic of the melancholic (25). Begun in 1620, the *Anatomy* continuously swells and bulges through its five editions during Burton's lifetime; a posthumous edition (1651) includes additions made up to his death in 1640. In his continuous writing and revising of the *Anatomy*, Burton appears motivated not so

35

much by the possibility of completion but rather by the endless deferral of completion; or perhaps, the act of writing about the subject of melancholy sustained Burton as a melancholy subject such that writing and being became indissoluble. Indeed, the introductory "Democritus to the Reader" often indicates the close relationship between the author and his subject; like Montaigne, Burton, is also the subject of his book. And yet, Burton claims that writing is the antidote to melancholy – "I write of melancholy, by being busy to avoid melancholy" (16) – as if the writing "I" could be imagined distinct from the melancholic subject. We might pause at this claim for a moment: is the articulation and inscription of melancholy the way "to avoid" the disease or, on a less apparent level, the basis for sustaining it? In other words, is melancholy *the* most profound danger to the masculine subject (as Burton passionately avows) or is it a necessary and enabling condition of masculinity? This chapter seeks to explain why the answer is both.

Such an analysis requires us to understand melancholy as a discursive practice (traversed by several other cultural narratives) in which Burton's text has the pre-eminent voice in this period, rather than seeing it as the autobiographical key to the author's psyche. The *Anatomy* encourages such an analysis since it is more accurately a vast compilation of other texts on the subject (ranging from Aristotle to Shakespeare) than a display of Burton's own unique discernments; it thus provides a register of both the long and short cultural history of melancholy and (less obviously) of the ways masculinity has been figured through melancholy. As Lawrence Babb points out, Burton "has absorbed almost everything that his cultural milieu has to offer."[1] To the extent that Burton's voice *is* available, it appears in occasional editorial remarks through the figure of Democritus Junior, his persona, or more subtly in the sequence and arrangement of his mostly borrowed material. Rather than locating Burton at the origin of his text, it is more useful to imagine a collective, abstract authorship – the cultural history of the idea of masculinity that surfaces in the *Anatomy* – wrestling with its own internal contradictions. In this way, we are better served by reading Burton's text as a register of prevalent fears and anxieties and as an attempt to construct a viable version of masculinity in the face of them.

We must also reject the view of melancholy as a clinical term describing a particular pathological condition, as if psychological categories and descriptions were somehow free of the cultures that develop and utilize them. By the same logic, any application of psycho-analytic categories of analysis risks erasing differences among histori-cally specific conceptions of the psyche. The ahistoricism involved in the use of psychoanalytic categories is particularly apparent in the case of seventeenth-century melancholy since the disease (like all mental and physical conditions) is rooted in a humoural conception of the body that does not survive in nineteenth- and twentieth-century formulations of subjectivity. In this attempt to historicize the emergence of modern subjectivity from its roots in humoural psychology, Gail Kern Paster's superb book, *The Body Embarrassed: Drama and the Disciplines of Shame in Early Modern England*, offers a variety of salutary new directions. As Paster observes, "the materials of early modern humoural theory encode a complexly articulated hierarchy of physiological differences paralleling and reproducing structures of social difference."[2] Certainly *all* conceptions of subjectivity are embedded in specific social formations and ideologies, including psychoanalysis, but Paster encourages us to think differently about the very relationship between physical and psychic states (or between material and immaterial aspects of subject), a distinction that does not exist within humoural psychology. I will address the considerable implications of this material aspect in Burton's understanding of melancholy (and subjectivity in general) throughout this chapter. For the moment, a general characterization of the medical disease of melancholy in the early modern period will be useful.

In its natural, healthy state – before it might become a disease – melancholy is simply the name given to one of the four primary humours that comprises the body. Its physical qualities are coldness and dryness, and its corresponding element is earth. This normative presence and function of melancholy in the body is capable of becoming a disease – indeed, in many discussions it is always on the brink – if the humour becomes abnormal or unnatural in quantity or quality. English writers use a variety of terms to describe melancholy as a disease, including unnatural melancholy, melancholy adust or black choler; Burton generally refers to it simply as melancholy, as I shall also do here. The transformation from natural melancholy to its diseased form may be caused by a wide variety of emotional, physiological or environmental factors (inseparable in humoural psychology) including, most often: diet, strong passions, too much thinking, too little or too much sleep, a hot climate – virtually anything that upsets the natural, balanced functions of the body's melancholy humour.[3] The potential causes of melancholy are so broad, derived from so many natural, everyday bodily functions and human experiences, that it is not inaccurate to say that melancholy becomes the overarching term for anything imbalanced or excessive – whatever is not normal. Although melancholy is widely described and studied in the most careful scientific terms, it would appear to have functioned, especially in Burton's text, as a discourse of otherness – an Other not beyond the pale but more insidiously present within.

Now, it is worth making the following provisional observations about the general character of the disease. First, on the level of the individual, humoural psychology assumes an essential sameness among the materials that make up the psyche; the considerable differences (including gender and forms of sexual desire) among individuals are the result of degrees and propensities of the same materials, or humours. Partly this is because the fluids that comprise the body are fungible; that is, they are transformable from one to another, as in the belief that semen derives from blood. In Paster's account, the body's fluids are "less conceptually differentiated" and thus "homologous" in their bodily functions.[4] This means that in theory everyone has the potential to possess or enact the entire spectrum of human characteristics and desires that derive from the balance (or imbalance) of fluids in the body. A potential contradiction emerges from this anatomical belief since early modern sociopolitical theory claims inherent differences (gender, status) whereas humoural theory expresses differences as gradations and degrees. Second, given the correspondences between microcosm and macrocosm, between the body natural, the family and the state, an individual's emotions, diseases and desires – everything that makes up the physical/psychological body – are *already* and by definition social and political qualities. This is slightly different from saying that one could *choose* to draw an analogy between, for example, the individual faculty of reason and the office of the king; the point is that such an analogy provides the conceptual possibility of both terms in the first place. Thus it is ahistorical to consider the individual psyche as a separate entity, or even as the product of social factors, since for the Renaissance the two realms are *a priori* linked and coterminous. Additionally, this also means that humoural theory will reveal somatic and psychic versions of the contradictions and tensions that exist in the cultural system; or, reciprocally, those contradictions will be played out in the struggle of the body's humours. In brief, to think within the system of humours is to think in terms of a series of linkages rather than in discrete units, relationally rather than atomistically. Humoural psychology, the science of fluids, is itself a remarkably fluid model.

Given this general framework, I read melancholy in Burton's text as a repository for those elements deemed contrary to a specifically masculine vision of social order and individual rationality. That vision would correspond to a model of normative humoural masculinity in which the body's fluids are carefully (and anxiously) regulated according to what is allowed to enter and what must be expelled and in which all members of the body act properly in accordance with their assigned places and designated functions – an idealized vision of the masculine body as well as a utopian political state. Read in this way, melancholy occupies an important and revealing place as the Other to early modern England's construction of "normative" masculinity and of the patriarchal state. Melancholy is thus not a clinical pathology but a term for the Other within, a behavioral category in which masculinity addresses its fears about itself, its individual and collective anxieties. As Burton writes, "[a]ll men are carried away with passion, discontent, lust, pleasures, &c.; they generally hate the virtues they should love, and love such vices they should hate" (61). It follows that representations of melancholy such as the *Anatomy* must do some kind of cultural work, if only to articulate and thus defuse these anxieties. As in my earlier discussion of jealousy and cuckoldry anxiety (both significant forms of melancholy in Burton's description), melancholy enables and sustains masculine subjectivity, despite its torturous effects, precisely because its articulation allows for the projection and disavowal of internalized forces that threaten masculinity. Put simply, the discourse of melancholy plays its part in the cultural construction of the early modern (male) subject by providing a mutable category against which masculinity may then (anxiously) define and defend itself. If Burton sees his book as an attempt to anatomize melancholy in order to purge men of its destructive symptoms, my own reading will argue that the category of melancholy itself provided a discursive scapegoat that shaped and supported a very unsteady construction of masculinity. The male melancholic suffers an especially acute volatility in his humoural distribution; he is especially vulnerable to the mercurial effects of the body's fluids and to the delicate balance between retention and evacuation. Following Paster's definition of humoural bodies as "so porous, vulnerable, various, or even bizarre that they seem to be created out of alien substance," Burton's masculine subject occupies the humoural body *par excellence.*[5]

In pursuing this reading of Burton's *Anatomy* I am also building on the brilliant foundation laid out recently by Juliana Schiesari in *The Gendering of Melancholia.*[6] Schiesari employs Freud's essay, "Mourning and Melancholia," and Lacan's account of male subjectivity in general, (especially "Desire and the Interpretation of Desire in *Hamlet*") to provide a largely psychoanalytic history of what she terms "a politics of lack."[7] Schiesari understands melancholy as a discourse that uses the idea of the melancholic to elevate men to the lofty level of literary, philosophical and artistic genius (following Aristotle's original claim) by providing "a way for men to talk about their exile, about their losses, and about their desire for a union that cannot be had but that points to some kind of truth."[8] The sustaining aspect of melancholy as a central discourse and performance of masculinity is that it transforms real or imaginary loss into a symbol and then converts that symbol into a sign of something positive, ennobling, and distinctive from the vulgar who do not share such a fine sensitivity. Melancholy thus functions to cover up or compensate for the fundamental condition of male lack, much like the function of the phallus in Lacan's symbolic. It thus perpetuates an economy of deferred desire (similar to the cultural work of Petrarchism) since "satisfaction is gleaned in the idealization of loss *as* loss, in the perpetuation and even capitalization of that sense of loss."[9]

According to Schiesari, the discourse of melancholy additionally functions at the expense of women and in support of a number of subordinating constructions of "woman" and "femininity." Mourning, for example, becomes an activity necessarily left to women since it responds to the loss of an actual rather than symbolic object, thus tying women to a material level and preventing them from reaching the sublime symbolics of loss accorded to the melancholic man. However, in the most negative tradition of melancholy, following the Galenic rather than Aristotelian tradition, there is nothing transcendent or recuperative about the symbolics of loss: it is a debilitating, degenerative humoural imbalance that must be cured by purgation, among other methods. In these depictions, Schiesari argues, woman often functions as the source of the disease, leading (or seducing) man down to the horrors of a debased, sexual corporeality – in these depictions, melancholy itself is gendered female. Such versions of melancholy are the most overtly misogynistic, often displaying, as in the medieval figure of Dame Melancholy, an inordinate fear of female sexuality as destructive, even castrating.[10] According to this logic, the discourse of melancholy displays the melancholic man as possessing many of the characteristics of the most misogynistic constructions of woman precisely in order to purify masculinity from this "feminine" disease. For reasons I think specific to the anxious sex/gender system in early modern England, Burton most closely follows Galen's version of negative melancholy, both in his inveterate misogyny and also in his portrait of the melancholic as in many ways feminine, or as potentially effeminized, as well as in the pervasive threat to masculine reason posed by melancholy excess. Although one does find in the *Anatomy* traces of the Aristotelian tradition, especially in the satisfaction Burton takes in counting himself among the privileged melancholics of the past, his *homo melancholicus* is by and large a figure of anxious masculinity.

Despite Schiesari's persuasive defense of her use of psychoanalysis to analyze earlier cultural paradigms, specifically through her commentary on Stephen Greenblatt's "Psychoanalysis and Renaissance Culture," her claim to be "historicizing the gendered appropriation of lack, sorrow, and loss in the poetic and philosophical traditions of Renaissance melancholia"[11] in readings of quite different texts and contexts nonetheless appears to me overdetermined by Freudian and Lacanian models. Especially in the brief but richly suggestive section on Burton's *Anatomy*, Schiesari invites a more historically determined account of how melancholy functions as "a politics of lack" that registers specific forms of cultural and sexual otherness in early modern England. As I have suggested, Burton's assumption of the well-worn homology between the psycho-physiological health of the individual and the political condition of the state encourages an analysis of melancholy as the site of cultural linkages and exchanges among ostensibly discrete practices and belief systems in early modern England. Indeed, Burton's representation of melancholy is so steeped in humoural psychology that any discussion of the physical body always and unavoidably possesses a political and social dimension, as exemplified in the following passage: "But whereas you shall see many discontents, common grievances, complaints, poverty, barbarism, beggary, plagues, wars, rebellions ... contentions, idleness, riot, epicurism, the land lie untilled, waste, full of bogs ... the people squalid, ugly, uncivil; that kingdom, that country, must needs be discontent, melancholy, hath a sick body, and had need to be reformed" (65). Such a expansive linkage of related spheres exemplifies the tradition of Renaissance *copia* (as many critics have noted), but that mode of writing is itself available within an episteme that presumes a vast network of homologies and correspondences – it is not merely a formal device. Even though the homology between the body politic and the corporal body is not unique to Renaissance England, the correspondence will always be invested with political elements specific to the culture that employs it. It would thus seem significant at the outset that Burton writes (and is widely read) during a period of increasing volatility in the political affairs of England. To cite a single example: the House of Commons is increasingly depicted as an unruly and ungovernable body (especially to the monarchist sensibilities of Burton), where reason no longer prevails – precisely the character of the melancholic.

A second prominent issue that locates the *Anatomy* in early modern England is Burton's lengthy discussion of marriage as one of several "remedies of love" that offer an antidote or way of preventing inordinate lust, the primary quality of "love-melancholy." Here Burton must be understood within the context of the Protestant (and Jacobean) valorization of marriage and the family as analogous to the patriarchal state and as the primary means to contain and legitimate male and female sexual desire. Burton supports this fairly new social development but his primary interest as a student of melancholy is (quite typically for this period) in the potential hazards of love and marriage for men, especially jealousy and cuckoldry anxiety: "marry a lusty maid," Burton reports, "and she will surely graft horns on thy head. All women are slippery, often unfaithful to their husbands" (829:III, 3). Here Burton echoes many sentiments and phrases from the "querelles des femmes" debate I discuss in subsequent chapters, including passages worthy of Joseph Swetnam's fearful misogyny printed five years before Burton began the *Anatomy*. He also offers the often stated sentiment that cuckoldry is inevitable, as if it were endemic to the gender system itself. Burton's misogyny is certainly illuminated by the psychoanalytic processes of projection and compensation that form the basis of Schiesari's study, but the intensity and excess of his discussions of matters pertaining to love, sexuality and gender register and exemplify specific agitations both in the political and the sex/gender systems of early modern England. Here it is useful to remember the popularity of the melancholic or malcontent in the late sixteenth century, specifically in the context of unrequited love. In the drama before 1580, Lawrence Babb finds "no instance in which melancholy is used in connection with love"; examples after this date abound.[12] In addition to Timothy Bright's first English treatise on melancholy printed in 1586, melancholy also emerges as a distinct feature in the fashion for sonnet writing that captivates the 1590s. Similar to my earlier discussion of Petrarchism, melancholy provides a discourse – for Burton, a revealingly copious one – that preserves the idealized objectification of the beloved as other and at the same time enables a compensatory narrative of masculine empowerment against the perceived threat of engulfment or loss.[13] Babb's observation that "Burton, then, offered a book on melancholy to a melancholy generation"[14] is not evidence of the particularly saturnine character of the age, nor is it simply a claim for the popularity of the genre. Rather, the fashion for melancholy emerges as a specific way to negotiate masculinity by imagining and representing its own dissolution. In other words, masculinity is allowed to stage discursively its own "regression" to a state of "femininity" within the framework of the safe – indeed, sometimes lofty – discourse of melancholy. It is ironic, if not contradictory, that this cultural work appropriates a *construction* of woman invented by men in the first place; thus, the discourse of melancholy alleviates masculine anxieties that are activated by the perceived necessity of imagining "woman" in particularly threatening ways, not at all on any real attempt to negotiate relations between men and women. The further complexity of this process is that it is operating within a "scientific" knowledge of the humoural body – a body characteristically "feminine" in its unruly fluidity and orificial vulnerability. For my purposes, this is an ideological matter, but for the Renaissance, it is a matter of anatomical fact.

"[O]ur style bewrays us" (21)

Before turning directly to these matters, I want to explore the isomorphic relationship between the anatomical body of the melancholy man and the textual body of Burton's *Anatomy*. There are many ways in which Burton's *Anatomy* feels as if it should have been written in the sixteenth rather than seventeenth century, if not earlier. It is the last example of the popular Renaissance anatomy genre and it recalls in form and structure the older idea of a correspondence between the book and the world. As I develop in the next chapter, Bacon's insistent claims for a new beginning, a clean break from the errors of the past, stand in contrast to the antiquarian Burton, who displays an almost worshipful allegiance to what has already been said and written: "[w]e can say nothing but what hath been said, the composition and method is ours only" (20). And in contrast to Bacon's aggressive self-positioning as the author of a new epistemology, Burton is content to submerge himself among a sea of contemporary and classical authors: in this way the *Anatomy* is very much a retrospective book, linked in form and sensibility to the period before empirical science and the age of reason. Indeed, if the Baconian perspective is most appropriately represented by the telescope, where nature becomes the object of man's scrutiny and control, the counterpart in Burton is the fluid body of humoural psychology, an explanatory system that lives in a world of correspondences and similitudes between human, natural and cosmic spheres, where texts resemble rather than signify the world.[15] The many formal analyses of the *Anatomy* have for the most part failed to situate the form and structure of the book in this older context, where resemblance and similitude are taken for granted rather than used simply as rhetorical devices. The form of the *Anatomy* must be historicized within an earlier conception of tropes and the place of language in the world in which resemblances were assumed rather than fashioned. In this regard we might recall the shift in understanding of tropes and metaphors that roughly occurs between the outset and end of Elizabeth's reign. Thomas Wilson's definition of similitude from the middle of the sixteenth century suggests likenesses that already exist among all things; the tropological comparison is thus a kind of discovery: "Therefore those that delite to *prove* thynges by similitudes must learne to know the nature of diverse beastes, of metalles, of stones and al mannes life."[16] Similitude can "prove" the pre-existent similarity and resemblance among the various things on Wilson's list because their "nature" is the same. Henry Peacham echoes this belief in *The Garden of Eloquence* (1557): "Necessity was cause that Tropes were fyrst invented, for when there wanted words to expresse nature of diverse thinges, wise men remembering that many things were very like one another, thought it good, to borrow the name of one thing, to expresse another ...."[17] In the *Anatomy*, Burton similarly assumes rather then argues for the relevance of examples of melancholy among plants and animals: "Melancholy extends itself not to men only, but even to vegetals and sensibles"; and in the following paragraph, "[k]ingdoms, provinces, and politick bodies are likewise sensible and subject to this disease" (65). Love-melancholy in particular "shews itself in vegetal and sensible creatures, those incorporeal substances ... and hath a large dominion of sovereignty over them" (643: III,2). By contrast, later rhetorics such as Puttenham's *Arte of English Poesie* (1589) appear suspicious of natural resemblance in the world, calling attention instead to a slippage between words and referents that anticipates Bacon's critique of the idols of the marketplace. In this later model, tropological relationships are characterized as the product of human artifice rather than by a natural or inherent affinity. The artificiality evident in Puttenham's famous definition of metaphors as "an inversion of sence by transport" exemplifies this change.[18]

In his account of the Renaissance episteme, Foucault articulates a hermeneutics in which "to search for the law governing signs is to discover the things that are alike." Language (like the book itself) partakes in this system of correspondences; it is not apart from the world, as Bacon suggests, but itself "a part of nature," according to Foucault.[19] If language and the book resemble as much as signify what they represent, the form and structure of a book such as the *Anatomy* can be understood as an imitation of the melancholy subject as well as a book about his psycho-physiological qualities. Language thus possesses a material quality not just graphically but also in the way it exemplifies, enacts and repeats its referents in addition to signifying them. Within this epistemic frame, the humoural body is embedded in the world through its shared fluids, elements and temperaments; bodies spill over into one another just as the fluids within the body are fungible. Conversely, the Baconian body is removed to a seat of empirical judgment, far less implicated in the material it studies. Following this logic we can recognize a series of homological relationships among the body of Burton's text, the psycho-physiological body of the melancholic, and the body politic. Once again it seems important to point out that the structural affinity among these bodies is assumed as if it were natural and God-given, like the network of resemblances and hierarchies described in, for example, the Elizabethan "Homily on Obedience," where a vast analogical web links the inevitable order of the seasons to equally immutable social hierarchies – this, at least, is the ideological structure that is supposed to hold the system in place.[20] If we place the *Anatomy* in this earlier epistemological framework, it makes sense that the book itself should enact the same conflicts as the melancholic: if the book struggles between structures of containment and the *copia* that overflow boundaries, the melancholic is engaged in a war between his capacity for human reason to order and regulate madness and an overwhelming surge of inordinate love and desire. Let us develop this idea more closely in terms of the book's structure.

In contrast (or complement) to the Rabelaisian body of the *Anatomy*, Burton draws up detailed tables organizing his vast material into partitions, sections, members and subsets, as if the entire treatise were governed by a precise logic. Many critics have been persuaded to view the tables as providing a carefully delineated structure, but if one tries to match each of the sections to the material contained within them, it becomes clear that the body of the *Anatomy* is at best loosely structured by its "skeleton." In Devon Hodges' analysis, "the order of the synoptic tables is a kind of mask that not only hides but also gives rise to the disorder so basic to the anatomy form.[21] Hodges suggests a general principle that applies to the thematic content of the book as well: forms of structure and containment seem to enable and encourage their transgression. The *Anatomy* thus exhibits a formal tension between overflowing its boundaries and respecting them, between an inordinate *copia* of material that swells in each successive version and a structure of containment based on reason and logic. But the important point is that these two impulses are not separate entities but rather mutually defined and dependent. When Burton appeals to reason as the antidote to melancholy excess, this reciprocity has considerable consequences, for the antidote is also the cause. In Schiesari's account, the "book is supposed to be the antidote but is also the source of melancholy; the disease inspires him to write but the writing aggravates the disease."[22] It is no wonder critics have found the *Anatomy* a "trackless jungle," on the one hand, "a medical treatise ... orderly in arrangement," on the other: they are reading two sides of the same coin.[23]

These competing impulses have usually been understood in terms of a dialectic between order and chaos, or reason and madness; the side one occupies marks different critics' interest in finding organic unity, on the one hand, or accepting the text's excesses, on the other. Ruth A. Fox exhibits the former sensibility in her celebration of the text's achievement of unity between aesthetic form and diverse content: "To see the wholeness of Burton's book, to see its diversity through the unity imposed upon multiplicity by the structure of anatomy, is essential to our understanding of the cutter's art."[24] Less persuaded by Fox's commitment to the cohesion of the *Anatomy*, David Renaker finds Burton influenced by the sixteenth-century logician Peter Ramus' precise method of spatial organization, but he then argues that Burton "took a curious revenge": "Everything that Ramus had sought to banish – digressiveness, inconsistency, copia, the fusion of rhetoric with dialectic – ran riot over and through the meticulous pattern of 'method.'"[25] More recently, Hodges suggests that the formal contradiction between Burton's "disorderly prose" and his carefully structured tables provides a thematic correlative in the book's articulation of the struggle between madness and reason, a struggle the author finally loses: "Instead of curing madness, Burton's *Anatomy* seems to create it."[26]

Hodges makes explicit what Renaker implies: that the form of structuring knowledge in the *Anatomy*, or perhaps more accurately, the failure of the form to structure knowledge adequately, is inseparable from the text's most significant preoccupation – the consequences of our inability to bound and control the passions, imagination, desire and madness. The *Anatomy* is indeed literally about the struggle between madness and reason, but it enacts the difficulty, perhaps impossibility, of containing those humoural forces that exist within men, the drives that threaten to overflow the tenuous boundaries constructed by reason, moderation, and morality. The body of Burton's text and the anatomical body he dissects are both perpetually in danger of overflow and transgression. It is a battle, one might say, between representing the body as "official" or "orificial." For the moment, I offer one example of the correspondence between Burton's textual and physical bodies – one in which the author appears to be futilely chasing after the end of his own sentence:

But this love of ours is immoderate, and not to be comprehended in any bounds. It will not contain itself within the union of marriage, or apply to one object, but it is a wandering, extravagant, a domineering, a boundless, and irrefagable, a destructive passion: sometimes this burning lust rageth after marriage, and then it is properly called Jealousy; it extends sometimes to corrivals, &c., begets rapes, incests, murders. (655:III,2)

Despite his claim to "call a spade a spade" (25), this passage exemplifies Burton's richly adjectival, heavily subordinated prose style – a style that appears most frequently when Burton characterizes the dangers of "immoderate" love and desire, those moments of "boundless," "destructive passion." Burton's prose cannot contain the excesses of the melancholic any more than the institution of marriage can contain erotic desire. At times the exuberance and richness of his lists of transgressions overwhelm any sense of possible containment by the forces of moderation and reason, as if the prose itself were enacting the struggle against the symptoms of melancholy. In the same way, Burton's frequent use of the et cetera sign serves notice that his long lists of passions and desires have no ending, as if a period would impart a false closure on what is, finally, uncontainable. Indeed, as Burton admits, "[o]ur style bewrays us" (21).

Michael O'Connell follows Burton's own directive ("I doubt not but these following lines, when they shall be recited, or hereafter read, will drive away melancholy," 30) in arguing that the copia of the *Anatomy* serves as a kind of "talking cure" for the disease: "Talk, whether counsel drawn from the ancients or ramblings among contemporary pharmacopia, has an efficacy in itself. Language is the truest antidote, the best physic to melancholy."[27] O'Connell points out that the articulation and anatomization of melancholy serve as a form of purgation. But this way of thinking assumes that language is an entity apart from the world and thus a medium through which to comment upon it without complicity. As much as Burton would like to think the *Anatomy* is such a tool of dissection and purgation (as his well-structured tables attempt to accomplish), more often the book displays the isomorphic relationship between language world that I characterized above. There are several instances in the *Anatomy* in which melancholy is likened to the potential chaos of language itself: for example, the "chaos of melancholy" is compared to the world of language after the Tower of Babel. In this discussion, after admitting his inability to "sufficiently speak of these symptoms," Burton adds: "the four and twenty letters make no more variety of words in divers languages, than melancholy conceits produce diversity of symptoms in several persons" (347: I,3). Here and elsewhere, the excessive symptoms of the melancholic resemble figurative language as much as they are represented by it: both are "irregular, obscure, various, so infinite, Proteus himself is not so diverse" (347: I,3).

If the body of Burton's text enacts and reproduces the body of the melancholic such that the language of the text displays an isomorphic relationship to the material of the text, what sort of corporal body *is* the subject of his anatomy? As I will argue in the following pages, the body dissected in Burton's text is an anxious male body, constantly under attack by the ungovernable forces within it, nervous about its own orifices, under siege by its own ("feminine") elemental fluidity, caught in a losing battle between reason and the seductiveness of its own over-whelming desires and, ironically, threatened by the very "Others" it has constructed to defend against these desires. This is most evident in the third partition of the *Anatomy*, "Love-Melancholy," where Burton discusses the causes, symptoms and possible cures of melancholy. It is useful at the outset to cite Fox's observation that in the third partition, "the structure of the work becomes not vaguely illogical, but definitely so."[28] As Burton turns to the form of melancholy derived from love and sexuality, "more eminent above the rest" (643: III,1), his own forms of order and containment are most dramatically challenged.

"A man in woman's apparel" (Democritus to the Reader, 11 p. 21)

To begin in this direction, let us pursue further the implications of Schiesari's case for the play of gender in the *homo melancholicus*. For Burton, and among many of the writers on melancholy whom Schiesari discusses, "woman" figures interchangeably as the source of melancholy and as the character of the melancholy man: taken together, the at least implicit consequence is that women cause men to act like women. As the cause of melancholy, "woman" is misogynistically and stereotypically understood as seductive, lustful, inconstant and deceptive – the subversive force (especially in the sense of a threat from within) that overthrows masculine reason and self-control, "so cunningly can they dissemble" (837: III,3). Thus Burton devotes a long section entitled "Artificial Allurements" to his (very commonplace) perception that women's apparel and cosmetics "incite men the sooner to burning lust" (692: III,2). Burton cites approvingly the conclusion of a man who lived in Brazil among women who wore no clothes at all: rather than "a provocation to lust ... their nakedness did much less entice them to lasciviousness, than our women's clothes" (684: III,2). By contrast, he asserts that "[n]akedness ... is an odious thing of itself, an antidote to love" (687: III,2) since "their outward accoutrements are far more precious than their inward endowments" (689: III,2).

Burton's fairly insistent claim that women's "beauty is more beholding to Art than Nature" shows a revulsion toward women's bodies similar to that exhibited by Hamlet. The corporal disgust directed at women that pervades the *Anatomy* leads Burton to passages of remarkably excessive prose that take the form of long lists of supposedly damning attributes. Under the section, "Symptoms of Love," Burton lists in a single sentence well over a hundred adjectives and adjectival phrases describing women's bodies as in various ways revolting (737–738: III,2). Burton's need to elevate himself through the act of writing above the corporeality and mortality he assigns to women is remarkably transparent in this passage, and quite similar to Hamlet's misogynistic rantings before the graveyard scene. He takes as axiomatic the connection between melancholia and mortality – "Melancholy is in this sense the character of Mortality" – then in the next sentence specifically links mortality to women: "Man that is born of a woman, is of short continuance and full of trouble" (125: I,1). The text reads as if the constructed, written expression of women's bodies in this way purges the author of the unacceptable materiality of his own existence.

Following this commonplace "logic" of Renaissance masculinity, the figuring of woman as sexuality itself threatens masculine transcendence: sexual desire for women drags men down to the level of base corporeality, dangerously equalizing hierarchies of gender and social status. Here the idea that the *Anatomy* is intended to purge men of the melancholy disease takes on particularly gendered implications. Burton utilizes an age-old construction of woman as linked to base corporeality in order to purify masculinity from its own sexual desire and from its own consequent vulnerability. In other words, sexuality itself is already gendered in the form of effeminizing vulnerability for men, supporting Stephen Orgel's formulation that "this is an age in which sexuality itself is misogynistic."[29]

We must keep in mind the context of humoural psychology as well as Renaissance notions of sexuality in developing this point, especially as they are shaped by the complex ideological function of blood, explored by Paster as "a deeply contradictory site of multiple, competing, even self-contradictory discourses."[30] Erotic desire (indeed, any form of passion) is perceived as a manifestation of humoural balance or imbalance, abundance or deficiency, in part because procreation requires the production of greater heat in the blood, more difficult for women than men because they are inherently colder. Semen is a form of rarefied, heated blood (a sort of ultra-blood) that, since Aristotle, represented the masculine principle. As Thomas Laqueur points out: "Sperma, for Aristotle, makes the man *and* serves as synecdoche for citizen."[31] In Jacques Ferrand's *Erotomania* (1612; English trans., 1640), the sperm is "nothing else but Blood, made White by the Naturall Heat, and an excrement of the third Digestion."[32] It is worth mentioning that this connection between blood and semen means that the Renaissance use of blood to figure purity or impurity in other "bodies" has a material, corporal basis. As the central figure for patrilineal bonds (dependent on procreation), national identity (as in King Henry's St. Crispin's Day speech), or status delineations (the required purity of the aristocratic female) – indeed, as the most significant trope of masculinity – blood functions simultaneously on figurative and literal levels. Semen is the most purified form of English, masculine and aristocratic blood: it is the very substance of masculine power as well as its signifier. Conversely, as Paster shows, menstrual blood is figured as a sign of women's inability to regulate their own fluids. It is discharged because it has no necessary function in the body.[33] We can surmise that this figuration of women's blood, as well as the belief in its sex-defining coldness, function by opposition to elevate male blood to its presumed level of seminal importance.

But the paradox in this cultural and anatomical code is that if the generation of semen (heated blood) is the most quintessentially masculine moment, it is also, finally, just a moment. Thus ejaculation represents the supreme moment of masculine disempowerment *and* vulnerability – a literal and figurative "emptying out" of the masculine principle. Put simply, masculine erotic desire generates the material of masculinity but also destroys it. Orgasm threatens masculine agency and self-control in part because it represents a "feminine" inability to regulate the flow of one's fluids: a struggle represented in the double entendre senses of "will" as volition and as desire. In William Vaughan's *Approved Directions for Health* (1600), for example, the loss of seed "harmeth a man more, then if hee should bleed forty times as much."[34] This logic provides a material explanation for the sudden transition in Shakespeare's sonnet 129: "A bliss in proof, and prov'd a very woe." And it may also have been the originally scientific basis for the still current folk belief that men should not have sex before any activity that requires aggressiveness, since orgasm diminishes their masculinity. In one scene of Robert DeNiro's portrait of Jake LaMotta in Martin Scorcese's "Raging Bull," this version of anxious masculinity is dramatized when, on the night before a big fight, the aroused boxer rushes away from his negligee-clad wife in order to pour ice water down his pants. Consummation is "devoutly to be wish'd," as Hamlet observes, but it also marks the dissolution of masculine identity. In Hamlet's case, that is exactly the point.[35]

In his discussion of the causes of love, Burton cites a theory that understands inordinate desire as the result of "certain atomi in the seed, such as are very spermatick and full of seed" (661:I II,2), following the general belief that all forms of passion and desire in the extreme are the result of an excess of a particular substance in the body. He then adds that "if they cannot be rid of the seed, they cannot stop burning, for which cause these young men ... are so subject to it [lust]" (661: III,2). If orgasm represents the loss of masculinity but is also an "evacuation" (Burton's term) necessary for psychological health, once again masculine desire unavoidably leads to and results in its own dissolution. And of course, this sentiment is everywhere in the culture's representations of masculine love and desire: gender and anatomy reciprocally shape and inform each other in part because the anatomical body is already a social and political body.

In the Renaissance, then, the idea that orgasm signifies a profound masculine loss has a very material basis; indeed, this scientific assumption may have provided the historical residue from which psychoanalysis translated the materiality of loss into the symbolics of loss. In studying the early modern period, if we only follow Schiesari's politics of loss from a primarily psychoanalytic point of view, we miss the historically specific politics of loss provided by Renaissance biology, the ways in which cultural anxieties were reciprocally represented as anatomical. And finally, it is neither necessary nor possible to resolve the question of whether or not the biological theory is merely the effect of a symbolic notion of masculine loss. In the Renaissance (as still today) we have only a culturally specific dialectic between biology and gender, one that still exerts a vestigial influence on our own period despite the absence of the humoural "facts" of biology. In the *Anatomy*, similarly, Burton poses the question as to whether melancholy "be material or immaterial," but he does not appear interested in answering one way or another (151: I.1), nor is he particularly concerned with what we would call crucial clinical distinctions: "And whether it be a cause or an effect, a disease, or symptom, let Donatus Altomarus and Salvanius decide, I will not contend about it" (148: I,1). In other places, Burton takes for granted the importance of discussions such as "how the Body works on the Mind" and how "the body, being material, worketh upon the immaterial soul, by mediation of humours & spirits which participate of both" (318: I,2). To summarize, his treatise assumes that all psychological states are simultaneously material and immaterial within a system of extensive correspondences and analogies.

In this system of material psychology the melancholy man in general, and especially the man afflicted with "love melancholy," is characterized by a higher proportion of blood in his system since passion (as well as imagination) produces black bile, the substance most characteristic of the melancholic. The liver is the organ that produces blood – the most abundant humour – and it is also the source of black bile. The greater proportion of blood causes the greater production of semen and thus the greater need to dispel it – resulting in the melancholic's unusual propensity for lust. He is thus particularly vulnerable to the dangers of masculine loss synonymous with masculine sexuality. Consequently, he is also most in need of embracing the misogynistic attitude of disgust toward women's bodies that serves to compensate for and displace the self-destructiveness of his own sexual desires. In this sense, *homo melancholicus* is the picture of masculinity and masculine desire *in excess*, since he possesses all those material elements that constitute masculinity, only in higher proportion.

The melancholy man thus plays out a heightened version of the masculine struggle to maintain reason and rationality in the face of the irrationality and excessiveness of passion and desire, represented as the unruly flow or imbalance of his humoural fluids. According to Burton, since the "rational resides in the Brain, the other in the Liver," the seat of passion and imagination (624: III,2), the melancholic's *psychomachia* is between specifically gendered factions within the male body: the feminine corporeality of the liver in its production of fluids continuously threatens the authority of the ethereal, masculine brain – the seat from which humoural fluids must be carefully regulated. In the following description of this struggle from the *Anatomy*, competing forces appear in an internecine war over control of the body and its psychological status: "according as the humour itself is intended, or remitted in men, as their temperature of body, or rational soul, is better able to make resistance; so are they more or less affected" (126: I,1). Since this struggle is between masculine and feminine elements within men, its "resolution" involves some form of purgation of the feminine, often accomplished through bloodletting, perhaps the most widely supported physical cure for melancholy. The letting of blood evacuates the "feminine" from within men afflicted with the disease but it also makes them resemble women, for whom the evacuation of blood is natural. Burton compares menstruation to melancholics who have difficulty letting blood: they "have had some evacuation stopped, as haemrods, or months in women" (352: I,3; see also 324: I,2). The comparison in this phrase is based on the shared "failure" in both women and melancholy men to regulate blood flow – a characteristic of women but a threat to men. Once again, the melancholy man in his excess of blood and in his need to discharge it resembles women. This is one way of explaining the strains of misogyny that characterize the melancholic, since the feminine element that is evacuated is constructed as dangerous and threatening. But it also explains the self-directed disgust, frustration and sometimes violence of the melancholic, since on some level he is always warring with forces from within. As Burton quotes Felix Platerus, "*after many tedious days*," melancholics "*at last, either by drowning, hanging, or some such fearful end*, they precipitate or make away themselves." Suicide is "a common calamity, a fatal end to this disease" (368–369: I,4).[36]

To summarize, the melancholy man's physical and psychological health (they are the same thing) within humoural science depends on a proper balance of material fluids as well as the continual discipline of the body by the brain. Melancholy is linked to so many functions and substances of the body that it is quite impossible to delineate a coherent system, but the central trope in every case is the maintenance of equilibrium over and against the dangers of excess – a homeostatic masculine body. This is accomplished in part by the proper regulation of what enters and leaves the body, the control of its borders, especially points of entry and egress. As I have suggested in regard to the body of the text itself, we can imagine this as a contest between an *official* body that tightly controls or conceals its openings and an *orificial* body whose boundaries are dangerously fluid, the latter figure most often represented as characteristically feminine.[37]

Melancholy can be caused or cured by too much bodily retention or evacuation – any failures in the body's self-regulation. Burton's interest in what enters the body results in lengthy discussions of diet as a cause of melancholy. In other examples: if too much wine enters the body, the blood will be heated, resulting in inordinate lust; "keeping in of our ordinary excrements" may cause melancholy, and a man who "never went to stool" became "grievously melancholy" (203: I,2); "one wounded in the head ... as long as the sore was open, was well; but when it was stopped his melancholy fit seized on him again" (205: I,2). Since the humoural system depends on different degrees of temperature and quantities of moisture in the body, virtually every physical and psychological state may be achieved or averted according to the addition or subtraction of hot, cold, moist or dry, substances – "*the manners do follow the temperature of the body*" (318: I,2). The exact recipes vary considerably: melancholy is either cold and dry or hot and dry according to the source one follows. But the important point is to maintain the right amount in relation to the others through the brain's strict regulation of what enters and leaves the body: "Now the chiefest causes [of melancholy] proceed from the heart, humours, spirits: as they are purer, or impurer, so is the mind, & equally suffers, as a lute out of tune; if one string or one organ be distempered, all the rest miscarry" (319: I,2). Or, as the basis for the remedy of blood-letting: "How should a man choose but be cholerick and angry, that hath his body so clogged with abundance of gross humours?" The body of the masculine subject requires attention to the purgation or retention of a variety of fluids and substances in order to maintain a physical state of purity and balance, but this proper balance is always perilously achieved in its ability to regulate what is essentially a "feminine" body.

As I have suggested, what is striking about the identification of this anxious masculine body, more acutely so among melancholics, is its affinity to the text's representation of women's bodies, another way of saying that the melancholy man is characterized by his feminine qualities. When the sexualized body of woman is described in contexts most threatening to men (jealousy, seduction to venery, infidelity), it is a body whose boundaries are unstable, whose fluidity appears potentially overwhelming and whose orifices (the site of what goes in and out) are not at all regulated – very much the body of Shakespeare's Cleopatra, figured by the ebb and flow of the Nile. If the ideal masculine body obtains proper governance and balance of its fluids in order to preserve its purity, the bodies of men and woman both fail in the same ways. And of course, given a similar corporeality, the same personality traits necessarily follow: inconstancy and changeability, moodiness, sullenness, an inability to be governed by reason, the excess of passion and imagination. Indeed, any one of Burton's misogynistic descriptions of woman could be applied to the melancholic. For example, under the member, "Remedies of Love," Burton advises his readers to look more closely at women in order to discover what they really are, advice intended to diminish the love-melancholic's passion: "See her angry, merry, laugh, weep, hot, cold, sick, sullen ... in all attires, sites, gestures, passions" (786: III,2). This is quite similar to the portrait of the melancholy man described earlier by Burton in his general discussion of the disease. Elsewhere, under the member, "Symptoms of Love," Burton makes the parallel explicit: love-melancholy is "full of fear, anxiety, doubt, care, peevishness, suspicion, it turns a man into a woman ... because fear and love are linked together" (728: III,2). This portrait is also nearly word for word the description of the jealous man. That jealousy is the most destructive subset of love-melancholy supports the idea that jealousy is an intensification of love rather than a perversion. The jealous or cuckolded man becomes what he most fears about love in the first place: the loss of self-control, potency, and castration; in short, he fears becoming like "woman."

In his discussion of the dangers of marriage, Burton typically describes woman as "like the Sea, their affections ebb and flow" (791: III,2) and as "so irregular and prodigious in their lusts, so diverse in their affections" (790: III,2). In a similar portrait, melancholy men are "not able to confine [their] desires within natural boundaries ... like overflooding rivers ..." (653: III,2) ... [one finds] "prodigious riot in this kind" (692: III,2). In the case of adultery, the melancholic himself enacts what is most fearful in his construction of woman. Burton writes, "[a]ll women are slippery, often unfaithful to husbands" (829: III,3). And among men, "of this Heroical passion, [another phrase for love-melancholy] or rather brutish burning lust of which we treat; we speak of wandering, wanton, adulterous eyes, which, lie still in wait" (683: III,2). The melancholic man also resembles the stereotypical construction of woman in his inability to use language and to interpret correctly, as if his privileged relationship to the symbolic were severed by the disease. In discussing the general symptoms of melancholy, Burton writes: "The first is false conceits and idle thoughts: to misconstrue and amplify, aggravating every thing they conceive or fear: the second is to talk to themselves, or to use inarticulate, incondite voices, speeches, obsolete gestures, and plainly to utter their minds and conceits of their hearts by their words and actions" (347: I,3). Finally, if woman is consistently constructed in the *Anatomy* as duplicitous and cunning, as if there were an inherent discrepancy between the actual and performative, outward show and inward essence, melancholics (such as the enigmatic Hamlet) "do not express themselves in outward shew" (345: I,3).

As Schiesari points out, one of the functions of the discourse of melancholy in Burton's text is thus to represent the melancholy man as similar to women in behavior and in physiological balance in order to appropriate feminine vulnerability and, in so doing, maintain compensatory control through representation itself – through the act of writing about the melancholy man as feminine and effeminized. In "wanting to extricate himself from the 'indecorous' subject of woman," Schiesari writes, "Burton betrays his own fearful identification with them."[38] Since this kind of appropriation requires the performance and/or discursivity of melancholy, it is not at all surprising to find in the *Anatomy* many examples of the lustful, love-melancholy man as a crossdresser. To play the part of woman requires gesture and costume as well as sensibility.

In his discussion of "Artificial Allurements," Burton gives examples (Antony is the most prominent) of men so vanquished and effeminized by their "burning lust" for women that they "go beyond women, they wear harlot's colours, and do not walk, but jet and dance, he-women, she-men, more like players, Butterflies, Baboons, Apes, Anticks, than men ... in a short space their whole patrimonies are consumed" (691: III,2). Corresponding to my earlier discussion of the generation and evacuation of semen, an excess of desire for women consumes and erases characteristics distinctive of masculinity, understood here in terms of apparel, carriage and inherited property, reducing men to the status of the very women who have seduced them unfairly through the guile of "artificial allurements." If reason is overthrown by lust, masculinity reverts to the inferior status of women, animals, players (presumably boy actors), but as this is the result of desire, the overthrow of masculinity is, paradoxically, something to be desired. Or at least, the line between the retention of masculinity and its dissolution is fluid, such that the desire for masculine self-control and agency engenders a desire for its own inversion. Indeed, according to Burton, the transvestite lovers play their part so well they "go beyond women."

Another example is the melancholy Alcibiades, whom Burton describes "dallying with wanton young women, immoderate in his expenses, effeminate in his apparel, ever in love" (663: III,2). In this sequence, immoderate love for "young women" leads Alcibiades to dress like women. In the case of the jealous melancholic, men are once again transformed into women, in manner and in dress. Burton quotes the following exemplary poem from Propertius:

> Each thing affrights me, I do fear,
> Ah pardon me my fear,
> I doubt a man is hidden within
> The clothes that thou wear.

He then adds the rhetorical question: "Is't not a man in woman's apparel?" (841: III,3). As Burton suggests in his list of the causes of male jealousy, even male anatomy is included as part of the theatrics of gender, since a common symptom of melancholy is impotence: "but when as afterward he did not play the man as he should do, she fell in league with a good fellow" (832: III,3).

If, according to this masculine "logic," woman is both cause and effect of the melancholy man, it becomes clear that the disease is what men fear becoming as much as what they fear *they already are*. In Schiesari's psychoanalytic account, "melancholia is driven by a *horror vacuus* that seeks to cover over that lack understood as sexual difference (namely castration) but that keeps rediscovering lack in the disintegrative quality of melancholy thought."[39] In this sense masculinity relies on the discourse and idea of melancholy to fill a fundamental lack by appropriating the projected quality of lack from woman; the melancholy man thus acts like woman in order to avoid becoming like woman. But he also takes pleasure in the control of the representation, in the ability to "go beyond women" – to stage the other so as to retain the very agency that is threatened by the essentially "feminine" body of the melancholic in the first place. The power of appropriating woman thus spills over into a form of pleasure in acting as woman; by contrast, *forcing* men to cross-dress would be the ultimate humiliation as it would represent the loss of agency. This is why representing such a debilitating persona as the melancholic (or jealous man) can function as an enabling discourse for the masculine subject – as long as the articulation and/or performance of melancholy is in the control of men. The loss of volition and reason occurs in the melancholic's inordinate lust is recouped by projecting its cause onto women and by articulating that loss through the discourse of the melancholy.

It is interesting from this perspective to consider briefly Burton's claim that beauty, in women, "is more beholding to Art than to Nature, and [that] stronger provocations proceed from outward ornaments, than such as nature hath provided" (684: III,2). Although such a sentiment is not unique to the *Anatomy*, Burton's repeated insistence of its importance is conspicuous. To cite a few examples: "the greatest provocations of lust are from our apparel; God makes, they say, man shapes" (687: III,2); "their [women's] outward accoutrements are far more precious than their inward endowments" (689: III,2); or, finally, "Nakedness ... is an odious thing in itself" (687: III,2). In Burton's Protestant sensibilities, the dangerous seduction by "artificial allurements" in women, by their painted rather than natural faces, their costumed rather than natural bodies, is comparable to Catholic idolatry, a point he makes several times. In this comparison, heterosexual desire appears fundamentally unnatural, "a mad and beastly passion" (657: III,2). The passage also allows Burton to dismiss in a very misogynistic way the materiality of woman's bodies since the erotic allurement of women is, finally, artificial. Thus love is "a kind of legerdemain, mere juggling, a fascination" (696: III,2). Once again, I think the masculine logic at work here is to attempt to purge from the melancholic man (through the discourse of melancholy) his own "unfortunate" materiality, to lift him above subservience to the melancholy excesses of his own body upwards to the airy realm of the brain. Masculine purity and transcendence would be compromised if Burton presented the love-melancholic as naturally attracted to women, or if women were by nature seductive. If what "God makes" is not the source of heterosexual desire, the procreative act, like the moment of consummation, is contrary to the masculine ideal. This contradiction may explain the pervasive fantasy of male parthenogenesis, including its encoding in Bacon's claims for the pure and untainted dissemination of knowledge, as we shall see in the next chapter. The artificiality of heterosexual desire articulated in these passages contradicts Burton's argument that sex within marriage is the only acceptable outlet for desire. In important ways, the "natural" and "unnatural" are not immutable categories; they are instead enlisted on behalf of different, sometimes opposing, arguments, especially in Burton's discussion of sodomy and homoerotic desire.

[A]cting both the man and woman at once

In the subsection entitled "Love's Tyranny," Burton discusses the multifarious ways in which masculinity is compromised, if not over-thrown, by inordinate lust. Once again the *Anatomy* is concerned with degrees of disorder: the worst sins are those furthest from the require-ments of moderation and reason – those sexual practices most inimical to procreation within marriage. Thus it is not surprising to find a severe condemnation of sodomy based on the usual Pauline injunction: "they will go headlong to their own perdition, they will commit folly with beasts, men 'leaving the natural use of women,' as Paul saith, 'burned in lust one towards another, and man with man wrought filthiness'" (651: III,2). In the previous section, we saw how inordinate lust for women effeminizes men, leading to their adoption of women's apparel, gestures and behavior; in this discussion, the sodomite is represented as extending the same matrix of desire further away from its "proper" bounds: he sins by degree, not by essence. Sodomy is represented in the *Anatomy* as a specifically heinous sin but also as yet another form of inordinate lust, a temptation to which the melancholic (which is to say, all men) is susceptible inasmuch as he is particularly vulnerable to the tyranny of desire. This apparent paradox is quite consistent with the framework of humoural psychology: since all men possess the same humoural system in varying degrees, all forms of desire are at least latently possible. Indeed, the virulence of Burton's condemnation of sodomy as unnatural may be explained by his own corporeal explanation of the "democratic" basis of desire in which homoeroticism is quite natural, at least in potential. In this way, masculine desire within the context of humoural psychology adds an important corroborating perspective to several recent historical studies of homoeroticism in the Renaissance, particularly those of Alan Bray and Jonathan Goldberg.

The emerging picture of early modern homoeroticism is well-known, but it will be of use to give a brief summary of those aspects pertaining to my discussion of the *Anatomy*. In *Homosexuality in Renaissance England*, Bray shows that homosexuality was neither a separate cate-gory of sexuality nor the basis for individual identity that it later became; instead, it was understood as one of several forms of debauchery that comprised "the disorder in sexual relations that could break out anywhere."[40] In Goldberg's definition, "sodomy was assumed to be a temptation anyone might succumb to, rather than a marker of identity."[41] Especially for Protestant England, marriage was supposed to provide the necessary containment of inordinate lust in all its forms.

Homoeroticism was an "abomination" among other forms of sexuality but it was also decried more aggressively than inordinate heterosexual lust because it was understood as most contrary to procreative sex within marriage. Homoerotic desire among men was not separate from other forms of desire – not the sexual Other it has become in the twentieth century. This apparent contradiction (from our perspective) perhaps explains why the charge of sodomy in the Renaissance is so often attached to more "secure" forms of otherness, like Catholicism, witchcraft or treason.[42] The charge of sodomy is linked to the non-sexual activities of those clearly contrary to the normative in order to give it a greater discursive precision than it would possess on its own. In other words, since desire is believed to be fluid and undirected, it must be attached to a crime that is clearly transgressive. Burton's condemnations of sodomy are always contextualized by a series of other sins – sexual and otherwise – in order to make the practice of sodomy an Other. As I have suggested, his particular anxiety toward sodomy (and thus his need to frame it in this way) is aroused by the fact that since his entire treatise is based in humoural psychology, all forms of melancholy disease are rooted in the natural substances of not only the body but also, by analogy, the earth, heavens, even plants and animals. If the function of sodomy was to figure the unnatural, the disorder lurking beneath the divinely ordered universe, Burton must resolve the fact that the sodomite is quite natural in his desires, only unnatural by degree. We should thus read the sodomite in the *Anatomy* in terms of its different linkages and associations rather than as possessing an inherently different sexuality.

Let us explore for a moment this idea of desire as "democratic" in Burton's text. It is impossible to overstate the depiction of melancholy as a universal malaise whose origins lie in the natural operations of the body itself. As Babb observes, "there is hardly a mental disease which is not associated with melancholic humours by one author or another."[43] Within a conceptual framework based on correspondence and degree, it is difficult to make absolute discriminations, since any given entity shares the properties of another, either by analogy or similitude, or because humans possess a shared physiology beneath their individual temperaments. Thus Burton regularly includes hetero and homoerotic practices in the same discussions of inordinate lusts; for example, "adultery, incest, sodomy, buggery" are all "prodigious lusts" (662: III,2). In the following passage, from the preface "Democritus to the Reader," Burton constructs an opposition between the mutability of culture and the essentiality of the humours and their effects:

We change language, habits, laws, customs, manners, but not vices, not diseases, not the symptoms of folly and madness – they are the same. And as a River, we see, keeps the like name and place, but not water, and yet ever runs, our times and persons alter, vices are the same, and ever will be ... we are of the same humours and inclinations as our predecessors were, you shall us all alike. (43)

This passage recognizes cultural and historical changes, but essentializes "folly and madness" as two of the "diseases" that are rooted in our shared, physiology – "we are of the same humours." The passage may also be read as claiming the universality of homoerotic desire inasmuch as desire knows no object: "laws" and "customs" may change but our "vices are the same." Here Burton articulates a struggle between universal or natural desire (independent of any specific object) and the mutable, constructed forms of social organization that are supposed to contain and regulate desire. In short, desire is a figure of universal anarchy especially, but not exclusively, homoerotic. The *Anatomy* is indeed quite broad in its catalogue of those cultures for whom sodomy is "common" practice: "Among the Asiaticks, Turks, Italians, the vice is customary to this day; sodomy is ... the Diana of the Romans ... Nothing more common among monks and priestlings ... And terrible to say, in our country, within memory, how much that detestable sin hath raged" (652: III,2).

And yet, at the same time, Burton's subject matter requires him to make important categorical discriminations between, for example, madness and reason, chaos and order, or "filthy burning lust [and] pure and divine love" (621: III,2). He is caught, one might say, between a moral system in which positive and negative values are ostensibly opposite in nature, and a relativistic system in which all humans have the natural capacity, even propensity, for the same "vices." In a frequently echoed sentiment, Burton writes: "All men are carried away with passion, discontent, lust, pleasures, &c.; they generally hate the virtues they should love, and love such vices they should hate" (61). Binary oppositions established between "virtues" and "vices" are overwhelmed by human passions. The *Anatomy* thus continuously struggles with the contradiction between categories that mark difference, distinguishing one from another, and difference that is a matter of degree, always threatening to exceed fragile lines of discrimination.

The contexts within the *Anatomy* in which Burton discusses sodomy are critical to our understanding of the place of homoeroticism in Renaissance thinking and in the text itself. The second section of the third partition defines and gives examples of "heroical Love," or "love-melancholy." This section proceeds with discussions of "love among the vegetals," "love among the beasts," "love of statues," then "love's tyranny," in which sodomy first appears. Although the anxious pitch of Burton's prose is greatest in the last part, he assumes a general correspondence among all categories of life in their relationship to love. In other words, all forms of life are anthropomorphized. Thus Burton relates exemplary stories about a jealous bear, fish that "pine away for love and wax lean" (647: III,2) and a "Palm-tree that loved most fervently, and would not be comforted until such time her Love applied himself unto her" (645: III,2). Yet despite this basic correspondence and sameness in the power of love and desire ("Love is so powerful ..." 644: III,2), Burton still tries to claim divisions by applying the categories "natural" and "unnatural," as in the following distinction: "Yet this is natural for one beast to dote upon another of the same kind; but what a strange fury is that, when a Beast shall dote upon a man!" (647: III,2). Given the collapsing of distinctions that characterizes Burton's discussion of love and desire, this attempt to engage an opposition between "natural" and "strange" is somewhat peculiar. Here Burton is once again caught between the indiscriminate tyranny of desire derived from the humours, its leveling of distinctions between species and objects of desire, and the need to apply some categorical standards. As we turn to the passages on sodomy, we find the same paradox at work.

The democratic nature of desire is exemplified in the following passage: "Semiramis with a horse, Pasiphae with a bull, Aristo Ephesius with a she-ass, Fulvius with a mare, others with dogs, goats, &c., from such combinations in ancient days were sprung monsters, Centaurs, Silvanuses, and prodigious sights to affright mankind. And not with brutes only, but men among themselves, which sin is vulgarly called Sodomy ..." (651: III,2). Once again the et cetera suggests a list that could continue indefinitely, as if Burton's own writing cannot contain his subject matter. But more importantly, sodomy is linked to, perhaps even worse than, a variety of combinations of bestiality that produce monstrosity. The sequence that ends with sodomy functions as a way to locate homoeroticism as unnatural and monstrous because (according to the *Anatomy*) it is so pervasive, so rooted in a universal desire (or lust) that knows no specific object. If sodomy were in *its own right* "monstrous," such a rhetorical strategy would not be necessary. The passage continues by listing once again the frequency of homoerotic practices: "this vice was customary in old times with the Orientals, the Greeks without question, the Italians, Africans, Asiaticks ..." (651: III,2). Nor is sodomy only the practice of cultural Others, as Burton's list finally comes home to reveal how frequently in England "that sin hath raged" (652: III,2). But even on the domestic front, Burton must still link sodomy to the Other: English "wenchers, gelded youths, debauchees, catamites,

boy-things, pederasts, Sodomites (as it saith in Bale), Ganymedes, &c."
are always found in the company of priests and votaries (652: III,2).

The following sequence of practices of inordinate love shows how
broadly and indiscriminately love tyrannizes over men *and* women:
"scourging each other with whips"; "a woman in Constantinople, being
mad in love with another woman ... went through the ceremonial of
marriage disguised as a man"; those "who couch with beautiful cada-
vers" and those who "are in love with idols and images"; "men with men
or women with women"; "men go with goats, swine, and horses," and
finally, women "inflamed with mad passion for beasts" (653: III,2). The
linkages among this sequence of erotic passions are based on the degree
to which inordinate lust is indulged, not on the specific practice involved.
Borrowing a contemporary term, Burton seems to believe that polymorphous perversity is at the core of human desire; what characterizes all of
the practices in his list is that "no part [is] free from lewdness, no orifice
not defiled and given over to shameful lust" (653: III,2). In all cases, the
temptation to these "nasty sins" is the result of an inability to "confine
your desires within their natural boundaries, but rather, like overflooding
rivers, bring about violence, filthiness, turmoil, and confusion of nature
in regard to love" (653: III,2). It should be remembered that Burton's
condemnation of heterosexual lust is at least as severe as his injunctions
against homoeroticism; in tone and content, these passages are in fact
interchangeable. In his discussion of the symptoms of heterosexual love,
Burton writes: "if once they be overtaken with this passion, the most
staid, discreet, grave, generous and wise, otherwise able to govern
themselves, in this commit many absurdities, many indecorums, unbefit-
ting their gravity and persons" (736: III,2). The opposition between
natural and unnatural sexual practice is thus not based on the object of
one's desire, as it will become by the end of the nineteenth century, but
rather upon the extent to which "love tyrannizeth over men," in the
continual struggle to contain desire with reason and self-control. But as
we have seen, "natural boundaries" is a vexed term in Burton's discussion since he repeatedly describes polymorphous desire as universal and
unavoidable.

For Burton, love in the form of inordinate lust is not only indiscriminate
in its object choices but omnipotent as well: "Human, divine laws,
precepts, exhortations, fear of God and men, fair, foul means, fame,
fortunes, shame, disgrace, honour, cannot oppose, stave off, or withstand
the fury of it, love overcomes all, &c." (656: III,2). Rooted in the
materiality of the humoural body, neither social forms of regulation nor
the exercise of human reason can contain it: "this fire of Love burneth

and scorcheth afar off, and is more hot and vehement than any material fire; 'tis a fire in a fire, the quintessence of fire" (733: III,2). Here Burton argues in Heraclitean fashion that the very essence of human life is the amorphous, uncontainable force of erotic desire, mutable in its forms and destructive of masculine reason and social order.

The body of the melancholic in Burton's account is thus Rabelaisian in nature, especially in terms of the subversive potential of that body as articulated by Bakhtin. Unable to contain the fluidity of desire, Burton's melancholic body is ungovernable by the individual authority of reason or by the social structures of law and marriage. As I shall explore in this section, Burton's discussion of melancholy in general and specifically of the melancholy man's susceptibility to the "tyranny of love" applies simultaneously to corporal and social bodies. Given the correspondence between microcosm and macrocosm, between the body and the world, or between the body natural and the body of the state, emotions, desires, diseases – everything that makes up the physical and psychological body – are *already* social and political qualities. To reiterate: it is thus ahistorical to consider the individual psyche as a separate entity, or even as the product or effect of social factors, since for the Renaissance the two realms are *a priori* coterminous. This is slightly different from saying that one could *choose* to draw an analogy between, for example, the individual faculty of reason and the office of the king; the point is that such an analogy is always there, providing the conceptual possibilities of both terms in the first place. And since humoural psychology is rooted in the material properties of the body, it is also ahistorical to imagine either male or female bodies as apart from the sociopolitical domain, although obviously not in the same ways. Whatever one *did* in private, sexuality and desire were not construed as private practices since the body itself was neither conceptually nor literally a private domain.

Given the high premium placed on reason and self-control as the most critical constituents of Renaissance masculinity, the discourse of love, passion and desire is nearly always cast individually in terms of psychic turmoil, and collectively as an insurrection against the state or as a challenge to social order and cohesion. It is important to read this correspondence metaphorically and literally at the same time; indeed, the distinction seems difficult to maintain if we remember those rhetorical treatises in which metaphors described the world as it always was – a world of pre-existent correspondences and similarities – rather than as the way to link disparate things or concepts. This way of thinking, as I have argued above, places the *Anatomy* within an earlier conception of tropes and the place of language in the world in which resemblances were assumed rather than fashioned.

Let us consider first the explicitly political metaphors engaged by Burton to represent the melancholy man's struggle to maintain a proper government of desire, remembering that these metaphors largely depend on a system of correspondences already in place. In the introductory "Democritus to the Reader," Burton first introduces the analogy (or perhaps "homology" better suggests the structural and isomorphic equivalence within the system of correspondences) between individual melancholy and the health of the state: *"the State was like a sick body which had lately taken physick, whose humours were not yet well settled, and weakened so much by purging, that nothing was left but melancholy"* (67). This similitude is not just a way of illustrating the disease of melancholy by way of political analogue; based on the correspondences between the humoural fluids that comprise the body and the various elements of the state, Burton assumes that the health of the body politic also requires proper balance. Typically, the body politic should be governed by and obedient toward those institutions that correspond to human reason – religion and the monarchy. Thus Burton cites the two most common causes of a "melancholy" of diseased state: "when religion & God's service is neglected" and the "[c]onfusion, ill-government, which proceeds from unskilful, slothful, griping, covetous, unjust, rash, or tyrannizing magistrates" (66). Any temptation to read the body politic only as an analogy or allegory for the melancholic body is dispelled by Burton's assumption that the bodies of princes literally affect the health of the body politic: "Whereas the Princes and Potentates are immoderate in lust, hypocrites, epicures, of no religion, but in show: what so brittle and unsure? what sooner subverts their estates than wandering & raging lusts on their subjects' wives, daughters, to say no worse?" (67). In effect, a monarch plagued by melancholy will produce the same symptoms of the disease in the state because the monarch's body is a synecdoche for the body of the state. And in a later passage: "As it is in a man's body, if either head, heart, stomach, liver, spleen, or any one part be misaffected, all the rest suffer with it; so is it with this economical body" (92). In both cases, social order depends on the proper governance of passion by reason, the body by the head. For Burton, this is a constant struggle: quoting Ovid, he writes: *"Reason pulls one way, burning lust another"* (737: III,2).

Indeed, the most common appeal throughout the *Anatomy* is to "[l]et Mercury, reason, rule thee against all allurements, seeming delights, pleasing inward or outward provocations" (779–780: III,2). It comes as no surprise that the army of "allurements" (located in the body's pleasures) that continually attack masculine reason are most often construed as female. Burton's understanding of the body politic thus upholds the construction of woman as governed by passions inherent in the body rather than by the seat of reason in the head. Interestingly, this is the case even in the expression of homoerotic seduction, since the point is that capitulation to one's own lust is an expression of "feminine" lack of self-control independent of the desired object. Additionally, as I have suggested above, Burton's belief that love and desire effeminize men is not at all unique to early modern masculinity, but his discussion underscores the fact that this danger was understood in terms of status and gender, or perhaps more accurately, in the context of status *as* gender. This way of thinking explains why desire is feminized regardless of the gender (or even species) of its object, since a monarchy of desire in any form overturns the authority of individual reason (the head) and the political authority of the king. Objections to James' homoerotic relationships were thus primarily based on two homologous sins: he is overruled by his passions and he was raised his favorites to positions of power in violation of the natural, hierarchical system.

In a paragraph under the subtitle "Symptoms of Love," Burton writes: "They [love-melancholics] are commonly slaves, captives, voluntary servants, a lover is the slave of his beloved ... his Mistress' servant, her drudge, prisoner, bond-man ... What greater captivity or slavery can there be ... than to be in love?" (742: III,2). Here Burton understands the loss of reason and self-control as a reversal of fortune and status, a version of the woman or the servant on top. This is made clear in the next sentence: "Is he a free man over whom a woman domineers, to whom she prescribes Laws, commands, forbids what she will herself?" (742: III,2). Using the well-worn analogy in which love and passion are specifically feminine qualities, Burton suggests that a man in love is a man ruled and enslaved by a woman. Indeed, this "feminine principle" threatens to overwhelm and dominate men as a kind of defilement in Burton's examples, as if masculine reason and feminine love/passion were wholly separate entities. "Your bravest soldiers and most generous spirits," Burton writes, "are enervated with it, when they surrender to feminine blandishments and defile themselves with embraces" (645: III,2). But the problem with construing these terms as warring factions within the body natural and the body politic is that they are not opposed but rather mutually dependent; they can only have meaning in relation to one another. Such a system requires the continual production of melancholy for the individual and the state in order to be able to imagine a healthy body natural or body politic. In effect, each side of the binary opposition may be said to *desire* the other in an endless deferral of resolution.

Here the logic of Burton's representation of love and desire as destructive but also enabling becomes clear. On the one hand, love and desire are internal, fundamental, humoural forces; on the other, they are turned into an external enemy against which the individual must always defend. Burton represents intrinsic forces as foreign enemies in order to combat them, but the enemy is always within. In other words, that which represents the most powerful threat to the construction of masculinity must be externalized, turned into an Other, but the presence of the same threat is also the *condition* of masculinity. The melancholic man plays out this model of otherness by living in a state of perpetual psychic and physical conflict and, in so doing, dramatizes and exacerbates the unavoidable tensions and anxieties of masculinity. The melancholic life is "full of agony, anxiety, fear, and grief, complaints, sighs, suspicions, and cares," as Burton writes, because masculinity knows itself only in the process of desiring the Other, not in its consummation of that desire: "there is no end of Love's Symptoms, 'tis a bottomless pit. Love is subject to no dimensions ..." (761: III,2).

Perhaps the best way to get at the unavoidable and enabling nature of this contradiction, given the way masculinity is constructed in the first place, is to look briefly at Burton's understanding of desire in the abstract. Early in the third partition, Burton introduces the definition of love and desire that underwrites all of his discussion: "Love is a voluntary affection, and desire to enjoy that which is good. Desire wisheth, Love enjoys: the end of one is the beginning of the other: that which we love is present; that which we desire is absent" (618: III,1). Burton then engages in a brief discussion, citing a variety of opinions from Plotinus, Plato, Ficinus and others, as to whether love is "a God or a Devil." In this discussion there are two models of desire and love at work. The first one involves the idea of consummation: desire is fulfilled once absence is replaced by presence. This is understood as divine love, connected to and inspired by God, since it is based on the idea of fullness and plenitude. One of the symptoms of the melancholic in general is that he is given to despair over the difficulty of attaining presence with God – the same paralyzing yet sustaining economy of desire articulated around love and erotic desire. Burton is never at rest with a model of desire that promises its own fulfillment, as suggested in the ambiguous phrase, "the end of one is the beginning of the other." If he means this reciprocally, not only is love the end of desire, but love is also the beginning of new desire, and so the cycle continues. This idea of desire as a perpetual, restless force is corroborated throughout the text. In a general discussion of desire from the first partition, Burton writes: *Desire hath no rest*, is infinite in itself, endless, & as one calls it, a perpetual rack, or horse-mill ... still going around as in a ring" (242: I,2). Or, in the context of love particularly: "I am deluded with various desires, one love succeeds another, and so on, that before one is ended, I begin with a second ... Mine eyes are so moist a refuge and sanctuary of love, that they draw all beauties to them, and are never satisfied" (660: III,2). In other words, desire by nature is always in excess of the object that would satisfy it. Or, to return to Burton's earlier opposition, absence and presence are not separate entities but mutually dependent on one another, reversible rather than discrete. "Desire hath no rest" because the circularity of presence and absence is "infinite," "still going around as in a ring."

This model of masculine desire as restless and insatiable, perhaps one could say self-destructive, will appear in several discussions in this book – different discussions account for its pervasiveness in a number of ways. For Burton, the salient aspect of desire as an "infinite" and "endless" force is that it continuously assails and overwhelms the boundaries represented by masculine reason, moderation and self-control. Burton himself relies frequently on spatial metaphors: lust is "a raging madness," and "a monster of nature" (651: III,2) that threaten to overflow the social boundaries constructed to contain it, such as moral injunction, marriage, the rule of reason. But the transgression of boundaries is also their enabling condition and their source. As Claudio realizes in *Measure for Measure*, "surfeit is the father of much fast" (I.ii.127). Even in describing the disempowerment and suffering of the melancholic, the *Anatomy* asserts its discursive authority by articulating the reciprocity of presence and absence, order and disorder, the rule of reason and the rage of lust.

By way of conclusion we can thus begin to consider the enabling function of Burton's conception of melancholy as a discourse of masculinity that incorporates – indeed, valorizes – the very contradictions and tensions that otherwise threaten the masculine subject. The masculine humoural body is by definition perilously close to becoming "feminine," always at risk of being overruled by its own lusts and passions, anxiously attentive to the balance of its own troublesome fluidity. In response to these anatomical "facts," Burton's *Anatomy* is a history of masculine vulnerability that offers the possibility of maintaining some control over the disease through representation, some comfort in recognizing himself and his readers within the shared plight of his gender. In other words, Burton stages the most dire visions of anxious masculinity in order to dispel them through an articulation of the knowledge and experience of melancholy. The ideological work of Burton's text is to disguise the cultural basis of masculine identity in the cloak of a psycho-physical disease caused by natural elements within the body; in short, nature is the explanation for ideology. But in Burton's own anatomy of the melancholy body as a body under siege, anxiously in search of an unattainable equilibrium, nature is not the serenely ordered work of God but rather a pressure cooker of volatile, combustible fluids. How can such potent internal pressure be released? By writing about it, externalizing it, and especially by assigning it to someone other than oneself. Perhaps the last word (if that were possible) belongs to Andre Du Laurens, whose medical treatise was translated into English in 1597: when a melancholic "see[s] three or foure talking together, he thinketh that it is of him ... being alwaies in feare, he thinketh verely that one or other doth lie in wait for him, and that some doe purpose to slay him."[44]

Purity and the dissemination of knowledge in
      Bacon's new science

... chaste, holy, and legal wedlock.
                              Bacon, "The Masculine Birth of Time"

In *Purity and Danger*, Mary Douglas argues that the "body is a model
which can stand for any bounded system . . . [whose] boundaries can
represent any boundaries which are threatened or precarious."[1] Her
analysis is dialectical rather than causal: The corporal body is both the
source of a culture's comprehension and delineation of its figurative
bodies, and the *site* of contestation between what is perceived as pure or
impure, normal or aberrant. As I have shown in my discussion of
Burton's *Anatomy*, humoural science provided one of the ways early
modern culture imagined different bodies in relation to one another,
especially in terms of their precarious boundaries and vulnerable orifices.
Douglas' broad, theoretical claim is thus particularly applicable in a
culture where homology, correspondence and similitude form the conceptual basis for comprehending virtually all aspects of the world,
including the physical body itself. This chapter proceeds from Douglas'
linkage of corporal and figurative bodies to analyze the rhetoric of
Bacon's "new science" in terms of the semiotics of female chastity in
early modern England and the purity claimed on behalf of an aristocratic
body whose boundaries were perceived as threatened. Baconian science
and the language of its dissemination reside uneasily at the intersection
of several discourses: the history of scientific investigation to which he
responds, but also domestic relationships, female chastity, the endangered royal prerogative and the increasingly porous delineations of
status. To situate Bacon's corpus at such an intersection acknowledges
and depends upon the circulation and exchange effected by the network
of analogies and homologies that characterizes early modern conceptual
frameworks – in this case, the circulation among a scientific body of
writing, an aristocratic body and a particularly apprehensive construction of women's bodies.
  Such an approach does not claim to provide a single interpretive key

to all of Bacon's widely ranging corpus, nor does it suggest a simply causal relationship between the period's sex/gender system and Baconian science. Instead, I want to show how Bacon's conceptions of knowledge and the written form in which he disseminated that knowledge are shaped and encoded by the symbolic capital accorded to female chastity in the early seventeenth century. This focus opens up an important reciprocity between gender and status: in early modern England, the masculine discourse demanding sexual chastity in women is always additionally shaped by an anxiety about the preservation or pollution of an ideal of class purity. Or, in other terms, a status system dependent on the "proper" dissemination of property and title between men literally and symbolically requires the assurance of female chastity and virginity. The fact that early modern delineations of social rank were considerably more fluid and open-ended in practice than they were in theory may have contributed to a even more urgent demand for symbols of class purity. In other words, the potential for "pollution" and instability of status boundaries that occurred at all levels would promote an increased employment of symbols intended to represent the "purity" of supposedly inherent class identities. Calvin's remark on the necessity of chastity in women is an early modern commonplace in terms of his linkage between female sexuality, property and status: "what else will remain safe in human society if license be given to bring in by stealth the offspring of a stranger? to steal a name which may be given to spurious offspring? and to transfer to them property taken from lawful heirs?"[2]

In this passage, Calvin paints by negation a clear and concise portrait of masculinity in the early modern period at the same time as he reveals perhaps its most pervasive anxiety. The proper and legal dissemination of property from father to eldest son in a patrilineal culture is the cornerstone of order in "human society," and it is thus one of the most fundamental ingredients of masculinity – without it, one's "name" is stolen. This dissemination is entirely an affair between men, both in its positive outcome (father to son) as well as in its disruption ("the spurious offspring" of a "stranger"). Thus, while it is accurate to say that Calvin's dire vision reveals an anxiety about wives' infidelity, he also worries that nothing will "remain safe" if economically proper relations between men (established through female chastity) are not sustained. In the homo-social economies of this period, a dyadic model of masculine identity in which "woman" is constructed as other is always, at the same time, a way of establishing relations between men.[3]

The rich complexities of this triangularity are considerable, especially in the case of Bacon. As a powerful player on both sides of the political and literary patronage systems surrounding the Jacobean court, and as one whose dealings in bribery ranged from high government figures to his own servants, Bacon clearly lived in that homosocial "network of influential patrons, of their clients and suitors and friends at court" so brilliantly studied by Alan Bray.[4] Bray uses Bacon's own essay on friendship to develop the economies of homosociality: Bacon, Bray writes, "says that such friendship as there is in this world is in truth between those who have the same material interests, those 'whose fortunes . . . may comprehend the one the other.' "[5] Such friendships, of course, are more likely to be between men in this period since they are necessarily between those of similar economic interests. The same can be said for the negative or competitive relations among men evoked in Calvin's remark about the necessity of female chastity. Shared material interests are the positive basis for male friendship in Bacon's essay; but according to Calvin, the sharing of property or heirs is the dreadful result of infidelity, a direct path toward social upheaval. A potential contradiction thus obtains in the homosocial economies of this period. In one direction of the spectrum of relations between men, we witness an antagonistic, competitive dynamic that is often played out through women; women are transacted property, or their chastity is a badge of honor for husbands, validated only when other men desire to steal it. But in the other direction, where women are not directly involved, the kind of friendship Bacon articulates would be more available, homoerotic or not. A literary example makes the point well. In Shakespeare's sonnets, Eve Sedgwick has argued, the presence of the dark lady in the later sonnets leads to a volatile atmosphere between the poet and the young man, displacing the much more congenial, affectionate relationship depicted in the earlier sonnets.[6]

Of course, the yet unmentioned element in the case of Bacon is his notorious reputation as a pederast or sodomite, the evidence for which would suggest more than just attempts to defame his character. Bacon almost certainly had sex with men, or boys.[7] If we assume Bacon's own homoerotic practices as well as his personal and professional travels along the homosocial pathways of power and patronage, how is it possible to read his corpus through the lens of early modern attitudes toward marriage and female chastity, given that neither of these social rhetorics should have apparently held much interest for him directly? The short answer is because the textual evidence is so overwhelming: Bacon's writings are suffused with metaphors from marriage, generative or destructive female sexuality (figures like "chastity" and "purity" are everywhere), and his epistemology is dependent upon often misogynistic constructions of "woman" that are commonplace in this period. Beyond this, the more complicated answer is that a male/female dyadic economy, as exhibited in Bacon's gendered rhetoric, is by no means in opposition to homosocial discourses, nor is it necessarily in opposition to homoerotic practices. Indeed, the figure of purity in Bacon's writing functions to set men apart from women (pure/impure) but also to bond men to one another, as in the pure dissemination of knowledge between males (father to son, mentor to student) Bacon imagines in "The Masculine Birth of Time." To read the early modern period in terms of such an opposition depends upon a homosexual/heterosexual distinction that was not yet established, as a considerable body of recent scholarship has shown.[8] Following this premise, it is important to realize that there was also not an independent rhetoric of homoeroticism (except in charges of homoerotic practices as a way to defame) inasmuch as there is not a distinctively homosexual identity. In other words, when Bacon thinks his epistemology through an early modern rhetoric of sexuality, none exists that is specifically or uniquely homoerotic – homosocial, of course, but nothing like what the twentieth century has developed.

Thus, if Bacon's new science is to be read from the standpoint of his own homoerotic practices, one would need to rely on signs and figures from his personal life rather than on an available public discourse. This is the method adopted by Graham Hammill in a recent article entitled "The Epistemology of Expurgation," where Bacon's epistemological project is linked to sexuality through the trope of purgation – purging false idols from the minds of his readers and purging the body with enemas and purging pills, as Bacon (not at all uncommonly) did. Hammill's arguments importantly introduce Bacon's own sexual practices into the analysis of his epistemology, especially in "The Masculine Birth of Time," where the dissemination of knowledge is figured in an incontrovertible homoerotic (or perhaps pederastic) vocabulary. But this should not lead us to the kind of opposition Hammill offers in concluding that "Bacon imagines these [forms of disseminating knowledge] not as an odyssey into the vagina but rather as wanderlusts into the anus."[9] This statement represents two distinct ways of sexualizing Bacon's corpus, an either/or proposition that is more aligned with a twentieth-century erotic economy than with the early modern period's. Bacon's homoerotic practices do not prevent him from figuring his new science in a heterosexual economy – that rhetoric was widely available and it has as much to do with status and class purity as it does with gender. In short, the early modern sex/gender system involves a homosocial/homoerotic spectrum as well as a male/female dyad – not as an opposition but rather as co-existent, sometimes mutually re-enforcing, vocabularies. This is especially true when we add to the analysis of Bacon's epistemology his belief that social order depended on maintaining clear status delineations.

Status considerations – or better, status anxiety – especially inform Bacon's reproduction of the symbolic capital of female chastity as if it were "natural" in order to legitimate his own scientific enterprise. In other words, his insistence on the chastity of "female" nature and on a "chaste and perfect style" of exposition results in a body of scientific writing that re-inscribes patriarchal and aristocratic authority already legitimated *through* and *by* the female body. At the same time, however, this insistence responds to the perceived endangerment of that authority – the perceived threat of "pollution" to the ideal of the masculine, aristocratic body whose patrilineal privileges were symbolically and actually confirmed by the regulation of female sexuality. At the outset, it must be recognized that my use of the term "aristocratic body" denotes not a readily distinguishable rank in early modern England (even the peerage could be increased by royal preferment, as James liberally demonstrated), but rather an ideal to which various degrees of the gentry might aspire, or a symbol that might legitimate newly acquired status as if it were inherent. Here it is useful to follow David Harris Sacks' understanding of the English aristocracy as "a *class* whose membership depended upon social determinants of honor and wealth, and not a *caste* established exclusively by blood." In drawing this distinction, Sacks portrays English social structure as a permeable, contested set of relations, not as a static hierarchy. Since female chastity could signify these variable "social determinants," the female body itself became a contested site of collective and individual masculine identities; anxieties about masculinity were projected onto female bodies and sexualities.[10] In Thomas Hoby's translation of Castiglione's *Book of the Courtier* (1561), for example, without female chastity, "the which children were uncertain, and the bond that naturally knitteth all the worlde together by bloud, and by the love that naturally each man hath to that is borne him, should be loosed."[11] As in my earlier discussion of Calvin's similar statement, female chastity is invested with the power to preserve or threaten the "bloud" that figures the purity of status distinctions that are simultaneously construed as the necessary bonds between men.

Such an investment is primarily a matter of concern to the landed gentry – those whose wealth and prestige would be most enhanced through selective marriage and protected through inheritance. And it was precisely this stratum of English society who found their own status most endangered by the new social mobility and redistribution of wealth. According to Lawrence Stone, "families were moving up and down in the social and economic scale at a faster rate than at any time before the nineteenth and twentieth centuries."[12] Stone also points out that the years between 1610 and 1620 witnessed the height of economic changes for the landed classes,[13] one result of which was "an arrogance revealing their basic insecurity".[14] Although Stone relies perhaps too heavily on a static model of the social hierarchy against which to measure these changes, his work underscores the need in this period to represent one's status as permanent or inherent even if that were not in actuality the case. Placed in this context, the fervent interest in regulating marriage and in insuring the chastity of wives may be seen as a compensatory tactic for preserving those status distinctions that were perceived as threatened or, alternately, newly achieved.

My purpose in sketching this cultural field involving class purity and female chastity is not to implicate Bacon directly in its manipulations. Indeed, as a second son, Bacon's status and mobility depended on his own merit rather than on his birthright, despite the potential yet unrealized advantage derived from his father's service to Elizabeth. Moreover, since Bacon married late in life to little economic advantage, he was not himself involved in self-advancement through the marriage market. Bacon occupied the broad category of "gentlemen" – defined by William Harrison in 1577 as "those whome their race and blood or at least their vertues doo make noble and knowe."[15] The ambivalence, if not contradiction, contained in Harrison's description applies exactly to Bacon's own very self-conscious aspirations: from his father's position as Elizabeth's chancellor, he felt *entitled* to rank and prestige because of his "race and blood," but he could only *achieve* that status by making his "vertues" known, which is to say, he relied on his own merit and the display of his status. However, it is plausible to argue that Bacon's own high aspirations combined with his lack of inheritance gave him an even more acute awareness of the class distinctions marking the landed wealth to which he aspired. As Keith Wrightson points out, the term " 'gentlemen' was employed by them as a group expression, implying a certain homogeneity of social position and identity of interests, perhaps even a collective consciousness, which was attributed to no other singular group – though they might on occasion speak broadly of 'the common people', or 'the poor'." Wrightson implies that the gentry represented itself as far more homogenous and insulated than it actually was. Because the "line dividing gentleman from the rest in the body of society was a permeable membrane,"[16] Wrightson continues, people like Bacon were more inclined to adopt a discourse of rigid class boundaries and pure class entities. While Bacon was not literally an aristocrat in "crisis," to borrow Stone's phrase, his ambitions were very much invested in a social order dependent upon the preservation of traditional class boundaries as well as the royal prerogative, which he felt guaranteed those boundaries. As Bacon was lifted to positions of power and prestige by James, this investment increased dramatically. Indeed, Bacon's political ambitions were inseparable from his scientific publication: the majority of his writing was done either at the outset of his expectations and solicitations for royal preferment under James (1603–1609), or at a time when he naively sought to regain favor following his impeachment (1621–1626).[17] Bacon's writing is always informed by the monarch whose favor he sought and, more generally, by his support of the social hierarchy in which he could achieve the power and prestige he felt he deserved.

In 1622, a year after his infamous impeachment by the House of Commons but still at a time when he believed he could be restored at court, Bacon wrote "An Advertisement Touching a Holy War." I quote the following passage at length in order to introduce in Bacon's thought and writing the inseparability of gender, female desire and a social order perceived as largely dependent upon patrimony, inheritance and the proper use of language:

Now let me put a feigned case . . . of a land of Amazons, where the whole government public and private, yea the militia itself, was in the hands of women. I demand, is not such a preposterous government (against the first order of nature, for women to rule over men,) in itself void, and to be suppressed? I speak not of the reign of women, (for that is supplied by counsel and subordinate masculine,) but where the regiment of state, justice, families, is all managed by women . . . in this there is only error of nature. Neither should I make any great difficulty to affirm the same of the Sultanry of the Mamaluches; where slaves, and none but slaves, bought for money and of unknown descent, reigned over families of freemen. And much like were the case, if you suppose a nation where the custom were, that after full age the sons should expulse their fathers and mothers out of their possessions . . . for these cases, of women to govern men, sons the fathers, slaves freedom, are much in the same degree; all being total violations and perversions of the laws of nature and nations.[18]

In this passage, the social hierarchy is legitimated by a hierarchical opposition between "the first order of nature" over and against "total violations and perversions." The analogous perversions Bacon imagines include the "preposterous" rule of women, the "reign" of "slaves . . . of unknown descent" as well as the overthrow of patrilineal inheritance by sons. Here Bacon reproduces the dire vision of the "Homily on Obedience," first promulgated under Edward VI and re-issued throughout Elizabeth's reign: "all abuse, carnal libertie, enormitie, synne and Babilonical confusion" will result if the natural order created by God is perverted in any of its analogous hierarchies.[19] But the leading hierarchy in Bacon's evocation of natural order (only available in such extreme terms once James replaces Elizabeth on the throne) is the necessary subordination of women to men. The rule of women is the "preposterous" and perverse violation of nature that preoccupied the male imagination in the Renaissance in its fascination with the always geographically remote state of the Amazons.[20]

The excessive terms (by the standard of non-polemical Renaissance prose) of Bacon's unruly vision – "violations and perversions" – reveal the persistent and always present threat posed by the subordinate categories in his hierarchies. Bacon's claim that the reign of women is "itself void, and to be suppressed," at once acknowledges the presence and threatening power of a female Other, simultaneously negated as "void" and, paradoxically, constructed as powerful enough to require suppression. In this revealing contradiction, Bacon demands subordination of the very female authority he describes as an absence, thus implicitly acknowledging an even greater threat posed by "the reign of women." Furthermore, Bacon's vision of a static social order derived from "the laws of nature created by God" (this is invoked by Bacon later in the dialogue) is undermined by the tension and violence of the terms he requires to express that order: a supposedly immutable social order is uneasily dependent on the subordinate terms that threaten it – the "void" that names the rule of women over men.[21]

Near the end of "An Advertisement," Bacon extends his sense of social order based on the "law of nature" to include the opposition between Christians and "barbarians." Drawing from Genesis, he presents religious unity in terms of linguistic communication: "for as the confusion of tongues was a mark of separation, so the being of one language is a mark of union" (35). This vision of unity is described as "the supreme and indissoluble consanguinity and society between men in general." The triangularity involving relations between men figured through a construction of a dangerous Other (women or non-Christians) is once again at work here as Bacon assumes that social order begins from the "union" among men. In effect, language that produces communication (rather than "confusion") is the medium that unites men in consanguineous bonds. Yet another hierarchy is thus added to those mentioned above: "one language" is set over and against the "confusion of tongues." The latter, in the form of misprision or what Bacon calls the "idols of the marketplace," always haunts and potentially subverts the former.

By taking all of these hierarchies in relation to one another, we see that Bacon has assumed an implicit analogy between the purity of language and a masculine purity of blood as the dual sources of a specifically aristocratic and masculine concept of social order. The "consanguineous bonds" among men who should rule are forged by patrimony, the subordination of "slaves," and the communicative power of "one language" – very much the conditions of the homosocial network in which the author operated. In Bacon's vision, proper language (frequently called "the chaste and perfect style") disseminates power, knowledge and authority between men, but only in so far as it can protect itself from the threatening mediation of women and the "confusion of tongues." This point corresponds to the terms of Bacon's attacks on earlier forms of scientific knowledge, which he repeatedly describes as both lacking masculine potency and as caught up in sophism. Aristotle "left nature untouched and inviolate, and dissipated his energies in comparing, contrasting and analysing popular notions about her."[22] In "The Masculine Birth of Time," Aristotle is "the worst of sophists stupified by his own unprofitable subtlety, the cheap dupe of words."[23] The trope that functions to unite these discourses is purity, evoked in the service of protecting boundaries against pollution. Bacon calls for a purity of knowledge that takes the form of his inductive method of scientific investigation, a masculine, aristocratic purity that must continuously suppress its subordinates, and a linguistic purity that is manifested in his nostalgia for those "primitive" languages (Chinese characters, hieroglyphics) that supposedly signified transparency.

But pure, linguistic dissemination must always, in the Renaissance male imagination, "pass through" women. As Evelyn Fox Keller points out, Bacon's metaphors for the dissemination of knowledge compensate for what he perceives to be the unfortunate necessity of involving women in procreation; purity functions tropologically as a way of avoiding the mediation of the female – it is "a way of doing without the mother."[24] This unfortunate mediation leads Bacon to a fantasy of male parthenogenesis that appears in "The Masculine Birth of Time" as a kind of homoerotic dissemination and conception. It also leads to an explicit distrust of figurative language, so often construed in the Renaissance as feminine. Such a threat once again shapes Bacon's formulation of order later in "An Advertisement": "Now if there is such a tacit league or confederation [between men]," he continues, "sure it is not idle; it is against somewhat, or somebody: who should they be? Is it against wild beasts? or the elements of fire and water? No, it is against such routs and shoals of people, as have utterly degenerate[d] from the laws of nature; as have in their very body and frame of estate a monstrosity . . ." (35–36). Bacon explicitly represents Christianity's Other in the very same terms he has previously employed to describe rule by women, adding "monstrosity" and "degenerate," both terms frequently applied to women (and, ironically, to sodomites) in a variety of pamphlets and sermons from the early seventeenth century. The "chaste and perfect style" for which Bacon campaigned is thus hardly a disinterested stylistic choice; rather, it reflects and discursively supports a broad ideological framework that includes early modern construction of gender, female desire and the "necessary" privilege of the upper classes.

Following this line of thinking, it is evident that Bacon's prose and his meditations on language are shaped by conditions quite different from those that preoccupy many studies of his style and poetics. Morris Croll's inclusion of Bacon in the "anti-Ciceronian movement" as one committed to objective "scientific realism" obscures the extent to which Baconian prose – precisely in its attempt to purify language of its Ciceronian excess – is deeply embedded in the politics of his scientific enterprise and more generally in the preservation of aristocratic and patriarchal prerogatives. In this sense, neither the production of knowledge nor its written delivery can be said to exist outside of an historically specific ideological network. Indeed, from a different critical perspective, Croll's own claim for Bacon's "virile realism" admits to the specifically masculinist character of Bacon's style.[25]

It is revealing that in the centuries of Baconian scholarship only two recent books have pursued the enormous implications of the sexualized and gendered language in which Bacon formulates his scientific enterprise. Even Foucault's crucial insistence that knowledge is fundamentally linked to forms of discursive and disciplinary power, including his later investigation of the "scientia sexualis," nonetheless does not explicitly explore the knowledge/power dynamic as a specifically gendered phenomenon. Genevieve Lloyd's *The Man of Reason: "Male" and "Female" in Western Philosophy* (1984) and Evelyn Fox Keller's brilliant *Reflections on Gender and Science* (1985), written almost concomitantly, trace the discursive history of western scientific knowledge as profoundly shaped by differing historical constructions of gender and sexuality.[26] Before returning to Bacon's own writings from this perspective, it is worth considering briefly some of the critical assumptions (besides the obvious fact of their anteriority to contemporary feminist analysis) which have enabled Baconian scholarship to maintain its own "purity" from Bacon's deeply sexualized and gendered conceptualization of the new science. This is a particularly notable omission inasmuch as so many studies of Bacon have dwelled extensively on his style and on the function of his rhetorical language – language completely suffused with metaphors about marriage, masculine power and the chastity or promiscuity of a feminized "nature."

It will come as no surprise to point out that before the work of Keller and Lloyd, most studies of Bacon approach his style and use of rhetorical language by way of evaluating whether or not his figures of speech and imagery accurately express his intensions. Brian Vickers' valuable *Francis Bacon and Renaissance Prose*, for example, suggests in his carefully argued methodological introduction that "our analysis of style . . . should consider the relation between the style of a particular passage and, loosely speaking, the argument or overall intention of the whole work, and indeed its degree of excellence."[27] Vickers' commitment to generally humanistic methods and precepts of scholarship is also apparent in his manner of historicizing a writer's language – once again, an intentionalist/expressionist model prevails: "a writer's work can be quite satisfactorily studied on its own or with reference to his own theory of style in so far as he consciously expresses it, but . . . such a study can gain much from viewing its subject in historical terms."[28] In many ways, Vickers argues from within the same framework of linguistic representation as Bacon himself; building on the work of Rosemond Tuve, he asserts that "Bacon's use of imagery corresponds to the traditional pattern in that it is used to express the writer's attitude to his subject in a direct and illuminating way, and is intended to persuade and convince his readers."[29] The operative model of language in Vickers' interpretive strategy is one in which the meaning and value of writing are understood as the direct and transparent communication of a writer's thoughts to his readership; even the most extended, "indirect" metaphors contribute to meaning only if they are vehicles for the author's intent and design, however difficult that intent is to identify. The most fundamental assumption of this model – exemplary of Derrida's discussions of logocentrism – is that subjectivity is anterior to language, thus upholding the authority of the subject who "writes" the world in a way analogous to and legitimated by God's own original inscription. Indeed, Bacon's own nostalgic model for his writing – unavailable since Babel – is Adam's pure and original naming of the things in the world.[30]

No doubt the kind of critical approach Vickers exemplifies promotes a very detailed analysis of many of Bacon's stylistic features, as well as an historical understanding of his place within Renaissance debates over the function of rhetoric and the use of figurative language. But at the same time, by working within a humanistic tradition that understands literary analysis as the discovery of a writer's ability to express his intent to a readership, such an approach reproduces many of the same interpretive categories in which Bacon himself wrote. Consequently, it becomes very difficult to "read against the grain" of Bacon's texts, the results of which is a kind of circularity between writer and critic in which the humanist assumptions of each are mutually validated. When Vickers suggests that Bacon's imagery reveals his subject matter in a "direct and illuminating way," for example, he reproduces Bacon's priority of "matter" over "words" as well as his persistent use of images of light and illumination as metaphors for revealing the dark and hidden secrets of nature. More telling is the way in which Bacon's own masculine author/ity is also reproduced in Vicker's criticism: He refers, for example, to "the potency of this poetic vision" and frequently to Bacon's "mastery of style."[31] As Keller and others have pointed out, "mastery" and "potency" become the key terms not just for Bacon's style but for the new scientist's relationship to nature as well.

And yet, Bacon is perhaps more sensitive to the possibility that writing – especially a highly figurative style – may lead his audience astray than many of his critics, thus potentially undermining the desired authority of the writer/scientist. John C. Briggs points out the "paradox" in Bacon's understanding of rhetorical language between "rhetoric as a theory and practice of communication" and "the idolatrous imagination [that] has misled all rhetoricians and their audiences."[32] Bacon defines the "idols of the marketplace" as "false appearances that are imposed on us by words." When he adds that although "we think we govern our words . . . yet certain it is that words . . . do shoot back upon the understanding of the wisest" (III. 396), the use of "govern" suggests the necessity to control the dangerous possibility that language may precede and thus shape our thoughts – perhaps the most profound threat to humanistic notions of the author/subject. Moreover, if the intended meaning of the writer is potentially lost through the medium of writing, responsibility for understanding is in part transferred to Bacon's readership – a kind of interpretive democracy Bacon could not tolerate.

My point is that we cannot begin to understand the profound ways in which Bacon's prose and his scientific method are embedded in Renaissance constructions of masculine authority until we suspend the kind of admonition W. K. Wimsatt makes against "the carelessness of thinking of words as separable from meaning," which "suggests play with words, disregard of meaning."[33] Instead, we may utilize the strategies of reading developed by much contemporary criticism in order to analyze "the play of words" as a very serious play that dramatizes the conflict between an individual writer's attempts to exercise mastery over language and the ways in which ideologically embedded language already informs individual thought. Bacon's desire to master both nature and language is characterized by his attempt to close the gap between words and meaning – in effect, to *enforce* logocentricity. Bacon's language becomes far more than a conduit for his intentions; it reveals the ideological underpinnings of his scientific project and of his particular construction of masculine authority within a larger historical network. In addition to reproducing

Bacon's own conditions of meaning, through this approach we can also realize what he appears to have feared most in his determination to subjugate imagination and rhetoric to reason and the "proper" use of words.

Baconian science emerges as a way to rediscover an immediacy between the mind, words and nature through a rigorous mastery of both nature and language. Instead of merely discovering such congruences, as Bacon believes an earlier period was able to do, in the new science "the greater reliance should be placed in the mechanical arts, because nature betrays her secrets more fully when in the grip and under the pressure of art than when in enjoyment of her natural liberty."[34] The "secrets" which nature only "betrays" under the coercion of the scientist are the correspondences and similitudes which God originally placed in the world, but which have been subsequently hidden and disguised. At the same time, the model of the new scientist places masculine subjectivity outside of and antagonistic to nature such that his very identity depends on his ability to master "her." As Bacon characteristically writes, "the mind may exercise over the nature of things the authority which properly belongs to it" (IV. 13). The space opened up by Bacon's perception that there is no longer an immediate congruence between the mind, words and nature is ideologically "filled" in his texts by the cultural assumption that man's natural position is one requiring direct manipulation of an historically specific construction of the feminine. By contrast, in his often waged attack on ancient philosophy and science, Bacon states that earlier scientific method "permits one only to clutch at Nature, never to lay hold of her and capture her" (IV. 13).

Understanding the politics of Bacon's new learning thus demands several levels of interpretation. The most apparent is his very deliberate statements in support of the royal prerogative and the preservation of social hierarchy. In terms of monarchy, Bacon construes proper authority as singular rather than plural, and in the case of a ruling gentry, governance should be restricted rather than dispersed. Both of these versions of power and authority are located in an original Father who in turn serves to legitimate different aspects of patriarchal authority. Such an interpretation we may ascribe to Bacon's own political ambitions and, reciprocally, to what we know of his political and social philosophy. However, even though Bacon and some of his critics would see him as the progenitor of a new science, his scientific corpus must also be situated in terms of the ways in which Bacon conceptualizes and articulates his thinking according to a set of assumptions about status and gender that do not necessarily come under the author's conscious evaluation. This level of analysis reaches a further dimension when we realize that Bacon's own concepts of language and style – ostensibly a politically neutral sphere meant to provide the best means of expression – depend upon the very same ideological assumptions as his more explicit politics. On this level, each of the tropes that shape Bacon's concepts of language – purity, immediacy, purgation – function to legitimate sources of authority whose preservation depends on the exclusion and debasement of that which is perceived as threatening. In his very efforts to draw a distinct line between the aristocratic, masculine subject and the "vulgar" or the "feminine," in the employment of these discrete elements as if they formed a mutually supportive confederacy, Bacon's texts reveal an anxious masculine prerogative.

Bacon devotes a considerable amount of his writing to the ways in which the mind seeking true knowledge must circumvent, or perhaps transcend, the illusions fostered by the necessity of understanding and representing the world through language. As any reader of Derrida will note, the paradox of this effort is that Bacon's "desire to eliminate the intervention of words," in Martin Elsky's phrase, can only be carried out by further writing – writing that seeks to strip away the "idols of the marketplace" such that nature can be apprehended purely and without mediation.[35] As I suggested above, Bacon's nostalgia for the innocence of Adamic language and his fascination with Chinese characters and hieroglyphics suggest that his ideal model of language is conceived as a desire to return to an original state of linguistic transparency and purity. Bacon writes in *The Advancement of Learning*, "God hath framed the mind of man as a mirror or glass capable of the image of the universal world, and joyful to receive the impression thereof, as the eye joyeth to receive light" (III. 265). In its most pristine state, the mind possesses a natural correspondence to the world such that an understanding of nature needs only to be discovered or remembered beneath the layers of false appearance and contamination acquired by civilization since its original fall. Language partakes in this system of correspondence and similitude as the means by which the world originally "written" by God can be discovered; consequently, it ought to function as a transparent medium that is homologous to nature. Bacon's new science thus derives from two seemingly contradictory impulses: on the one hand, he presents an epistemological rupture from the errors of the past; on the other, he constructs an imaginary past characterized by a sense of purity among the mind, language and nature. Bacon's use of "instauration" – denoting a new beginning as well as a restoration – implies both of these impulses.

"Knowledge ought to be delivered," he argues, "*in the same method wherein it was invented*" (III. 404, Bacon's emphases). The inductive method is intended to produce such a congruence through reasoning by gradual ascent from the particulars of nature to its most general laws. Bacon's critique of Aristotle, among others, is based on the latter's imposition of forms and categories (including language itself) that do not derive from nature but rather from the scientist himself; as a result, Greek philosophy is "childlike" and "incapable of begetting works."[36] In opposition, Bacon's scientific method and the language by which scientific knowledge is "delivered" allows the scientist to reside "purely and constantly among the facts of Nature" (IV. 19). The "barren" philosophies of the ancients are replaced by Bacon's "fruitful," unmediated relationship between the scientist and nature, a relationship metaphorically construed as a way "to unite [his pupil] with things themselves in a chaste, holy and legal wedlock."[37] Nature is objectified not only as female but more specifically as a chaste bride whose sexual purity is the basis for the propagation of knowledge by Bacon's masculine scientist/ subject. His position toward ancient philosophy and science is thus to construct the past's relationship to nature as impure and adulterated in order to advance his own pure, chaste "marriage" to nature. This strategy parallels Protestantism's claim to return to an original scriptural purity before the corruption of Catholicism. In Protestant histories such as John Foxe's *Acts and Monuments*, the new church needed to clear away centuries of Catholic "mediation" (idolatry, Latin, the clergy, for example) in order to rediscover its pure origin.[38] Bacon proceeds analogously by clearing away the centuries of supposedly impotent science caused by Aristotle and Galen's enslavement by words and superstition.

Bacon's own semiotic theories are directly explored in books two and six of *The Advancement of Learning*, where he discusses the two kinds of signs. The "Notes of Things," also called "the cogitations of things," "are of two sorts": *ex congruo* signs "hath some similitude or congruity with the notion," including hieroglyphics, gestures and emblems; *ad placitum* signs are words "having force only by contract or acceptation," a term similar to Saussure's sense of the arbitrary nature of the sign (IV. 400, 439–440). In the latter case, words are "deficient" according to Bacon because they depend only on convention; elsewhere, he suggests that they are impure because of their public circulation among the "ignorant." In a passage that anticipates Saussure's own argument against the illusion of a "natural" relationship between signifier and signified, Bacon writes that "words are the tokens current and accepted for conceits, as moneys are for values, and that it is fit men be not ignorant that moneys may be of another kind than gold and silver" (III. 402). But while Saussure accepts the necessarily social and conventional aspect of language, Bacon sees it as leading to deception, misrepresentation and finally, social dissolution. This point is emphasized in Bacon's above reference to the steady debasement of English coinage beginning in the reign of Henry VIII, ending the immanent or iconic relationship between monetary signifier and its signified value. Language, according to Bacon, is an analogous symbolic system inasmuch as words have come to possess an assigned rather than intrinsic value; like coins, they are no longer "congruent" with what they represent but instead dangerously related only by a "contract" democratically circulated among the "vulgar."

Bacon begins his dedication to James of the second book of *The Advancement of Learning* by extolling the King's "royal issue, worthy to continue and represent [him] for ever," and by advising that "those who are fruitful in their generations, and have as it were the foresight of immortality in their descendants, should likewise be more careful than other men of the good estate of future times, to which they must transmit their dearest pledges" (IV. 283). In the next paragraph, he turns to the question of "what has hitherto been done by kings and others for the increase and advancement of learning," a question that demands "a style active and masculine, without digressing or dilating" (IV. 284). In these brief quotations, three elements of Bacon's project coalesce: the virtue of patrilineal descent, the importance of the pursuit of knowledge and the "masculine style" in which that knowledge should be disseminated. Bacon's construction of these elements as validating one another depends upon analogous and particularly early modern constructions of the "feminine" or "female" as a necessary but potentially dangerous figure of mediation; consequently, according to this logic, patrilineal descent requires the chastity of wives, knowledge is represented as the mastery of "chaste" nature, and proper writing – frequently extolled by Bacon for its "chastity and brevity" – should not be misled by figurative or "dilating" language. In Bacon's writing, each of these three privileged terms owes its identity to the "feminine principle" which it repeatedly seeks to exclude, avoid or appropriate. But ironically, Bacon's own "dilations" and digressions on the importance of these terms at the same time reveal their tenuous dependence on a masculine construction of the "feminine" as threatening in the first place. In other words, the deliverance and representation of knowledge reproduces and reinforces the exclusions and anxieties apparent in its manifest claims for the "natural" dominion of man over nature.

Bacon's attitudes toward rhetoric and figurative language are not unique among the many treatises on the subject printed in the second half of the sixteenth century. As I described in my discussion of Burton's *Anatomy*, the early modern period witnesses an increasing suspicion of

what Puttenham calls the "lengthy transport" of metaphorical signification to convey intended meaning.[39] Richard Sherry's sense in 1550 that
metaphors "sheweth the thynge before oure eyes more evidently" utilizes
an older tradition of iconic language: metaphors were considered pictures
of ideas to which words possessed an intrinsic connection. The writings
of both Bacon and Shakespeare, over fifty years later, indicate the extent
to which by the end of the century and following, such a connection had
become either a nostalgic ideal or the source of considerable anxiety.
While Shakespeare's plays often provocatively explore this sense of a
"fallen" language, Bacon and others appear determined to insure, if only
by authorial vigilance and mastery, the connection between words and
things. As I suggested earlier, this effort often seeks to naturalize itself by
drawing from other discourses; in effect, linguistic transparency now
requires an ideological support system. This determination is more and
more frequently manifested by representing metaphors, in their capacity
to mislead signification, as feminine.

In *The Artes of Logicke and Rhetorike* (1584), Dudley Fenner describes
the proper use of metaphors in terms of courtship and marriage: "This
change of signification muste bee shamefest, and as it were maydenly,
that it may seeme rather to be led by the hand to another signification,
then to be driven by force unto the same. Yet sometimes this fine manner
of speech swerveth . . ."[40] It is ironic that Fenner's metaphor for
metaphorical transport, at least to twentieth-century readers, considerably complicates the "change" from one signification to another such
that the transport is perhaps more compelling than the final "signification." Fenner's metaphor draws a parallel between a metaphorical
transition and a woman's passage from maidenhood to marriage. Proper
meaning or "signification" is achieved if the "father" benevolently leads
(rather than forces) his chaste "daughter" to the hand of her "husband."
One could further suggest that metaphorical "change of signification" is
represented by Fenner as the dangerous possibility of female volition and
desire that must be controlled in its moments of temporary freedom,
something like the liminal space opened up in the forest scenes of *A
Midsummer Night's Dream* before the play returns, slightly altered, to the
patriarchal authority of Athens.

Patricia Parker's *Literary Fat Ladies*, from which my analysis of
Fenner's metaphor is drawn, provides an extensive and fascinating
account of how women are "figured in discussions of rhetoric in ways
which evoke links with the 'far-fetched,' with uncontrollable and even
indecent garrulity or speaking out, and with the 'movable' transportability of certain tropes." "What is even more important," she adds,
"than the linking of women with the deceit, doubleness, or movable

nature of tropes, and the social as well as sexual implications of such transportability . . . is the question of the position of women in relation to the ordering of discourse itself."[41] Part of Parker's answer to this question involves the Renaissance notion – taken largely from Aristotle's discussions of generation – that language ought to order and discipline "female" matter: she cites Thomas Wilson's *Rule for Reason* for its "emphasis on disposition as shaping and bringing order and rule to a 'matter' which . . . calls attention to affinities between this language of the control of matter in discourse and the reigning gynecological conception of the male as 'disposing' the female in generation, 'wandering,' uncontrollable, and excessive *materia*."[42]

The analogy Parker draws between the discursive and scientific control over "feminized" matter deeply informs Bacon's writing of the new science: the "chaste and perfect style" is designed to reproduce "the same method wherein [knowledge] was invented" (III. 404). Once again, the original Word of God or its earthly manifestation in Adamic naming is the idealized form of "delivery" to which the scientist should aspire. When Bacon considers the question of the origin of the world, he follows Plato and Aristotle's representation of matter as a "common harlot" that is "entirely despoiled, shapeless, and indifferent to forms" (IV. 320). After having rejected a number of pre-Christian explanations for the creation of the world, Bacon suggests that "Pan [the nature of things] is the offspring of the *Divine Word*, through the medium of confused matter" (IV. 320). The creation of nature is understood as a form of divine writing, a discursive ordering of nature through the "medium" of chaos, or "matter." Moreover, God's writing of the world transforms matter, the "despoiled harlot," into chaste nature, the same paradigm of "rightful" masculine domination over nature that underscores Bacon's own formulation of the new science. One might say that Bacon's project is legitimated by the extent to which it reproduces this original model of creation; in both instances, the chastity of nature is insured through its discursive and scientific "disposition" by a masculine subject. Indeed, Genevieve Lloyd describes the relationship between the Baconian scientist and nature as the "right kind of nuptial dominance" in which scientific knowledge requires and produces "by force" a kind of sexual restraint in nature.[43] In Bacon's words, "nature betrays her secrets more fully when in the grip and under the pressure of art than when in her natural liberty."[44]

When this paradigm of masculine domination is played out in terms of the proper language of science, more is at stake than Bacon's insistence on a "chaste and perfect style." Rhetoric is understood as potentially "uncontrollable" not just because of its lengthy transport but additionally because it is, according to Bacon, "subservient to the imagination" (IV. 454). In this sense, imagination is the agency of "feminine" rhetoric that must be controlled by "masculine" reason. Bacon writes that "it is no small dominion which imagination holds in persuasions that are wrought by eloquence; for when by arts of speech men's minds are soothed, inflamed, and carried hither and thither, it is all done by stimulating the imagination till it becomes ungovernable, and not only sets reason at nought, but offers violence to it, partly by blinding, partly by incensing it" (IV. 406). Imagination is represented in erotic terms as a kind of siren that threatens to seduce and overthrow masculine self-control; in this sense, ungoverned imagination dangerously effeminizes men because it makes them like women. Here we might recall Burton's characterization of the melancholy man as effeminized by his flights of fancy and imaginative excess. In Bacon's case, metaphorical language is to blame; for Burton, the danger derives from the inescapable fluidity of the male body. The fact that both nonetheless partake in and depend upon these "feminine" perils once again exhibits the process of con-structing as feminine those characteristics that must be purged from one's (male) self.

In effect, Baconian rhetoric thus functions according to two competing impulses: either it is enslaved by imagination, in which case it is debased by its connection to the body, female sexuality and deception; or, alternatively, it is ennobled by the proper governance of reason. In the former case, rhetoric calls attention to the mediational aspect of language linked to post-lapsarian corruption; in the latter, rhetoric is a means of illumination modeled after God's inscription of the world. "Man still strives," writes Bacon, "to renew and reintegrate himself in those benedictions of which by his fault he has been deprived" (IV. 441). This dualistic understanding of rhetoric reflects and legitimates Bacon's representations of nature as possessing a great deal of power that must be carefully controlled in the name of scientific knowledge. Similarly, rhetoric has the "power to move men's wills," but only in the proper, "upward" direction if one is able to "apply and recommend the dictates of reason to the imagination" (IV. 455). Bacon's famous and often quoted definition of rhetoric – "to apply Reason to Imagination for the better moving of the will" – is thus hardly as disinterested a statement as critics of Bacon's style have frequently assumed.

Furthermore, if we take "will" to mean both violation and desire, it becomes clear that the masculine subject position is shaped by and dependent upon the construction of objects of knowledge and truth that remain elusive such that the Baconian scientist is always *in pursuit*. Such a model functions on several levels in Bacon's work: it begins to explain the characteristically "unfinished" nature of his corpus; it informs his discursive representations of nature as just beyond the "grasp" of the scientist such that Bacon's writing is always about "process" rather than "content," in Timothy J. Reiss' words; and finally, this model pervades Bacon's wrestling with the problem of rhetoric and signification inasmuch as he depicts language as continuously in pursuit of signification, rarely as consummated.[45] The emergence of a masculine subjectivity in Bacon's writing is thus motivated by the cooperative functions of purity and desire: the former is marked by exclusion and purgation, while the latter perpetually seeks to produce an external reality which, in turn, will reproduce the subject *as subject* in pursuit of knowledge and domination over the world he has constructed. Both are formulas for anxiety if only because they are constantly defending themselves against an enemy they have constructed.

Although many commentators on Bacon may be accurate in representing his ostensible project as, in Benjamin Farrington's phrase, "the subduing of nature to the satisfaction of the necessities of mankind," Bacon himself frequently underscores the extent to which epistemological satisfaction is elusive.[46] In *The Advancement of Learning*, he suggests that "the two principal senses of inquisition, the eye and the ear, affirmeth that the eye is never satisfied with seeing, nor the ear with hearing" (III. 264). This is due to the fact that in Bacon's formulation nature frustrates her inquisitors by withholding "her secrets." "The greatest obstacle which a man meets with," writes Bacon, "is his inability to vex matter unrestrainedly without permitting some part of it to escape" (V. 428). This particular aspect of Bacon's figuring of Nature as the scientist's chaste wife is shaped by the pervasive anxiety, often expressed in popular drama and treatises on jealousy and cuckoldry, in which men frequently acknowledge that despite continual surveillance and scrutiny, they can never be certain of their wives' fidelity. Such an anxiety toward unrestrained female desire is reproduced in Bacon's demand for nature to be "chaste" through a kind of inductive "ocular proof," to borrow a key term from *Othello*. Since knowledge is figured in Baconian science as process and pursuit rather than as consummation, nature must in turn be constructed as at least partially resistant to the scientist's interrogation and manipulation. This construction of external reality as never fully knowable in turn produces a masculine subject position marked by perpetual desire and, consequently, by the instability and anxiety that derives from the perceived need to control what is always elusive. Once again, the deep irony of this model is that the deferral of masculine satisfaction is the necessary result of a masculinist construction of nature and scientific method in the first place.

When Bacon imagines knowledge satisfied, it is only as a kind of ephemeral, physical pleasure derived from a concupiscent involvement with nature rather than the "chaste and holy wedlock" he so frequently invokes for the new science. Only when nature is "under constraint and vexed" rather than left "free and at large" does Bacon's scientist arrive at true knowledge; as such, "knowledge that tendeth but to satisfaction" is figured as a "courtesan" (III. 222). By privileging the figure of knowledge derived from nature as a chaste wife rather than as a "courtesan," Bacon's scientist is in the position of observing and interpreting – not without some anxiety – the "female" object of his desire.

Moreover, as I suggested above, Bacon's representation of the proper and most "fruitful" relationship between the scientist and nature echoes an emergent Protestant valorization of women as chaste wives rather than as virgins. He is thus poised between two extreme traditions: an earlier idealization of female virginity (recall that Aristotle, according to Bacon, "left nature herself untouched and inviolate") that does not produce generation, on the one hand, and a representation of "feminine" nature as deceitful and promiscuous, on the other. Neither relationship produces what Bacon calls in *The Masculine Birth of Time* "the legitimate passing on of knowledge."[47] Instead, the proper dissemination of knowledge between men requires the "chaste and lawful marriage" so frequently advocated in Protestant marriage and conduct manuals of the late sixteenth and early seventeenth centuries. Bacon's dissemination of knowledge thus requires the same regulation of female sexuality that was supposed to insure legitimate patrimony and inheritance. As *The Masculine Birth of Time* further reveals, this dissemination between men is specifically from one generation to the next in the figurative form of patrilineal inheritance. "My dear, dear boy," Bacon writes to the passive figure in this dialogue, "what I plan for you is to unite you with the things themselves in a chaste, holy and legal wedlock; and from this association you will secure an increase beyond all hopes and prayers of ordinary marriage, to wit, a blessed race of Heroes or Supermen."[48] The chaste marriage Bacon promises is secured by the proper dissemination of knowledge from the scientist to the boy and reciprocally, the dissemination of knowledge between men is secured by female chastity. But what emerges from this figuring of female chastity, in an age where paternity uncertainty is a commonplace sentiment and a biological fact, is of course an increased anxiety on the part of men.

It becomes clear in Bacon's writing that properly focused desire aspires to a kind of spiritual knowledge whose model is God's original writing/ creating of the world. Inasmuch as complete knowledge of God's forms is not only impossible but sinful (as a version of Faustian pride), Bacon transposes his model of perpetual desire for the knowledge of nature onto a vertical axis in which the object becomes knowledge of God. This transposition is made evident in the first book of *The Advancement of Learning* where Bacon argues that "in all other pleasures [except learning] there is satiety, and after they be used, their verdure departeth; which sheweth well they be but deceits of pleasure, and not pleasures; and that it was the novelty which pleased, and not the quality" (III. 317). Bacon immediately follows this passage by suggesting "that by learning man ascendeth to the heavens and their motions, where in body he cannot come . . . let us conclude with the dignity and excellency of knowledge and learning in that whereunto man's nature doth most aspire; which is immortality and continuance; for to this tendeth genera-tion, and raising of houses and families" (III. 318).

In the latter passage, the sacred and the secular commingle in mutual validation: knowledge produced from the scientist's "marriage" to chaste nature leads man to God; and reciprocally, aspiration to divine knowl-edge validates Bacon's figuring of nature as a chaste wife over which man possesses "natural" dominion. Any satisfaction of knowledge is tainted by the fact that it derives from an impure association with "promis-cuous" nature; at the same time, complete knowledge of God must remain just beyond the reaches of moral man. In effect, Bacon can only imagine masculinity in *pursuit* of knowledge; "satiety" or consummation would mark the death of the masculine, desiring subject.

Finally, we can return once more to the homologous realm of Bacon's language of the new science in order to suggest that a similar economy of desire functions in terms of writing as well as in the pursuit of knowledge. Bacon's nostalgic desire for the linguistic transparency of Adamic language, Chinese characters and hieroglyphics in the "de-livery" of knowledge can never be fully actualized, yet the scientist "by force of will" can begin to approximate this ideal state if he sufficiently cleanses his mind and masters the always imminent revolt of his own imagination and affections. The Baconian subject's "will" (as desire and volition) is produced in the act of subduing those elements of language which mediate between the mind and writing, or between the facts of nature and their "delivery" in language. As we have seen, Bacon's "plain style" is very much a phallogocentric fantasy inasmuch as these forms of mediation are repeatedly cast as "feminine" and as threatening to a social and political hierarchy Bacon depicts as if it were natural. Such an economy is reproduced in Bacon's call for the mastery of "feminine" nature by man's knowledge; in both cases, the "feminine" principle is granted considerable power, which in turn positions a masculine subject uneasily and perpetually in pursuit of something he cannot completely subdue.

"If you are wise," Bacon writes in *The Advancement of Learning*, "seek something to desire; for to him who has not some special object of pursuit all things are distasteful and wearisome" (IV. 487). Bacon's "object of pursuit" is repeatedly articulated as a mastery of nature that leads to immortality: "the entrance into the kingdom of man, founded on the sciences, [is] not much other than the entrance into the kingdom of heaven" (IV. 69). But this object of desire and knowledge does not exist independent of the economy of desire that produces it. That economy is thoroughly embedded in Renaissance figurations of "the feminine" as the "ground" upon which masculine knowledge and power is built and propagated. By insisting on the chastity of nature, the regulation of metaphorical excess and the subjugation of imagination by reason, we can understand this economy as staged in Bacon's writing through the anxious exclusion and subjugation of the possibilities of "feminine" agency.

Bacon's distrust of the mediational aspect of language additionally conditions and shapes his formulation of a pure, aristocratic body. This argument relies on the early modern sense of language as both "the instrument of society," in Ben Jonson's phrase, and a model or analogy for society, especially as it was embodied in the book.[49] When Thomas Wilson discusses similitudes, as I mentioned in chapter one, he understands the relationships between words as corresponding to pre-existent relationships in the world: tropes and figures were invented because things already corresponded to one another. Now it is possible to argue that the idea of language as corresponding to the world was giving way to the more familiar (to us) sense of language as a signifying medium during the period of Bacon's life; indeed, this duality seems to preoccupy Shakespeare considerably. But however nostalgic this model may be by the early seventeenth century, there still exists the at least residual idea that *how* language means in the early modern period is already a social and thus political issue. This is simply another way of stating what I have been arguing throughout this chapter: for Bacon to dwell on the transport from a word to its sense is simultaneously to ask whether or not the world is inherently ordered. An example of this concern in Shakespeare's drama occurs in the second part of *Henry IV*, where the voice of "Rumour" opens the play in order to represent the breakdown or unreliability of linguistic transport. Thus Bacon is not explaining linguistic communication through his analogy to the social order – that analogy is already in place. The question is what *sort* of communication or dissemination best exemplifies or embodies the vision of order Bacon embraces. His theories of language consequently embody and seek to authorize a particular understanding of the social hierarchy – one in which, among other things, governance should be the prerogative of the few.

Thus, in addition to the threat posed by feminine, figurative language, Bacon also insists that language should avoid contamination from its circulation among the "multitude." If language circulates as freely as public currency, the authority of those like Bacon to regulate meaning is dangerously compromised. At the same time, the threat posed by women is linked to the threat posed by the multitudes since proper linguistic dissemination must avoid any kind of dependence upon those assigned to subordinate status. Any form of circulation through "feminine" meta-phoricity or by way of popular convention contaminates Bacon's notion of truth and displaces the "natural" authority of those fit to disseminate that truth. The enforcement of transparent language, the "plain and simple style," thus provides a model and method of excluding or circumventing a broader, more participatory form of power and authority.

In *Thoughts and Conclusions on the Interpretation of Nature*, and frequently elsewhere, Bacon suggests that the "idols of the marketplace" owe their corruption to the fact of their circulation among the "vulgar": "Words are a kind of currency, which reflect vulgar opinions and preferences, for they combine or distinguish things according to popular notions and acceptations, which are for the most part mistaken or confused."[50] Bacon's allegiance to what we might call intellectual elitism is not at all surprising in such a hierarchical culture, especially given his own privileged birthright and the extent to which his fortunes often rested on his ability to preserve royal authority in the face of the Commons' challenges. Indeed, part of Bacon's project is to lay claim to the privileges of birth by advancing his own intellectual and political status. More telling are the instances in which Bacon's rhetoric belies a fear of any power and authority deriving from a multitudinous rather than singular source – a fear, in other words, that the actual practice of language may not live up to the theoretical model he demands.

In the *Aphorisms*, for example, having again stated that "words are imposed according to the apprehensions of the vulgar," Bacon adds that "words plainly force and *overrule* the understanding, and throw all into confusion, and lead men away into numberless empty controversies and ideal fancies" (IV. 55, my emphasis). In order to see the underlying distinction between singular and plural sources of authority, consider an earlier statement made around the time Bacon's fortunes under James were just beginning to be realized: "the word, sacred, hath been attributed to kings because of the conformity of a monarchy with a divine Majesty: never to a senate of people."[51] Words that acquire their meanings according to custom and popular currency are set in opposition to the King's embodiment of the divine word; once again, Bacon invokes proximity to God as a kind of logocentric basis of legitimacy for his own delivery of knowledge. Appointed Solicitor-General in 1607, Bacon's political activities would increasingly be committed to supporting the endangered royal prerogative, often according to a principle that may be described somewhat paradoxically as a pragmatic defense of the divine right of kings. Whether out of political conviction or personal aggrandizement, both Bacon's service to the Crown and his formulations of the new science were inseparable and often mutually validating projects. And the political vision he supports in this service appears under siege by the "multitudes" – by the capacity of language to mislead and misrepresent, to stir "idle fancies" and the imagination rather than to promote reason.

Contrary to his own project, Bacon often represents the old science as governed by popular belief and superstition. In *The Great Instauration* he argues that it was based on "the judgment of the time and the multitude" such that "if any contemplations of a higher order took light anywhere, they were presently blown out by the winds of vulgar opinion" (IV. 15). If in this example words and popular judgment mediate between the human mind and the truth of nature, Bacon additionally argues in a number of his texts that Aristotle's formulation of *a priori* categories "made us slaves to words," in effect preventing the scientist's direct apprehension of nature.[52] In this remark on Aristotle, Bacon's objection is not so much that people in general are slaves to words, but that the *wrong* people ("us") are. In both cases, linguistic mediation is understood in political terms as the "unnatural" overthrow of authority based on the primacy of reason; in other terms, mediation usurps the proper place of reason.

Indeed, Bacon's theories of language often seem shaped by the very metaphors he uses to represent them – metaphors drawn repeatedly from fearful visions of disobedience, social disorder and political rebellion. This point becomes strikingly clear in his discussions of rhetoric in *The Advancement of Learning*: "For we see that the government of reason is assailed and disordered in three ways: either by the illaqueation [OED: "entrapping in argument"] of sophisms, which pertains to Logic; or by the juggleries of words, which pertain to Rhetoric; or by the violence of the Passions, which pertains to Ethics" (IV. 455). Bacon develops the last point in the same text: "if the affections themselves were brought to order, and pliant and obedient to reason, it is true there would be no great use of persuasions and insinuations to give access to the mind, but naked and simple propositions and proofs would be enough. But the affections do on the contrary make such secessions and raise such mutinies and seditions . . . that reason would become captive and servile" (IV. 456). In this passage, Bacon casts the struggle between oligarchy and an early modern version of democracy (and by extension, in his own mind, between king and parliament) as an opposition between "reason" and disobedient "affections." In terms of language, "naked and simple propositions" should, in theory, retain a natural supremacy over the "persuasions and insinuations" that dictate the capricious loyalty exhibited by the populace in, for example, Shakespeare's *Julius Caesar*. And, as we have seen, when Bacon imagines sedition, he attaches the same terms of linguistic misuse ("Passions," "juggleries of words" and "affections") to the unruly multitude as he does to women. Indeed, it often seems that the gendered hierarchy is subsumed by Bacon's anxieties about status. Far from a disinterested stylistic choice, Bacon's "plain style" supports his vision of social order against a very poignant sense of potential insurrection that might rise from any of the bottom terms in his analogous set of social hierarchies.

Furthermore, as Bacon suggests elsewhere in a passage borrowed from Aristotle, "the mind has over the body that commandment which the lord has over a bondsman [and] reason has over the imagination that commandment which a magistrate has over a free citizen" (IV. 406). The subordinate elements in Renaissance social hierarchies are typically figured as corporeal and irrational elements of the imagination. Citizens, women and parliament should therefore naturally obey the reason inherent in a male aristocracy headed by the king. Since the opposition between reason and imagination is so fundamental to language, Bacon's position is an implicit claim for lucidity as the basis of aristocratic, masculine and absolutist authority. Even though in practice aristocratic and monarchical authority were often at odds, Bacon links the two as supportive forms of oligarchic government over and against the threat of the "multitudes," that large and unruly body for whom language is the medium of imagination, ideal fancy and irrationality rather than the single authority of reason and logocentric purity.

In the preface to *The Great Instauration*, Bacon makes no less a claim for his philosophical and scientific project than the "total reconstruction of sciences, arts, and all human knowledge" (IV. 8). Bacon's ambitious project both initiates and records what a number of scholars in different disciplines have generally understood as a profound epistemological transformation in early modern Europe around the beginning of the seventeenth century. This transformation newly conceives the relationship between man and nature such that the latter is objectified "to the eye of human understanding," in Bacon's own words, as "a labyrinth; presenting as it does on every side so many ambiguities of way, such deceitful resemblances of objects and signs, natures so irregular in their lines, and so knotted and entangled" (IV. 18). If an earlier conception of the natural world revealed resemblances and similitudes as divinely ordered "signatures" – Foucault's "prose of the world" – Bacon's position leaves the enforcing act of human knowledge and interpretation as the basis for establishing order among nature's "deceitful resemblances of objects and signs."[53] Nature is thus cast in an antagonistic relationship to human knowledge; the former is a potentially "deceitful" body that must be controlled and manipulated – even penetrated – in order to reveal its truths. Once nature is constructed in this fashion, Bacon's conceptualization of the new science is inevitably shaped by other, central discourses of the early modern period which also represent contestatory relationships based on domination and subordination: specifically, the inseparable discourses of gender and status difference. But more than merely exerting a shaping influence, gender and status both limit *and* enable the ways in which Bacon could conceive his "total reconstruction of sciences, arts and all human knowledge." The enabling aspect of this dynamic allows Bacon's scientific project to appear "natural" and inevitable through its appropriation of a supposedly immutable social formation.

However, the rhetoric in which Bacon represents the new science, as well as his own theories of language and style, suggest anything but an immutable social formation whose divisions may be taken as natural. Instead, as I have argued, Bacon's attempts to legitimate his own enterprise, his efforts to enforce a distinct line between the aristocratic, masculine subject and the "vulgar" or the "feminine," reveal in their most authoritative moments an anxious masculine prerogative whose preservation depends on the exclusion and debasement of that which is perceived as threatening.

Purity is the operative trope for each of the positive terms in the hierarchies that govern Bacon's understanding of the scientific enterprise and the language in which it should be represented. As a result, Bacon's new scientific knowledge may be read as a defense of masculine, aristocratic purity against potential contamination from the "vulgar," from women and "feminine" passivity, and from pluralistic rather than singular sources of authority. Similarly, he argues for a pure and simple style of writing in order to maintain the authority of those who should "properly" disseminate knowledge. But the "paradox of the search for purity," as Mary Douglas points out, "is that it is an attempt to force experience into logical categories of non-contradiction."[54] Indeed, Bacon enforces logic and reason as the "natural" agents of his entire enterprise, but it is an enterprise whose agitated categories are always tenuously balanced against the possibility of their contamination and dissolution, an inevitable result of the fact that the privileged categories are themselves defined by and thus dependent upon their oppositional terms.

Although Douglas offers perhaps a universal model of analysis, any application of her terms requires close attention to historically specific constructions of purity and contamination, normal and aberrant. And while it is true that every culture constructs its personal and collective identities by marking such distinctions, it is no less true that every culture fills these categories with its own entities differently valued: what is pure in one culture may be impure in another. Bacon's science is very much a product of the social tensions and contradictions of Jacobean England – it is shaped by the social complexities and anxieties that resulted from that period's re-negotiation of the status of women and its resultant concern with female chastity, by the shifting landscape of a social hierarchy whose degrees were fluid and often indeterminate, and by the monarch's tense relations to a Commons that steadily encroached upon the royal prerogative. By tracing the specific historical condition of Bacon's new science, we discover the origins of western culture's belief in our assumed dominion over nature as well as the formative terms of an anxious masculine subjectivity that knows itself only in the act of subordinating the Others it constructs.

3   Publishing chastity: Shakespeare's "The Rape of Lucrece"

In this chapter my discussion is organized around the circulation of three critical figures in the rhetoric of early modern masculinity: honor, publication and desire. In a specifically poetic context, I will look closely at the function of these figures as the bases for Shakespeare's representation and critique of masculinity in his early poem, "The Rape of Lucrece." In a broadly cultural context, I will consider how the poem's preoccupations and problems rehearse several distinctively Elizabethan discursive practices and belief systems involving honor among men as an often contradictory basis of male identity. By moving simultaneously in both directions, my discussion enacts the reciprocal circulation (rather than rigid demarcation) between the aesthetic and social which is especially characteristic of this period. But it also enacts a series of analogous reciprocities between: private and public spheres, private reading and public declaration, the enclosed and the *dis*closed, domestic space and the social arena, and finally, between what might be abstractly called inherent and circulated value. My arguments throughout this chapter thus reside at the contradiction between a cultural imperative to mark such binary differences and the impossibility of doing so; it interrogates, in this sense, some of the culture's *interstitial* anxieties. Lucrece herself poses a version of this question as she gazes forlornly at a mural depicting one of the West's most influential and potent myths – the story of Troy: "Why should the private pleasure of some one / Become the public plague of so many?"[1]

I intend the term "honor" to embrace all its multivalent significations in the early modern period, including often synonymous words such as reputation, credit, fame and opinion. Although all of these terms are used for both men and women, they nearly always circulate around sexuality (specifically virginity and chastity) in reference to women, for whom chastity and honor are virtually synonymous. By distinction, the range of referents for masculine honor is considerably more broad.[2] It perhaps goes without saying that in the early modern period, honor (in men) and chastity (in women) are the most definitive attributes of identity. But it is also true – and herein lies one potential source of anxiety – that both attributes are assigned by others rather than inherent, matters of public opinion rather than intrinsic possessions. Of course, this is simply to state the obvious: that identity is a social construction, conferred rather than innate. Still, it is not always realized that this formula rests on a paradox, or at least a possible tension: one *is* one's reputation, but one's reputation must derive from others. Since, in the early modern period, masculine identity is typically dependent upon and figured through female chastity (or its absence), this paradox is frequently the cause of considerable anxiety. Husbands are dependent on their wives' reputation for chastity – that is, dependent on something ultimately beyond their control, despite considerable effort to the contrary.

The second operative figure in my analysis – "publication" – also functions in several ways. On a literal level, I mean to suggest the material practices of editing, printing and the public circulation of texts as well as, in the case of Shakespeare, writing supported by a relatively private relationship to his patron, the Earl of Southampton. More broadly, I use the term to signify the transition from a private to public sphere – a "making public" that might take several forms of circulation and dissemination as in, for example, Collatine's "publication" of Lucrece's virtue at the outset of the poem, an act which initiates a series of publications of private acts throughout the poem.[3]

My use of "desire" in this triad is neatly delineated in Valerie Traub's recent book, *Desire and Anxiety*. Blending Lacanian psycho-analysis and Foucault's understanding of discursive power, Traub asserts that "desire is always (1) a matter of both minds and bodies; (2) implicated in interpretive networks, signifying systems, discursive fields; and (3) substitutive, founded on a lack, and hence, always the desire for the other."[4] With such a broad definition in mind, desire is no longer just the name for specific attractions to people, or to things; rather, it marks the very basis of culturally constructed subjectivities. "Ultimately one loves one's desires," Nietzsche wrote, "not the desired object."[5] We might take this aphorism to mean that we are most self-aware in the act of desiring – most profoundly ourselves – rather than in the completion of that act. If our forms of desire are also forms of enculturation, desire may be said to embody or "interpellate" indivi-duals, much in the same way Althusser understands the role of ideology: to know oneself as a subject is to recognize oneself and to be recognized as a desiring subject. In this way, we may say that desire is an active agent of ideology.[6]

But if desire motivates, explains and enables human action in a given culture – turns individuals into subjects – it must also threaten and destabilize, since desire is inevitably produced in and by a contradictory discursive field. Desire may be the social "glue" that holds subjects in place, but it is also a potentially anarchic energy that exposes the contradictions beneath the surface, the rents and tears behind a supposedly seamless social fabric. Throughout this book my focus on the circulation of masculine desire in a historical period especially marked by tension and anxiety along gender lines is intended to expose some of these contradictions. By tracking masculine desire – its motivations, directions, objects and consequences – we uncover the places where different ideologies of patriarchy do not fit together, where they conflict with one another to foster the anxieties inherent in early modern patriarchy.[7]

To take a paradigmatic example from Shakespeare's "Lucrece" (one that has also figured in my discussion of Burton's *Anatomy*), masculine desire appears as the supreme example of self-assertive will *and* as the agent of a complete loss of self-control. In other words, masculine desire is exercised in the name of conquest, possession and domination, but it also overthrows reason and leads to destructive excess. Paradoxically, then, desire is simultaneously the energy behind the most active and passive aspects of masculinity. Once again, Shakespeare's sonnet 129 succinctly develops this paradox: desire is "lust in action" (activity) but very quickly becomes "a swallowed bait / On purpose laid to make the taker mad" (passivity).[8] In other words, the desire to possess leads to a state of being possessed by one's desire. Most importantly for my purposes, this masculine "psychomachia," here in the form of an aggressor/victim conflict, is very often "played out" through women. Men project the conflict onto women or onto their relations with women; thus, the now-familiar formula in which love and desire effeminize inasmuch as they overthrow masculine reason; or, conversely, "woman" functions for men as the (transcendent) symbol of self-control in her embodiment of the figure of chastity. In the poem, Lucrece and Lucrece's body become the battleground for this struggle: at first, she is the symbol of Collatine's honor, truth and fortune; then, she is the "site" where Tarquin's psychological war between his reason and lust is played out; and finally, her suicide allows her to function as the transcendent symbol (and origin) of the new, repurified, republican Roman state.[9]

Understood in both their cooperative and antagonistic relations to one another, these three figures – honor, publication and desire – reveal the fundamental contradiction that anxiously manifests itself in Shakespeare's poem. Masculine honor, fame and reputation (and thus identity) require publication among other men; indeed, honor and its cluster of related terms have meaning only if they are publicly circulated, confirmed and celebrated. If female chastity functions as the basis of masculine honor, both terms accrue value only within a public exchange system – they must be published. But the rather obvious problem arises when we see that female chastity must at the same time remain the private possession of men, indeed of women too. A women's chastity should have intrinsic value – in and of itself – but since it functions as the basis for socially conferred identities, it cannot remain a private affair. In terms of masculine honor, the chastity of one's wife must be paradoxically (and indeed, impossibly) confirmed by other men *and* represented as intrinsically valued, published for other men yet controlled exclusively by the publisher, privately owned by the husband yet circulated beyond his dominion. The narrator of "Lucrece" poses this contradiction in the fifth stanza of the poem:

> Beauty itself doth of itself persuade
> The eyes of men without an orator;
> What needeth then apologies be made
> To set forth that which is so singular?   (29–32)

If we add the third term – masculine desire – this unstable paradigm becomes even more viciously circular and inescapable. Since desire is aroused by impediments to its fulfillment, spurred by the prospect of conquest, the publication of chastity – even the idea of chastity alone – contains within it the "seeds" of its own corruption.[10]

The paradigm with which I began – the circulation of honor, publication and desire – derives in part from the foundational influence of Rene Girard's theory of mimetic desire, especially as developed in his early book, *Deceit, Desire and the Novel*. The theory's latest incarnation appears in Girard's later book on Shakespeare, *A Theater of Envy*, in which envy operates as the agent of mimetic rivalry. In his brief discussion of Shakespeare's early awareness and formulation of this model, Girard writes:

The proudest men want to possess the most desirable objects; they cannot be certain that they have done so, as long as empty flattery alone glorifies their choice; they need more tangible proof, the desire of other men, as numerous and prestigious as possible. They must recklessly expose their richest treasure to these desires . . . Like a gambler, [this] anxious desire desperately attempts to rejuvenate itself.[11]

In this brief passage, Girard encapsulates the contradiction behind the self-defeating demand to publish chastity: the desire for individual possession versus the "desire of other men" to confirm the value of those possessions. He also articulates what we might call the addictive quality of this "anxious desire to rejuvenate itself," as if in these matters volition were entirely at the mercy of desire.

But Girard's discussions of Shakespeare consistently move in the opposite direction from my own once this initial paradigm is set in place. *A Theater of Envy* advances Girard's ambition to show that his triangular model of mimetic rivalry is the "fundamental source of human conflict."[12] He additionally measures Shakespeare's genius and dramatic success by the increasing extent to which Shakespeare recognized and depicted this deep structure throughout his career. Girard displays his debt to structuralism by arguing that literature and myth function as particularly sensitive registers of what is truly a theory of human nature, thus preventing historically specific critiques of the way power and authority are distributed among the gender of the players in Girard's triangle. Because Girard's model seeks to display what is "fundamental," it consistently moves toward structural equilibrium, even though its parts involve conflict, aggression and rivalry. As such, systematic or ideological contradictions are largely beyond its scope.

In this critique I am following Eve Sedgwick's discussion of the uses and limitations of Girard's work as developed in the beginning of *Between Men*. Sedgwick points out that "Girard's account, which thinks it is describing a dialectic of power abstracted from either the male/female or the sexual/non-sexual dichotomies, is leaving out of consideration categories that in fact preside over the distribution of power in every known society."[13] Sedgwick wants to particularize the operations of Girard's abstract model by applying it specifically to gender and sexuality. A further specification would take up the categories of gender and sexuality as themselves produced by the triangular model both Girard and Sedgwick promote. Girard's "dialectic of power" does not just describe the way things work; in the specific context of early modern England, we can see now its functions to shape masculine subjectivity in the first place. For my purposes, then, Shakespeare's "Lucrece" is not just a register of triangular desire, nor merely a representation of the exclusion of women from a system of male exchange, but most importantly a text that displays and reveals the contradictions and anxieties of the culture that author(ize)s it on the level of masculine subjectivity itself. Although the cultural work of the poem may be understood as an attempt to stage anxiety in order to contain it through aesthetic form, closure and resolution, my point will be that the resolutions themselves only further reveal the conditions that precipitate further anxieties.

Honor

> Honor therefore ys a certaine testemonie of
> vertue shining of yt self, geven of some man
> by the judgement of good men . . .[14]
>
> –Robert Ashley, "Of Honour" (1596)

[Man] cannot claim for himself ever so little beyond what is rightfully his without losing himself in vain confidence and without usurping God's honour, and thus becoming guilty of monstrous sacrilege.[15] (Jean Calvin, *Institutes*)

The above quotation from Ashley's essay exemplifies what might be called, borrowing from Raymond Williams, the "residual" or traditional notion of honor during the period of Shakespeare's lifetime, while the passage from Calvin represents the "emergent."[16] In the former, honor is the public conferral of virtue among "good" men (presumably men of some status), the socially acknowledged "testemonie" or circulation of virtue characteristic of shame cultures. In the same sentence, however, Ashley states that honor is also the name given to "vertue shining of yt self," as if the term signified an intrinsic quality independent of social assignation. Although one might say that "honor" is merely the linguistic confirmation of previously earned "vertue," it is reciprocally the case that virtue may not exist without its public nomenclature. Ashley himself raises this possibility when he later asks, "For how can vertue stand if you take away honour?"[17] If honor is confirmed publicly and through language, it functions as a signifier whose referent is assigned rather than inherent – this is indeed Shakespeare's critique as carried out in the figure of Falstaff, for whom honor is a mere "word."

Calvin confutes Ashley's notion of honor by suggesting that its reliance on social approbation usurps God's singular authority and thus leads to human vanity. This alternative use of the word is consistent with Puritan claims for the priority of one's conscience over and against obedience to secular authority. In this way of thinking, honor is more likely to be understood as a matter between God and individuals; it can be said to possess an "intrinsic" or private character rather than a social and public one. Or perhaps it is more accurate to say that Calvin and Puritanism internalize social approbation and assign it the name of God.

In any case, both notions of honor represent different strains in the early modern period, sometimes in conflict with one another, and either one could be said to *function* in the service of different political or religious positions. Fulke Greville stages this conflict in his long poem, "An Inquisition Upon Fame and Honor," where he more or less occupies (by the end of the poem) the middle position. On the one hand, honor

("Fame") is little more than human vanity disguised in the cloak of moral conscience:

> For Fame they still oppose even from those grounds,
> That prove as truely all things else as vaine.
> They give their vertues onely as humane bounds,
> And without God subvert to build againe.
> Refin'd *Ideas*, more than flesh can beare,
> All foule within, yet speake as God were
> there.[18]   (stanza 22)

But at the same time, honor may also provide a necessary sustenance, even though it is an entirely human construction:

> Of which three baytes, yet Honour seemes the chiefe,
> And is unto the world, like a goodly weather,
> Which gives the spirits life, the thoughts reliefe,
> Delight, and travell reconciles together:
> So as the Lean'd, and Great, no more admire it,
> Then even the silly Artisans aspire it.   (stanza 2)

Greville thus maintains the importance of socially granted honor, but critiques the idea that it is completely apart from any referent, as Falstaff wryly suggests. And although Greville values the importance of faith above any secular success, he nonetheless recognizes the idealism of Calvin's position in the face of man's inherent weakness, the result of which is an inevitable, pragmatic defense of the traditional version of honor and fame:

> For to be good the world finds it too hard,
> And to be nothing to subsistence is
> A fatall, and unnaturing award;
> So as betweene perfection, and unblisse,
> Man, out of man, will make himself a frame,
> Seekes outward helpe, and borrowes that of Fame.   (stanza 19)

In other words, since it is too difficult to live in the state of "perfection" suggested in Calvin's "intrinsic" version of honor, man "seekes outward help" by constructing a "frame": the system of socially conferred "fame" and reputation published among men. Greville thus wrestles with what he sees as an ideal notion of honor conferred only privately, from within, and a more realistic acknowledgment of the need for worldly recognition. His poem is very much a register of the way Puritan interiority challenged an older conception of public sanction as the basis of identity.

In his statistical study of the usages of honor and its associated words on the English stage, Charles Barber also finds the "beginnings of a tendency for honour to mean an inner conscience rather than an external reward."[19] He locates three definitions of honor and charts the frequency of their appearance on the public stage according to an either "gentry" or "non-gentry" context. Additionally, he adds a separate category for the growing instances of the *reputation* for possessing each of the three definitions. Although Barber's data is drawn exclusively from theatrical texts, he nonetheless provides a useful anatomy of at least public understandings of the word, perhaps at the expense of their religious sense. Despite new evidence of Calvin's sense of honor, Barber maintains that the most important idea circulating around the word at this time is still its knowability – the sometimes slippery concept of reputation. The second most prominent use of honor involves status, privilege and nobility, followed closely by references to honor in terms of women's chastity, construed as both "mental purity and the physical state,"[20] also a matter of perception rather than actuality. Although the third category refers specifically to women's own honor, it is important to realize that the first two categories, both of which refer to honor among men, rely heavily on the reputation of one's wife. Although the different uses of the word circulate in relation to one another, there is still a double standard at work, since wives' honor (chastity) is critical to their husband's reputation, but not the opposite.

Barber demonstrates a steady rise in the use of honor to refer to chastity in women (their own and as reflected upon their husbands) beginning in the first decade of the seventeenth century, where he finds a frequency six times greater than in the 1590s. During the same period, there are considerably fewer references to chastity in non-gentry women on the public stage (for example, in 1611–1620, there are eighty references among gentry and only two among non-gentry) and the numbers remain fairly stable. Barber's explanation seems persuasive: the increase in the use of honor shows "the process whereby the gentry . . . developed a distinctive code of behaviour to mark themselves off from the rest of society, and especially from the professional and commercial classes . . . and from those with puritanical leanings."[21] Barber's statistics may more accurately reveal a representational rather than behavioral pattern, but his general point remains important: honor as indicated and defined by chastity was of primary interest to those of property, and it functioned to distinguish that status from non-propertied classes during a period of increasingly perceived (and actual) threats to status boundaries. In general, masculine honor and female chastity were figures employed more frequently when status delineations were perceived as less secure by those who would most likely feel that insecurity.

Shakespeare's "Lucrece" registers and struggles with these multivalent definitions and functions of honor, providing an aesthetic field in which competing definitions of male and female subjectivity are played out. For example, the poem consistently describes the masculine prerogative of possessing women's chastity (as a commodity) in economic or mercantile terms. If honor is "geven of some man by the judgement of good men," as Ashley wrote, the system in which that judgment is valued is a competitive marketplace. Lucrece's chastity is a "rich jewel he should keep unknown / From thievish ears, because it is his own" (34–35). After the rape, Collatine is the "hopeless merchant of this loss" (1660). This vocabulary is most evident in Collatine's description of his wife during the crucial exchange among the men at the outset:

> For he the night before, in Tarquin's tent,
> Unlock'd the treasure of his happy state;
> What priceless wealth the heavens had him lent
> In his possession of his beauteous mate;
> Reck'ning his fortune at such high proud rate,
> That kings might be espoused to more fame,
> But king nor peer to such a peerless dame.   (15–21)

In this stanza, Lucrece's chastity is represented as a commodity whose value is established in the discursive exchange system between men; Collatine's publication of his "possession" confers his "fortune" at a "proud rate." But at the same time, her chastity is also "lent" by the "heavens," revealing the conflict between intrinsic and socially conferred systems of value. In effect, Collatine paradoxically employs the idea of the intrinsic value of Lucrece's God-given chastity in the social arena, very much the way of the world to which Greville resigns himself. As Nancy Vickers writes in her discussion of the *blazon* in "Lucrece": "Within this economy of competition, of course, wealth is not wealth unless flaunted, unless inspiring envy, unless affirming superiority."[22]

As her chastity is described as "priceless wealth the heavens had him lent," the suggestion is that Collatine has merely borrowed what truly belongs to "the heavens." According to Calvin's understanding of honor, Collatine's appeal to public approbation of his wife's honor in order to validate his own would be a "monstrous sacrilege," since he has usurped God's judgment. Lucrece's chastity should be neither possessed nor published by her husband, nor traded among men; its value is intrinsic. The final couplet underscores this position: although "kings might be espoused to more fame" (the residual definition of honor), Lucrece is a "peerless dame" whose virtues transcend even the highest social rank. According to this logic, Collatine's honor could not be compromised under any circumstances since his wife's chastity cannot be possessed nor acknowledged by anyone other than God.

The tension between these two opposing uses of honor is repeatedly reproduced in the poem's own unresolved conflicts. As Tarquin's "foul desire" begins to overtake him, the world of the poem becomes a rapacious marketplace, replete with militaristic terms, in which Tarquin's desire is instigated and compelled by his acquisitiveness and insatiability. Following a three-stanza blazon describing Lucrece (386–407), "new ambition" is "bred" in Tarquin: "Who, like a foul usurper, went about / From this fair throne to heave the owner out" (412–413). Here the conceit involves Tarquin's desire to usurp Collatine's rightful ownership of Lucrece's "unconquered" (408) body.

The extent of Lucrece's guilt or innocence is measured according to whether her own chastity is defined inside of or apart from this market-place. In regard to this issue, Coppélia Kahn argues that the poem distinguishes between a "materialistic conception of chastity" (the fact of physical pollution) and "a Christian ethic which disregards material circumstances and judges an act wholly according to the motives and disposition of the agent," which in Lucrece's case are completely pure.[23] In the former, Lucrece's honor and chastity are wholly defined in a social, material context, but in the latter, she may be judged according to a transcendent authority. Lucrece does condemn herself according to the former standard, but not by the terms of the latter: "Though my gross blood be stain'd with this abuse, / Immaculate and spotless is my mind" (1655–1666). This opposition reproduces a dualism between mind (or soul) and body: agency can only be judged by God, whereas "material circumstances" are publicly visible and accessible – they are marked by others. Here we have the woman's counterpart to the two versions of honor described at the beginning of this section, at least to the extent that women may have internalized a thoroughly masculine economy. If chastity is the female counterpart to male honor, Lucrece sees herself as guilty in terms of Ashley's "social" definition (even though her "shame" is "invisible") but innocent before God following Calvin's "intrinsic" understanding, as long as she can maintain in her own mind the soul/ body distinction, which at times proves difficult.

Indeed, where Lucrece blames herself, she often invokes terms borrowed from the masculine rhetoric of honor, internalizing its conditions of value in terms of ownership, competition and publication. She describes her chastity as the "treasure stol'n away" (1056), her husband as the lord of "that dear jewel I have lost" (1191), and her verbal and written publication of the crime as intended to "urge my impure tale" (1078). From these examples, it becomes clear that to the extent Lucrece measures herself according to the "public" conception of honor, she believes she is to blame. But her solace lies in the extent to which she can appeal to a Calvinistic conception of honor, to God rather than to others as the ultimate judge. It is the latter version of honor that makes sense of her suicide, since she has sacrificed her body for the preservation of her soul:

> "My honor I'll bequeath unto the knife
> That wounds by body so dishonored.
> 'Tis honor to deprive dishonor'd life,
> The one will live, the other being dead.
> So of shame's ashes shall my fame be bred,
>   For in my death I murder shameful scorn;
>   My shame so dead, mine honor is new born.   (1184–1190)

In this passage, Lucrece's physical death is the death of dishonor and "shame," suggesting quite literally her transcendence of the "shame culture" in which Ashley's version of honor predominates. Out of "shame's ashes" rises the phoenix-like "new born" honor advanced by Calvin.

In this way, Lucrece's suicide, which the poem seems to endorse (if not celebrate) as a "proper" solution, given what has happened, appears to offer an alternative to the socially based system of masculine honor which initiated the rape in the first place. In other words, if only Collatine had realized that Lucrece's value was intrinsic, not requiring publication, Tarquin's competitive, conquest-driven desire would not have been provoked, and the tragic sequence of events would not have begun. But except for Brutus' very late reference to "this chaste blood so unjustly stained" (1836), none of the men recognize Lucrece's claim that true feminine virtue is intrinsic – separate from whatever "pollution" her body has endured or from the public shame she has accrued on the marketplace of masculine honor. Indeed, just the opposite occurs: Lucrece's new, symbolic honor achieved in her death is quickly re-circulated and made to function in very familiar ways.

Thus, although Shakespeare clearly intends to show the emptiness and self-destructiveness of Tarquin's rapacity, there is little suggestion of a way out of the wolfish marketplace in which masculine desire is spurred to violent extremes by the fetishization of chastity. Indeed, as many critics have observed, the poem ends with a verbal duel between Collatine and Lucrece's father over who feels the most grief at her death, followed by another battle between men for figurative control of Lucrece's honor in the war of revenge launched by Brutus against Tarquin. In this way, the poem reproduces the conditions of the rape in its conclusion; despite its condemnation of the rapist, Lucrece is still the fetishized object, even more so as a transcendent symbol supposedly above the marketplace. In the final reckoning, her reputation in death is made to carry an even greater weight of masculine honor.[24]

Consequently, however we might argue that Shakespeare's "solution" – his possibility for egress from the dialectic of masculine honor and desire – appears in the idea that Lucrece's idealized chastity exists in a realm outside the marketplace of male rapacity, this is not how the poem ends. Like Greville, Shakespeare's version of intrinsic honor is impossible in the mercantile world in which he lives. But more importantly, the "solution" to the poem relies on yet another construction of "woman" as pure and inviolable, above the polluted marketplace in which masculine honor and desire are circulated. And this construction is of course not the opposite of the idea of the polluted female body but its necessary and enabling other half. As Lucrece observes, "But no perfection is so absolute, / That some impurity doth not pollute." It is precisely the representation of Lucrece's "absolute" purity, the suggestion that her intrinsic virtue transcends the exchange system, that fires Tarquin's desire in the first place. Lucrece is trapped in a masculine fantasy that leaves little room between idealization and debasement. What appears as an exit is in fact an infinite regress.

Barber's explanation for the greater frequency of references to honor (defined in terms of female chastity) among the gentry suggests that chastity among propertied women played a greater symbolic role in delineating status differences once those differences were perceived as permeable. As Lawrence Stone has shown, a number of factors contributed to the real and perceived sense that older status distinctions were under siege, including the increasing wealth and social mobility of mercantile and professional classes and, beginning in 1603, James' liberal conferring of new titles.[25] In a supportive literary context, Frank Whigham has argued in his essay on *The Duchess of Malfi* that regulation of women's marriages and sexuality served to ensure endogamous marriage and to symbolize class purity. The fascination with the contamination and purity of women's bodies and sexualities, so frequently enacted in the Jacobean theaters, functions to stage anxieties about class as much as about sexuality; indeed, the two are inseparable, at least on a symbolic level.[26] If "Lucrece" relies on the residual definition of honor as denoting reputation among the privileged in order to demarcate status differences increasingly dissolved by professional and mercantile classes, it is certainly ironic that its rhetoric of chastity is so replete with economic, mercantile terms. In other words, Lucrece's chastity is intended to figure the purity and difference of the landed classes, and yet this crucial symbol is infected by the rhetoric of those it is intended to exclude. Once again, the poem reveals the mutual dependence rather than exclusivity of its binary terms.

A more important contradiction arises when we recall from Barber's analysis that one of the primary connotations of honor involved personal title and nobleness of mind. Title or rank could be linked to honor inasmuch as social status carried with it supposedly innate personal qualities. As the son of the king, Tarquin sits at the apex of this social hierarchy, in theory the highest embodiment of the honor inherent in his position. This exemplary status becomes the basis for one of Lucrece's unsuccessful appeals to her assailant:

> This deed will make thee only lov'd for fear,
> But happy monarchs still are fear'd for love.
> With foul offenders thou perchance must bear,
> When they in thee the like offenses prove.
> If but for fear of this, thy will remove;
>   For princes are the glass, the school,
>   the book,
>   Where subjects' eyes do learn, do read,
>   do look.   (610–616)

Lucrece continues:

> And wilt thou be the school where Lust shall learn?
> Must he in thee read lectures of such shame?
> Wilt thou be glass where it shall discern
> Authority for sin, warrant for blame,
> To privilege dishonour in thy name?
>   Thou back'st reproach against long-living laud,
>   And mak'st fair reputation but a bawd.   (617–623)

Lucrece's point is that not only will Tarquin destroy his own honor, but that he will additionally corrupt the entire code of ethics, "reputation" and masculine honor he is expected to exemplify as well. (This is one of what Tarquin calls "lets" – further incitements to his lust.) But the paradox of Lucrece's argument is that honor (through female chastity) is only conferred among men of high standing through a system of competition in which the greater the status of the conquered, the more prestigious the victory.

Elsewhere Lucrece urges Tarquin "[b]y knighthood, gentry, and sweet friendship's oath . . . [t]hat to his borrowed bed he make retire / And stoop to honor, not to foul desire" (569, 573–574). ("Knighthood" is repeated several times in the poem to describe the bond between the two men, perhaps a nostalgic appeal to an earlier model of allegiance.) The bonds among men that she employs to persuade Tarquin of his allegiance to her husband are at once the same bonds upon which their rivalry is based, and they are the very terms used to unite the men in their revenge at the end: the men are "as bound in knighthood to her imposition" (1697). For Tarquin to cuckold Collatine is to destroy both men's honor but it is also the supreme act of conquest, and thus the accrual of honor for himself. The use of "stoop" in the next line seems tantalizingly close to admitting the reversibility of these terms, for it is possible to read the line as if it were saying that men debase themselves in front of *both* "honor" and "foul desire" at the same time.

Tarquin's theft of Collatine's prized possession is thus a "logical" outcome of the symbolic capital accorded to chastity by members of the nobility. In short, Tarquin *gains* honor by raping the wife of someone as powerful as Collatine at the same time as he *destroys* his own honor. This contradiction is certainly made explicit in the poem through Tarquin's tortured *psychomachia* between the preservation and corruption of his own honor – desire, or lust, is the agent that tips the scales toward the latter. But it seems to me that his overwhelming, inescapable desire is really standing in for the inherent contradictions of a system in which men receive honor from their peers in reciprocal relationships, on the one hand, yet also receive honor in their conquest of the same peers, on the other. As I suggested in the previous chapter, mutuality and rivalry are sometimes competing dynamics in the homosocial network. When Tarquin is described as "[p]awning his honor to obtain his lust" (156), or when the poem states "he hath won what would lose again" (688), it is not just because "lust" and "honor," winning and losing, are enemies in a Manichaean struggle, but due to the reversibility and mutual infection of one term by the other. The witches in *Macbeth* deserve to speak the equivocal coda to this part of my discussion: "When the hurlyburly's done, / When the battle's lost and won" (I.i.3–4).

Yet another important aspect of masculine honor involves the paternity of both Tarquin and Collatine. As countless examples attest, men in the Renaissance – especially men of property, if Barber is correct – felt a particularly acute anxiety toward the fact that women controlled whether or not their sons and heirs were legitimate. Paternity anxiety – the unfortunate fact that patrilineal succession needed to "pass through" women – may very well be at the heart of husbands' obsession with their wives' chastity.[27] Again, this anxiety would be especially exacerbated in a period when status distinctions were more porous, since patrilineal inheritance is the primary means by which families and ranks maintain their class endogamy. However persuasive this explanation, it seems to have operated on a mostly symbolic level, since there are few (at least literary) examples of women cuckolding their husbands with men of different rank – *The Duchess of Malfi* providing a notable exception. In any case, it seems quite obvious that paternal legitimacy was a powerful component of masculine identity for both fathers and sons, and that women (and women's sexuality) were perceived as the very unstable fulcrum upholding that identity.

Early in the poem, Tarquin imagines the complete unraveling of his pedigree if he rapes Lucrece:

> Yet though I die, the scandal will survive;
> And be an eyesore in my golden coat;
> Some loathsome dash the herald will contrive
> To cipher me how fondly I did dote;
> That my posterity, sham'd with the note,
>   Shall curse my bones, and hod it for no sin
> To wish that I their father had not been.   (204–210)

A few lines later, he compares the cost of selling "eternity" for the "fleeting" pleasure of "one sweet grape who will the vine destroy" (214–215). Why should Tarquin's paternity be destroyed by his own adultery, since presumably the heirs he has already produced are legitimate? Or, to put it differently, why should the rape of another man's wife threaten to cause his own sons to "wish that I their father had not been"?

The most obvious answer is that Tarquin will have committed a crime so heinous, "so black a deed," that his general reputation, and by extension his children's, will be destroyed. But I think the more complicated logic behind this moment in the poem is revealed when Tarquin, immediately after considering the severe price he is about to pay, turns his attention to the consequences of the rape for Collatine. In the third of three stanzas devoted to Tarquin's anticipation of the crime as an act against Collatine, he wonders:

> Had Collatine kill'd my son or sire,
> Or lain in ambush to betray my life,
> Or were he not my dear friend, this desire
> Might have excuse to work upon his wife,
> As in revenge or quittal of such strife;
>   But as he is my dear kinsman, my dear friend,
> The shame and fault finds no excuse nor end.   (232–238)

On one level, Tarquin believes that his proximity in friendship and status to Collatine makes the rape inexcusable. One is reminded of Leontes' jealousy in *The Winter's Tale*, where he irrationally fears that "[t]o mingle friendship far is mingling bloods" (I.ii.109). The closeness between Leontes and Polixenes since childhood seems to contribute to his jealous fantasy, suggesting that intimate friendship and rivalry among men are two sides of the same coin.

Similarly, in the above stanza from "Lucrece," Tarquin refers to Collatine as his deadly foe but then, immediately following, as his "dear kinsman, my dear friend." Casting Collatine as his arch-enemy would justify the rape, but in the same lines Tarquin also places himself in Collatine's position: to paraphrase, he wonders: what if Collatine were to destroy *my* paternity? This is one of several moments in the poem where the two men are depicted as almost interchangeable, at once each other's friend and enemy. The poem strongly suggests, as I have mentioned (following several other readers of the poem), that Collatine is initially responsible for the rape by advertising Lucrece's virtues. Now, as Tarquin imagines his own son having been "kill'd" by Collatine (figuratively what the rape does to Collatine's son), the rape would then possess a legitimate "excuse." Once again, the same contradictory effects of the masculine honor code are at work: Collatine is at once Tarquin's "kinsman" *and* rival, "dear friend" *and* enemy. It would seem that within a code that confers honor among men, the rape is a violation but also an extension of male bonds. This is clearly part of the masculine "logic" underlying Catherine Stimpson's observation that "[b]ecause men rape what other men possess, rape becomes in part a disastrous element of male rivalry."[28]

Both as kinsman and rival, Tarquin's rape destroys Collatine's honor as well as his own. He is, in effect, doing the same thing to himself as he is to Collatine, whose infamy is described by Tarquin to Lucrece in terms very similar to the fate he himself will suffer:

> So thy surviving husband shall remain
> The scornful mark of every open eye,
> Thy kinsmen hang their heads at this disdain,
> Thy issue blurr'd with nameless bastardy;
> And thou, the author of their obloquy,
>   Shalt have thy trespass cited up in rhymes,
>   And sung by children in succeeding times.   (519–525)

The consequences of the rape are very similar for both men: "disdain," illegitimacy surrounding children already born, and infamy for generations to come among their "kinsmen." But Tarquin's threat to Lucrece is specifically that she will be known as the "author" of her children's "obloquy," a charge which Lucrece in part internalizes after the rape. Although Tarquin is trying to persuade Lucrece of her responsibility at this moment in order to convince her to remain silent, the idea that Lucrece is at least partly to blame, as I have suggested, runs through the poem, as well as through its critical history.

The "logic" behind this assignation of blame in this case involves a male projection of paternity anxiety on to Lucrece. For if Collatine initially "issued" (in the sense of published) Lucrece's chastity in order to advertise and circulate his own honor, to assure his kinsmen that his own "issue" are legitimate, now Lucrece must be made to bear the responsibility for their "nameless bastardy." To play out the double entendre further, Collatine's preliminary, public "issue" destroys his biological "issue." In order to avoid admitting his own responsibility for this self-destructive sequence (which would mean exposing the fetishized role of female chastity in the first place), responsibility is projected onto Lucrece. In other words, placing the blame on Lucrece maintains the initial construction (and publication) of the importance of female chastity, despite its destructive consequences for both men.

But the poem is far more ambivalent toward the question of blame; indeed, Shakespeare turns responsibility back on both men at the same time as he reproduces the idea that Lucrece's suicide has meaning only if she is at least partly guilty. In the process of weighing the relative responsibility for the rape, the poem initiates a critique of the masculine economy of desire and honor that I have been addressing, but its conclusion (as in the sources) defers any resolution. This ambivalence is evident early in Lucrece's own lengthy narration: "Yet I am guilty of thy honor's wrack; / Yet for thy honor I did entertain him" (842–843). Because "thine honor lay in me," as Lucrece says in the preceding stanza, she understands herself as "guilty." But in the second line, an important qualification is introduced: not only did Lucrece uphold her husband's "honor" by entertaining Tarquin at Collatium, but if we read "entertain" to refer also to the initial dialogue between the men, Lucrece might be said to have dutifully entertained Tarquin *in absentia* through her husband's verbal encomium. In the case of both references, Lucrece is guilty only inasmuch as she has functioned "properly" in a masculine economy of desire and honor.

As I have suggested, the end of the poem conspicuously places the men as still very much within the same honor system with which the narrative began; even more, the ending incorporates Lucrece's "transcendent" suicide back down into that system. Immediately following the suicide, Lucrece is depicted as "that late sack'd island" around which "two slow rivers" of red (purity) and black ("stain'd") blood flow (1738–1744). Perhaps evoking an analogy between London and Rome, the image serves to ignite the men's nationalistic fervor, as well as establishing bonds and allegiances among them. Let us look more closely at the function of Lucrece's suicide as the key term in this homosocial triangle.

Lucretius' first lament is for the loss of his own paternal identity:

> That life was mine which thou hast here deprived.
> If in the child the father's image lies,
> Where shall I live now Lucrece is unlived? (1753–1755)

He continues to bewail the loss of the "broken glass" from which "my image thou has torn" (1758, 1762), reminding us that Lucrece's virtue in life served to reflect her father's honor and identity as well as her husband's. Given the poem's focus on chastity, it is possible to read Lucretius' desolation as partly due to *his* now corrupted patrilineal bloodline, the third man to suffer such a fate. Although his grief is primarily over her death, not her sexual violation, affective bonds between a father and his daughter are inevitably involved in paternity. Tarquinius' grief is not, of course, quite the same response as fathers who suspect their daughters of sexual impropriety: in *Othello*, Brabantio cries "O treason of the blood" when he first hears of Desdemona's supposed transgression (*Othello*, I.i.171). And Leonato's response to accusations against Hero in *Much Ado* are pathological, even by Renaissance standards:

> . . . Could she here deny
> The story that is printed in her blood?
> Do not live, Hero, do not ope thine eyes."
> (*Much Do About Nothing*, IV.i.120–122)

But the possessiveness Lucretius displays in the "grief contest" with Collatine, in which " 'my daughter' and 'my wife' " (1804) are interchangeable claims, draws Tarquinius into the same economy of exchange and possession.

The competition of grief between husband and father once more figures Lucrece's body as the battleground of competition among men, and once again utilizes a rhetoric of property and mercantilism:

> The one doth call her his, the other his,
> Yet neither may possess the *claim* they lay.
> The father says "She's mine." "O, mine she is."
> Replies her husband. "Do not take away
> My sorrow's *interest*. Let no mourner say
>   He weeps for her, for she was *only mine*,
>   And only must be wail'd by Collatine."
>
> "O," quoth Lucretius, "I did give that life
> which she too early and too late hath spill'd."
> "Woe, woe," quoth Collatine, "She was my wife,
> I owed [owned] her, and 'tis mine that she hath
> kill'd."   (1793–1804; my emphases)

Finally (and not a moment too late for this reader), Brutus interrupts the men's *lachrymachia* in order to issue the call to arms for revenge against Tarquin. Abruptly, the battle between Lucretius and Collatine turns into a relationship of comrades-in-arms, suggesting for the last time the reversibility of rival and ally. In good Roman fashion, Brutus appeals to the others' masculine honor, striking "his hand upon his breast," urging them to swear a "vow" of revenge in order to purify Rome from the pollution of tyrants. Just as the poem began, bonds between men are united around the idealized figure of Lucrece, her now "re-purified" body stirs and incites masculine honor, and we are promised a return to another battlefield, only this time the allies are rivals.

In the final stanza, the cyclic nature of the poem (its "eternal return," one might say) is even more striking:

> When they had sworn to this advised doom,
> They did conclude to bear dead Lucrece thence,
> To show her bleeding body through Rome,
> And so to publish Tarquin's foul offense;
> Which being done with speedy diligence,
>   The Romans plausibly did give consent
>   To Tarquin's everlasting banishment.   (1849–1855)

In the initial "publication" of Lucrece, her inviolable body was advertised in order to confer masculine honor and fame; now, her "bleeding," *violated* body and the purity of her soul have become the fetishized objects. Indeed, the poem can only end with yet another publication of Lucrece's body, for it is a body inevitably written among men in order to confer masculine honor.

Publication

> LEONATO: I might have said "No part of it is mine;
> This shame derives itself from unknown loins"?
> But mine, and mine I lov'd, and mine I prais'd,
> And mine that I was proud on, mine so much
> That I myself was to myself not mine,
> Valuing her – why, she, O, she is fall'n
> Into a pit of ink, that the wide sea
> Hath drops too few to wash her clean again,
> And salt too little which may season give
> To her foul tainted flesh!(*Much Ado About Nothing*, IV.i.134–142)

Gazing at a painting depicting the Trojan War, Lucrece wonders to herself: "Why should the private pleasure of some one / Become the public plague of many moe?" (1478–1479). Or, to imagine what is behind Leonato's confused tirade in the above passage from *Much Ado*: how can my daughter, so widely renowned and publicized as chaste, silent and obedient, have suddenly "fall'n into a pit of ink"? As I have suggested, the answer to these questions lies in the fact that the "private" has no value if it *remains* private according to a masculine system of publicly conferred honor. Publishing the private enables a system of bonds and exchanges between men, but it also necessarily produces the anxiety of the cuckold, the rage of the father whose own blood is "corrupted," and the violence of Tarquin. In this section I will pursue some of the implications of publishing chastity in the context of "Lucrece," but also extend my investigation to include the figurative uses of the private/ public boundary. For the latter course, I follow Stephanie Jed's observation in her brilliant work on the functions of the Lucretia story for humanism in Renaissance Italy: "we can begin to see this rape not as an inevitable prologue to Rome's liberation but as a historical figuration, formed and reformed to serve various interests and needs in different historical moments."[29]

Early in the course of his attack, Tarquin offers Lucrece a compact by which if she yields to him, he will keep the rape secret. This offer is based on the logic (according to Tarquin) that the "fault unknown is as good as a thought unacted" (527). The paradox behind this suggestion is that it completely defies the circumstances that brought Tarquin to Lucrece's chamber in the first place. Were it possible for Lucrece's body to remain unpublished and "unknown," Tarquin's violent lust would not have been aroused. Indeed, the most striking aspect of Tarquin's proposal is that Lucrece's acceptance of it would be *more* dangerous to masculine honor and identity than the publication of the rape – not so much for the characters within the poem but according to a broader cultural logic. For as I will argue more fully in the last chapter, the prospect that women's sexuality could remain secret, that their bodies could remain simply bodies rather than "texts" carefully scrutinized and anxiously interpreted by men, threatens the foundations of male identity and the masculine economy that enables it. The parallel often drawn between Collatine's publication of Lucrece's chastity and Tarquin's penetration of her chamber and subsequent rape is generated in part by this masculine "need to know," to make public what cannot remain private.

But it is precisely the ultimate secret of women's sexuality that keeps driving masculine desire for knowledge – in both senses of the word. As Tarquin makes his way to Lucrece's chamber, he encounters a series of deterrents ("locks," "threshold grates," "each unwilling portal," "vents and crannies"), each of which heightens his desire by deferring it:

> But all these poor forbiddings could not stay him;
> He in the worst sense consters their denial.
> The doors, the wind, the glove that did delay him,
> He takes for accidental things of trial,
> Or as those bars which stop the hourly dial,
>   Who with a ling'ring stay his course doth let,
>   Till every minute pays the hour of his debt.   (323–329)

In the next stanza he adds, "these lets attend the time . . . / To add a more rejoicing to the prime" (330, 332). The privacy Tarquin is about to invade (Lucrece's chamber and her sexuality) is constituted as desirable – as requiring conquest – by the series of deterrents he confronts. Each "trial" announces the secrecy and privacy (thus creating the transgressive appeal) of the crime he is about to commit.

In its lengthy description of Tarquin's path to Lucrece's chamber, the poem maps parallel paths between the invasion of her geographical space and the final penetration of her body. As Peter Stallybrass observes, citing several sixteenth-century examples, the "surveillance of women concentrated on three specific areas: the mouth, chastity, the threshold of the house"; later, he adds: "silence and chastity are, in turn, homologous to women's enclosure within the house."[30] But not only "surveillance": the *a priori* masculinist construction of women's bodies and their domestic spaces as private, requiring constant regulation of their openings, additionally impels masculine desire to transgress those boundaries. The prior establishment of such boundaries induces their violation just as the publication of Lucrece's chastity is not only a figurative rape but also an inducement toward the literal rape. As Jed points out, "[e]fforts to 'protect' these cut-off spaces will never deter acts of violence against women, for sexual violence is, in some sense, upheld by the way in which these spaces are represented."[31]

Shakespeare's "Lucrece" is itself a text "in which these spaces are represented" and its narrative must be understood as another version of publishing her chastity and violation analogous to Collatine's within the poem. Indeed, it seems undeniable that part of Shakespeare's intent was to stir erotic desire in his (male) readers through identification with Tarquin even though he simultaneously condemns the rape. The poem is decidedly written from a male point of view, and the gender of its intended audience is suggested in the phrase, "their gentle sex" (1237).[32] But this authorial complicity is especially evident in the long, Petrarchan catalogue of Lucrece's body when Tarquin first sees her (interspersed with references to her virtue) – as if Shakespeare were filling in readers who unfortunately missed Collatine's earlier discourse.

The last of these stanzas merits closer attention:

> Her breasts like ivory globes circled with blue,
> A pair of maiden worlds unconquered,
> Save their lord no bearing yoke they knew,
> And him by oath they truly honored.
> These worlds in Tarquin new ambition bred,
>   Who, like a foul usurper, went about
>   From this fair throne to heave owner out.   (407–13)

The conceit of this passage sets up Lucrece's breasts as "worlds," "unconquered" except by Collatine, and it reveals Tarquin's desire as predominantly "ambition" for Collatine's possession rather than for Lucrece herself.[33] For the male reader, the stanza blends descriptions of Lucrece's arousing physical beauty with statements of her unavailability, both conditions of the traditionally Petrarchan object of desire. In the lines following this stanza, the narrator states: "What could he see but mightily he noted? / What did he note but strongly he desired?" (414–415). The "text" of Lucrece's virtue and beauty is once again published: seeing and noting are almost coterminous with desirous.

In this way, Shakespeare "places" or identifies his male readers with male characters by presenting Lucrece as a "text" within the poem. This meta-narrative constructs an implicit parallel between writing and interpreting Lucrece in the poem, and the act of reading. It additionally provides another way in which the poem wages the battle between the publication of Lucrece's chastity (thus circulating her in the marketplace of male desire) and Lucrece's own resistance to her objectification. In the following passage (and elsewhere), she is primarily concerned with the publication of her ruined reputation following the rape:

> Make me not object to the tell-tale Day.
> The light will show, character'd in my brow,
> The story of sweet chastity's decay,
> The impious breach of holy wedlock vow.
> Yea, the illiterate, that know not how
>   To cipher what is writ in learned books,
>   Will quote my loathsome trespass in my looks.   (806–812)

In this stanza Lucrece imagines herself as a transparent text whose "character" will be easily discerned even by the "illiterate." Lucrece wants to control the dissemination of what has happened in order to preserve Collatine's honor, as the next stanzas make clear: "Let my good name, that senseless reputation, / For Collatine's dear love be kept unspotted" (820–821). In this sequence the contradiction inherent in publishing chastity is once again exposed. Earlier, Collatine's honor demanded the public circulation of his wife's "good name"; now, his honor depends on controlling the dissemination of his wife as text. Paradoxically, masculine honor requires the re-purification of a text it "corrupted" in the first place if Collatine's honor is to become once again "unspotted."

Ownership and publication, privacy and circulation, exist in a tense dialectic "resolved" by Lucrece's suicide. She transcends the marketplace that corrupted her in the form of a renewed symbol of purity that is,

however, circulated back into the marketplace as a new text, once again
interpreted in order to generate masculine honor:

> My resolution, love shall be thy boast,
> By whose example thou reveng'd mayst be.
> How Tarquin must be us'd, *read it in me*.   (1193–1195, my emphasis)

By figuring Lucrece as a re-purified text, the poem symbolically
removes the corruption of Tarquin's rape and, in a sense, returns Lucrece
to her original, pure state. In the context of Italian humanism, Jed argues
that the return to and recovery of original Greek and Latin texts were
motivated by a similar desire to restore lost purity. In her discussion of
Salutati's *Declamatio Lucretiae*, original purity figures the humanist
enterprise of translating and correcting ancient texts: "In order to
distinguish themselves from corrupters and violators who stained and
contaminated texts," Jed writes, "the humanists invented a language
which excised from the representation of their activities the signs of their
own relationship of contact with texts. They accomplish this by claiming
to restore what they thought were original, 'untouched' readings." Jed
recognizes this project as inherently flawed since "every castigation is
also a contamination"; that is, every re-purification reveals the signs of
its own restorative work.[34] In other words, humanist scholarship needed
to expunge earlier editors' "contact" with the texts and then disguise
their own manipulations. By extrapolation, the text serves as a battleground among men, or as a field on which men compete for the right to
plant their own seed. This is not at all unlike Bacon's aggressive
dismissals of earlier scientists and philosophers, the function of which is
to clear the field for his own dissemination of knowledge. We have seen a
similar dynamic in Bacon's repudiation of ancient science as barren and
impotent.

Jed shows the way in which an earlier text of Lucretia functioned
simultaneously in the service of humanist ideology and in the founding
myth of Rome. In a roughly similar way, Shakespeare's "Lucrece" may
also have figured the idea of a pure English state: England fashioned
itself as the descendant of Rome, and Elizabeth's virginal body was made
to represent England's impenetrability, as depicted in the Armada
portrait. Indeed, the poem follows closely enough on the heels of the
English defeat of the Spanish Armada for it to be possible to locate the
figure of purity in the poem as part of the renewed nationalism that
spawned, for example, Shakespeare's history plays. In the poem, this
identification is suggested when Lucrece is metaphorically described as
"a late sack't island" divided by "two slow rivers" (1738, 1740). But any
historical parallels we may find between Lucrece and either England or

Elizabeth herself must be tracked on a more figurative than direct level, since Lucrece's violation and re-purification contrast sharply with the pervasive symbol of Elizabeth's impenetrable virginity. In his discussion of Elizabeth's Armada speech, Louis Montrose argues the comparison as follows: "Unlike Lucretia, the Roman matron who submitted and was polluted, whose suicide was necessary for the cleansing of the social order, the royal English virgin will defend and preserve herself and her state."[35]

Perhaps a more fruitful historical moment may be found in the 1560s, a time of considerable uncertainty toward the viability of the new and untried Elizabethan state. The early fragility of Elizabeth's rule was exacerbated by her own questionable legitimacy, the rise of the northern earls in 1569, the constant threat of a Spanish invasion, and England's recent history of religious turmoil, in which Protestantism understood and defined itself as the recovery of the original purity of the Church, corrupted since by Catholicism. In such moments of perceived vulnerability, concern over boundaries, transgressions and figures of purity reach their most heightened pitch.

With this brief historical context I want to introduce the earliest Elizabethan story of Lucretia, one almost certainly unknown to Shakespeare. This version anticipates Shakespeare's representation of Lucrece as a corrupted text re-purified in order to advance the authority and legitimacy of its 'rightful' owners. I quote at length the richly allegorical preface to the 1570 edition of Sackville and Norton's *The Tragedie of Ferrex and Porrex, or Gorboduc* written by the printer, John Day:

Where this Tragedie was for furniture of part of the grand Christmasse in the Inner Temple first written about nine yeares agoe by the right honourable Thomas now Lorde Buckherst, and by T. Norton, and after shewed before her Majestie, and never intended by the authors therof to be published: yet one W.G. getting a copie therof at some yong mans hand that lacked a little money and much discretion, in the great plage. an[no] 1565 about [five] yeares past, while the said Lord was out of England, and T. Norton farre out of London, and neither of them both made privie, put it forth exceedingly corrupted: even as if by meanes of a broker for hire, he should have entised into his house a faire maide and done her vilianie, and after all to bescratched her face, torne her apparell, berayed and disfigured her, and then thrust her out of dores dishonested. In such plight after long wandring she came at length home to the sight of her frendes who scant knew her but by a few tokens and markes remayning. They, the authors I meane, though were very much displeased that she so ranne abroad without leave, whereby she caught her shame, as many wantons do, yet seeing the case as it is remedilesse, have for common honestie and shamefastnesse new apparalled, trimmed, and attired her in such forme as she was before. In which better forme since she hath come to me, I have harbored her for her frendes sake and her owne, and I do not dout her parentes the authors will not now be discontent that she goe abroad among you good readers, so it be in honest companie. For she is by my encouragement and others somewhat lesse ashamed of the dishonestie done to her because it was by fraude and force. If she be welcome among you and gently entertained, in favor of the house from whense she is descended, and of her owne nature courteously disposed to offend no man, her frendes will thanke you for it. If not, but that she shall be still reproched with her former missehapp, or quarelled at by curious persons, the poore gentlewoman wil surely play Lucrece's part, and of herself die for shame, and I shall wishe that she had taried still at home with me, where she was welcome: for she did never put me to more charge, but this one poore blacke gowne lined with white that I have now given her to goe abroad among you withall.[36]

Day's explanation for publishing a new edition of the play utilizes an extended metaphor borrowed from the story of Lucretia. An originally pure text that had been put forth "exceedingly corrupted" in the edition of William Griffith some years earlier is compared to Lucrece, a "fair maid" whom the printer "berayed and disfigured," and then "thrust . . . out of dores dishonested." The metaphor authenticates John Day's "newly appareled" edition by suggesting that he is redressing a moral wrong in restoring the text's original "honesty," as if he were acting out of moral obligation rather than self-interest.

Like Shakespeare's "Lucrece" and its antecedents, Day's preface is ambivalent about the extent of the Lucrece-text's culpability: "she" is the disobedient daughter who "ranne abroad without leave, whereby she caught her shame, as many wantons do." But at the same time, Lucrece is represented as a victim, whom the Tarquin-like printer "enticed into his house . . . and done her villainy." Day's Lucrece-as-text metaphor thus places himself in a competitive relationship toward Griffith, whom he vilifies as the corrupt printer. Day is the avenging angel who re-purifies the text and thus removes the stain of its earlier corruption. Of course, since all editions are ineluctably corrupt, Day duplicates the earlier "rape" in the name of re-purification – he wipes away earlier traces of mediation only to leave his own. In other words, he removes the stain of Griffith's edition only to replace it with his own or, in another way, he removes the seed of his competitor in order to plant himself. W. W. Greg's claim that Griffith's edition was not, in fact, "exceedingly corrupted" encourages this metaphorical analysis.[37] Indeed, one contemporary editor has compared Day's alterations to Griffith's and concluded that "the new apparel with which Day clothed the text did not quite cover the 'dishonested' body beneath."[38] In the competitive marketplace of London printers, "Lucrece" figures the struggle between men to disseminate the text of *Gorboduc*. The restoration of "Lucrece" to the state of her original purity is the condition of Day's own subsequent violation, his own mastery. This is evident in the preface as Day suggests that his "new apparelled" edition is once again ready for circulation since he has restored her "honesty": "her parentes, the authors will not now be discontent that she goe abroad among you good readers." But of course, Day's newly "chastened" text is now once again available for another corruption, and so the cycle continues, despite his claim to having produced the definitive edition.

For the "parentes" of Lucrece-as-text, the parthenogenic authors Sackville and Norton, Day's re-purification restores their proper ownership and right to disseminate themselves through her. This sequence is very similar to the plot of *Much Ado*: Leonato's excessive grief at the supposed corruption of Hero and the catastrophic loss of his filial possession are restored through Hero's staged death and resurrection. Day's use of the Lucretia story is also attentive to the same anxieties as he restores her back to the patrilineal fold: she is returned "in favor of the house whense she is descended." Thus Day's efforts may be understood allegorically to return a wayward daughter now domesticated to her rightful parents so that she may circulate in the marriage market to their economic advantage. According to Day, Sackville and Norton should be pleased to see their "daughter" "go abroad among you good readers, so it be in honest company." Day has restored their ownership, cleared their name and reputation, and prepared their daughter/text for profitable circulation among the public. If she is not accepted "in such form as she was before," Day warns, "the poore gentlewoman wil surely play Lucrece's part, and of herself die for shame."

Once again, Jed's model is instructive. She writes: "For the corruption of a text, in the minds of humanists, was not unlike a rape. The threat lay not so much in the actual violation but in keeping the rapist's seeds from reproducing."[39] Griffith's mediation in the textual dissemination of the play must be removed in order to allow yet another mediation on the part of Day. But to admit this process as such would be to give the lie to the claim that each new edition receives its legitimacy and value by reproducing an unmediated version of the original. Day needs to engage the figures of original purity in order to obviate the inadmissible fact that all editions and translations leave signs of mediation; they are all, in an absolute sense, corrupt. Thus, the story of Lucretia functions as an allegory of corruption restored to original purity. For if Day dresses his editorial enterprise in the clothes of a woman whose re-purification marked the founding of republican Rome, the most famously corrupted symbol of purity in his cultural lexicon, his own small claim to textual authenticity may itself appear inviolable. Day plays the part of Brutus, invoking the figure of purity in the service of his own authority and as the means by which men "properly" reprint themselves.

Before leaving this first Elizabethan version of the Lucretia story to return to the last, it is worth mentioning briefly the play Day's narrative so suggestively introduces. Like the printer's preface, *Gorboduc* stages a drama of transgression and corruption in which supposedly inviolable boundaries are under siege. In the play, "Britain land" is in the throes of a violent civil war. The country is referred to repeatedly in maternal terms as, for example, "the common mother of us all" (V.ii.) and as a "wretched mother" (V.ii.). Through this metaphor, the violation of the country is at least implicitly understood as a rape threatening the "female" purity of the state and the legitimacy of its patrilineal bonds. Eubulus, the sage counselor whose advice is ignored, imagines the consequences of the insurrection as follows:

> In the meane while these civil armes shall rage,
> And thus a thousand mischiefes shall unfolde . . .
> Loe he shall be bereft of life and all,
> And happiest he that then possesseth least,
> The wives shall suffer rape, the maides defloured,
> And children fatherlesse shall weep and waile . . .
> women and maides the cruell soldiers sword
> Shall perse to death . . .   (V.ii.)

Although this is not at all a unique depiction of the spoils of war, it does seem conspicuous in light of the material history of the text as told by Day in his preface. The invasion of Britain is depicted as rape followed by the consequent destruction of patrilineal bonds. The "text" of Britain is corrupted by "cruell soldiers" who penetrate it. As a tragedy, *Gorboduc* does not enact any form of restoration analogous to Day's textual rehabilitation. But near the ending it suggests by negation the terms of re-purification required of the mother country: 'These are the plages, when murder is the meane / To make new heires unto the royal crowne (V.ii.).

Although *Gorboduc* ends with this dire vision, it implicitly promises a re-purification of the state, analogous to Day's corrected text once the rebellion is ended. In drawing a parallel between these two texts, I am not proposing a direct link, as if Day's editorial allegory were consciously shaped by the contents of the play, but rather a shared rhetoric in which textual and political purity or contamination finds expression through the figure of the chaste woman. More importantly, the very construction of material texts and political states as "chaste" spaces in the first place functions to threaten what it intends to protect. The rhetoric of purity does not so much maintain impermeable boundaries as invite and enable their violation.

Desire

> Duke: O, when mine eyes did see Olivia first,
> Methought she purg'd the air of pestilence!
> That instant was I turn'd into a hart,
> And since my desires, like fell and cruel hounds,
> E'er since pursue me.   (*Twelfth Night*, I.i.18–22)

In this passage from Shakespeare's late Elizabethan comedy, Duke Orsino comically invokes several of the terms of my discussion thus far. Olivia, who is beautiful, virginal, unavailable (and rich) – indeed, able to purify the air itself – incites the Duke's desire upon his first visual apprehension of her. At once, as if the two moments were inseparable, this desire is no longer his own but instead turns against him in the form of an independent, tortuous force. In this final section I track the peculiarly masculine "logic" behind this libidinal sequence.

Collatine's lust is heightened by Lucrece's verbal resistance in a metaphor that naturalizes this particular narrative of male concupiscence:

> "So, so," quoth he, "these lets attend the time,
> Like little frosts that sometime threat the spring,
> To add a more rejoicing to the prime,
> And give the sneaped birds more cause to sing.
> Pain pays the income of each precious thing;"   (330–334)

At the outset of the poem, the "little frosts" that both impede and inflame Tarquin's desire are Collatine's praises of his chaste and virtuous wife. Thus, an economy in which the private "jewel" must be advertised in order to confer honor constitutes masculine desire; reciprocally, masculine desire enables and maintains the economy, even though the result (in the poem) is a figure like Tarquin who, "pawning his honor to obtain his lust" (156), "scowls and hates himself for his offense' (738). In short, the conditions of masculine honor are at the same time the source of its destruction. In "Lucrece" and elsewhere, Shakespeare appears particularly attuned to the vicious circularity of this model of desire; its inescapability is tersely captured in the final couplet of sonnet 129: "All this the world well knows; yet none knows well / To shun the heaven that leads men to this hell."[40]

As I shall argue more extensively in the next chapter, masculine desire is enabled by the impossibility of its own satisfaction or consummation, even though that impossibility is so often represented as hellish. This is simply because if masculine desire is impelled by conquest and acquisitiveness, if it is aroused by impediments or "lets," the economy at work needs continuously to generate new objects of desire in order to maintain itself in a perpetual state of unfulfillment. And because the masculine subject is coincident with his desire – that is, he exists so long as he desires – consummation raises the terrifying prospect of not-being, imagined after orgasm as *la petite morte*.

One way to understand the pervasive construction of "woman" as either transcendent or debased is to recognize both as responses to the circularity and inevitability of the masculine economy at work here. On the one hand, the idealized figure appears to promise an escape to the level of spiritual consummation; "woman" functions both as the symbol and the means by which "man" reaches beyond the mundane. Thus, Beatrice guides the pilgrim Dante through hell, St. Augustine transforms his carnal lust into spiritual desire (interestingly achieved through his mother), and Plato represents wisdom as Sophia, a kind of chaste goddess. Or, as I will discuss in the next chapter, Berowne states in *Love's Labor's Lost* that women are ". . . the ground, the books, the academes / From whence doth spring the true Promethean fire (IV.iii.299–300). On the other hand and in the opposite direction, the equally pervasive construction of "woman" as debased serves as a projection of the "hell" of masculine frustration on to women as if they were its source. Examples of this hardly require delineation, but surely Lear's misogynistic ranting, Hamlet and his father's charges against Gertrude, as well as the fiend-like descriptions of the Dark Lady in the sonnets ("to win me soon to hell, my female evil," sonnet 144)[41] are among the most prominent in Shakespeare's corpus. It perhaps goes without saying that this kind of projection sets women up as scapegoats, as if it were possible to "cleanse" masculinity by debasing women. But in both responses what appears as a way out of an economy that tortures its male members is in fact endemic to the economy in the first place – the construction of "woman" as transcendent or debased is supposedly the way out, but it is also the founding construction.

My point in drawing attention to this dynamic in both Shakespeare's work and in his culture is to understand the double-edged construction of "woman" not as merely false and dangerous, nor simply as enabling masculinity, but as enabling it in a way that perpetuates masculine instability and anxiety. As I argue throughout this book, anxiety is the condition of masculinity in such a patriarchal economy quite simply because its "solutions" to its anxiety are always returned to the economy in the form of generative causes – a gendered version of Sartre's "no exit."

Throughout this chapter I have tried to uncover and explain the ineluctable link between masculine desire and anxiety by showing some of the inherent contradictions that develop when masculine identity defines itself among men and through its various constructions of women. This way of thinking takes as axiomatic Valerie Traub's statement that "[d]esire and anxiety thus involve *fantasies* of the other, fantasies that transform and recombine elements in the existing social framework."[42] Traub sets up a reciprocal relationship between desire as "constituted in relation to social practices" and the effects of desire that in turn shape those processes. In this way of thinking, desire is coterminous with masculine subjectivity; it "inhabits" subjectivity and in so doing enables, motivates, but also threatens individuals.

Shakespeare's "Lucrece" enacts some of the "social practices" that shape and are shaped by the masculine, desiring subject, particularly as it understands itself in relation to one of western culture's most durable fantasies: the chaste, self-sacrificing woman. In my reading of the poem, masculine desire lies at the heart of a fundamental and, for Shakespeare, unavoidable contradiction: it generates and sustains the masculine subject, on the one hand, but also exposes and imperils it, on the other. Perhaps, if we follow Lacan, this is the fundamental quality of masculine desire: the perpetual deferral of satisfaction, the construction of new desired objects that maintain the subject in pursuit, the terror that desire should come to rest in consummation. In Lacan's thinking and in Shakespeare's poem, the masculine subject is by definition in pursuit, a restless signifier whose completing signified is always within sight but never reached. Consider the following description of Tarquin early in the poem: '. . . nothing in him seem'd inordinate / Save sometime too much wonder of his eye, / Which, having all, all could not satisfy" (94–96). Once woman is constructed as Other (as fetishized, idealized or debased), once the gap or lack between man and himself is in place, the self-torture of a Tarquin or Othello is inevitable.

As Shakespeare probes this model of identity and desire in "Lucrece," the poem comes up against the contradictions – what Traub calls the "structural impossibility" – of the model itself.[43] Desire emboldens Tarquin to assert his masculinity in his competitive relation to Collatine, but it also turns to "foul desire," the agent of his destruction. The object of masculine desire must be published for it to accrue honor and value for its owner, but the very same publication leads to the loss of ownership and honor. Since desire acts to destroy the ideals it constructs as desirable, the curious practice of re-purification ensues in order to maintain desire's endless pursuit.

It seems that everywhere we turn in "Lucrece" we come up against an endless circularity between the desire to possess and the equally unavoidable possession by one's desire, between (for Tarquin) the "sundry dangers of his will's obtaining; / Yet ever to obtain his will resolving" (128–129). The dilemma is developed more fully in the following stanza:

> Those that much covet are with gain so fond,
> That what they have not, that which they possess
> They scatter and unloose it from their bond.
> And so, by hoping more, they have but less;
> Or, gaining more, the profit of excess
>   Is but to surfeit, and such griefs sustain
>   That they prove bankrupt in this poor rich gain.   (134–140)

The more one desires, the less one values what one already possesses, thus desire leads to loss. On the other hand, if one's desires lead to increased possession, the result is "surfeit." Desire functions only as a destabilizing force; it swings inexorably between wanting (lack and desire) and losing, with only the briefest of stops at having. Or once again, in sonnet 129: "Past reason hunted, and no sooner had / Past reason hated . . ."[44]

"The Rape of Lucrece" attempts to find a way out of this circularity by in effect removing the Other, the constructed object of desire who, in the masculine economy of the poem, can only generate contradictions like "poor rich gain." Lucrece's suicide becomes a way out of this economy as she is transformed and elevated from object of desire to transcendent symbol: "My shame so dead, mine honor is new born" (1190). Her suicide is enacted as an imitation of the crime against her; she reproduces the act of Tarquin's penetration as if the rape itself killed her, as if her death could finally end and envelop the cycle of desire that preceded it.

But the final irony is that Lucrece still functions as a symbol in the male economy; she is every bit as much the Other when she is dead as when she was alive. Before the rape, Tarquin sees Lucrece in her chamber,

> Between whose hills her head entombed is;
>   Where, like a virtuous monument, she lies,
>   To be admir'd of lewd unhallowed eyes.   (390–392)

Entombed as a symbol of chastity (the preserve of male honor) while she is alive, her symbolic renewal is hardly more than a repetition of the same. Thus when Brutus takes the bloody knife with which Lucrece stabbed herself and promises to use it against Tarquin in order to "revenge the death of this true wife," and "so to publish Tarquin's foul offense," we are left with only slight variations on a theme: the continuing, inescapable cycle of desire, masculine honor, and its publication.

4   The anatomy of masculine desire in *Love's Labor's Lost*

As we have seen in each of my discussions thus far, sexual desire is a paradoxical if not contradictory drive: it impels the masculine subject toward conquest and possession, but at the same time, it threatens to dissolve the very subjectivity that desires in the first place. There are many ways to identify and to explain this paradox as a constituent element in masculinity. Desiring and being are inseparable because desire locates the individual in a series of relations to others and to other things – it apprehends and negotiates the world. But from this it follows that consummation, although "devoutly to be wished," is nonetheless the mark of not-being: for Hamlet the solution to his restless desiring (although not specifically sexual) is death. Or, following the logic of Duke Orsino's early speech in *Twelfth Night*, men hunt with their desire, but they are also hunted *by* it. We have seen this paradox expressed in physiological terms by Burton in his portrayal of the melancholic as consumed by his own excessive concupiscence; his masculine reason is overthrown by his feminine, desiring fluidity. Or, if Bacon's new scientific enterprise is to subdue a feminine nature, he nonetheless constructs nature as never completely knowable, protective of its secrets, thus leaving the scientist continuously in pursuit. And in Tarquin's version of this narrative, he is impelled by his desire to conquer what is most elusive (Lucrece's chastity) at the same time as he knows it will destroy him. In this dialectic of presence and absence – desiring to have and being afraid to have – masculinity is endemically at odds with itself – always already its own worst enemy.

The fact that this economy of desire is so pervasive in the early modern period and that it is so ineluctably self-destructive demands explanation on the level of ideology, for surely it is not a matter of individual volition or self-control. To know oneself as a man, to be interpellated by early modern culture as a male subject, is already to embody that culture's paradoxes – one of which is the self-destructiveness of desire. This is why it is so difficult for the texts of this period to imagine an outside, an escape, from the cultural forces in which they are embedded. In the many

textual representations of this economy of desire, "solutions" often take
the form of newly appareled articulations of the original paradox, as in
the refiguring of Lucrece's body after her suicide. Or, they transform
masculine anxiety into aesthetic or literary form, as if representation
itself – the putting into words – could serve in a compensatory fashion to
empower the threatened subject. The main focus of this chapter is the
ways in which an early Shakespearean comedy – *Love's Labor's Lost* –
grapples with and tries to resolve the paradoxes of masculine desire as
they are exemplified in the tradition of romantic love. But since deferral
will be such a key term in my analysis of the play, it seems appropriate to
begin elsewhere: across the channel to Montaigne's essays, then to the
long history of Petrarchism that was so popularly "englished" in the
1590s.

Montaigne's lengthy meditation on gender and sexuality is translated
by John Florio in 1604 as "Upon some verses of Virgil."[1] In this essay,
Montaigne offers his readers a sometimes rambling collection of observations, anecdotes, classical *exempla* and personal confessions on such
matters as cuckoldry anxiety, male impotence, constancy and inconstancy in marriage, the nature and causes of jealousy among both men
and women, and the social conditions and conventions of heterosexual
desire. The essay appears motivated by Montaigne's paradoxical recognition that sexuality, "so naturall, so necessary and so just," is nonetheless
rarely talked about "without shame." The silence regarding sexuality,
Montaigne further suggests, may very well promote rather than inhibit
sexual desire: "Is it not herein as in matters of books, which being once
called-in and forbidden become more saleable and publik?"[2] In part,
Montaigne's essay thus represents an attempt to empty out the "forbidden" appeal of sexual discourse by writing about it with candor and
honesty.

"Upon some verses" is also motivated by Montaigne's stated conviction that the essentials of sexuality and desire, once stripped of particular
conventions, are more similar than different among men and women. In
the essay's final paragraph, Montaigne writes: "*I say, that both male and
female, are cast in one same moulde; instruction and custome excepted,
there is no great difference betweene them.*" Despite this egalitarian claim,
the essay is very obviously presented as a dialogue between its author
and a male readership, and it offers distinctly masculine constructions of
female sexuality, desire, constancy, infidelity, and so on. Frequently, this
masculine perspective is precisely the subject of Montaigne's investigation. He admits that "women are not altogeather in the wrong, when
they refuse the rules of life prescribed to the world, forsomuch as onely
men have established them without their consent."[3] And in other places,

he implies that the "rules of life" prescribed by men for women may, in fact, contribute to a good deal of suffering and anxiety *by* men. Indeed, Montaigne's insistent self-critique throughout the *Essays* leads him to an unusual awareness of at least some of the inherent contradictions in early modern patriarchy.

For example, after an extended depiction of the jealousy of wives (a "tempestuous scholding humor"), Montaigne suggests that husbands, or at least the "obligation they place upon their wives, may contribute to *their own* cuckoldry:

Let us also take heede, least this great and violent stricktnes of obligation we enjoyne them, produce not two effects contrary to our end: that is to wit, to set an edge upon their sutors stomacks, and make women more easie to yeeld. For, as concerning the first point, *enhancing the price of the place, we raise the price and endeare the desire for the conquest.*

Here Montaigne articulates the "contrary effects" of publishing Lucrece's chastity at the outset of Shakespeare's poem, including the marketplace sensibility ("the price of the place") in which a male-enforced "obligation" of female chastity circulates. A few lines later, having mentioned that Venus "herselfe . . . cunningly enhanced the market of her ware," Montaigne wonders if "wee not be lesse Cuckoldes if we lesse feared to be so?," explaining that "according to womens conditions . . . inhibition enciteth, and restraint enviteth." In these passages, Montaigne suggests that heterosexual desire among both men and women is inflamed by the "inhibition" or "obligation" placed upon women. From Montaigne's male perspective, the patriarchal "rules of life prescribed to the world" produce an erotic economy based on the valorization of female chastity, virginity, modesty, and so on. This economy encourages male concupiscence and, paradoxically, the desire among women to transgress the restrictions placed upon them, one result of which is male jealousy, or cuckoldry anxiety, "the most vaine and turbulent informity that may affect a man's mind."[4]

Montaigne is well aware of the inherent contradictions produced in such an economy of desire. At one point, he announces that the "very Idea we forge unto their chastity is ridiculous." And in several instances, he exposes the double standard as serving the "interrest" of men:

Let us confesse the trueth, there are fewe amongst us, that feare not more the shame they may have by their wives offences, then by their owne vices; or that cares not more (oh wondrous charitie) for his wives, then his own conscience . . . Both we and they are capable of a thousand more hurtfull and unnaturall corruptions, then is lust or lasciviousnesse. But we frame vices and waigh sinnes, not according to their nature, but according to our interrest; whereby they take so many different unequall forms. The severity of our lawes makes womens inclination to that vice, more violent and faultie . . . and engageth it to worse proceedings then is their cause.[5]

With a different vocabulary at his disposal, Montaigne might have said that women's infidelity is a social trope that functions in the service of patriarchy: it is not condemned on the basis of "nature" but rather in terms of men's "interrest." What "interrest" does the "ridiculous" valorization of female chastity, modesty and restraint serve men? Certainly it is utilized in the service of a more general oppression of women. It is also, as Montaigne suggests here, the basis of masculine honor – men fear the "shame they may have by their wives offences." This observation is very much in line with the arguments I pursue throughout this book, especially in the concluding chapter: the economy that fetishizes female chastity constructs and sustains men as desiring subjects whose identities depend upon an anxious, sometimes volatile, relation to "objects" of knowledge and interpretation that are forever outside their mastery. As we have seen so often, such an economy produces a masculine subjectivity always in pursuit, one that requires the very conventions of deferral it also seeks to circumvent. Chastity is thus one of several "necessary" or enabling social tropes – Tarquin's "lets" – that provokes *and* defers male satisfaction.

In order to set up further my interpretive paradigm for reading *Love's Labor's Lost*, let us pursue further the masculine, erotic economy described above. Sexual desire is encouraged and inflamed by the perceived value of the desired object in an economy that requires the deferral or repeated renewal of desire. This volatile economy, according to Montaigne, depends upon inconstancy: "*it is against the nature of love, not to be violent, and against the condition of violence, to be constant.*" Here he is referring directly to female inconstancy, but he includes his male readers in the next sentence: "And those who wonder at it [i.e., female inconstancy], exclaime against it, and in women search for the causes of this infirmity, as incredible and unnatural: why see they not how often . . . themselves [i.e., the men] are possessed and infected with it?" I am inclined to read Montaigne's assertion that violence and inconstancy form the very nature of love as the projection of a masculine model of sexual desire and dissatisfaction onto women. The quoted passage appears amid three examples of women of notorious sexual appetites, examples clearly fashioned out of masculine sexual fantasies and anxieties: Thalestris, Queen of the Amazons, Venus, and Ione, Queen of Naples, who strangles her husband when she finds "neither his members nor endevours answerable [to] the hope shee had conceived of him," as Montaigne reports.[6]

Montaigne continues: "*If no end be found in covetousnesse, nor limit in ambition, assure your selfe there is nor end nor limit in letchery*. It yet continueth after saciety: nor can any man prescribe it or end or constant satisfaction: it ever goeth beyond it's [*sic*] possession, beyond it's [*sic*] boundes."[7] Once again, I would argue that the impossibility of satisfaction assigned to women in this passage may additionally function as an avoidance of a *fear* of satisfaction among men. In the sexual sense, satisfaction represents to the male imagination not just a "little death" but also a moment of loss and vulnerability – it figures an end to the desiring subject that must be resurrected through another "conquest." As I explored in my discussion of Burton's *Anatomy* and humoural psychology, this vulnerability also has a material, physiological basis: the evacuation of semen meant the loss of the masculine principle. Such masculine vulnerability finds its compensatory articulation in the creation of monstrous or unnatural *female* sexualities, a projection Montaigne warns against but to which he also succumbs.

Montaigne writes directly of this aspect of masculine desire in an earlier part of the essay: "Take away hope and desire, we grow faint in our courses, we come but lagging after. Our maistery and absolute possession, is infinitely to be feared of them: After they have wholy yeelded themselves to the mercy of our faith and constancie, they have hazarded something: they are rare and difficult vertues: so soone as they are ours, we are no longer theirs." In this passage Montaigne ominously reveals the dangers to women inherent in this masculine economy of desire. Men desire "mastery and absolute possession" only to resent its negation of the *process* of desiring; the "conquest" that results is threatening to women ("infinitely to be feared") because men project the source of their own inevitable dissatisfaction onto women, the result of which is anger, sometimes violence, against them. Montaigne concludes this section by telling the story of Thrasonides, who "was so religiously amorous of his love, that having after much sute gained his mistris hart and favour, he was refused to enjoy hir, least by that jouissance he might or quench, or satisfie, or languish that burning flame and restlesse heat wherwith he gloried, and so pleasingly fed himselfe."[8] Thrasonides fears satisfaction because his masculine identity exists only in the process of desiring; he must avoid satisfaction lest the "burning flame" that feeds and sustains him be extinguished. In the more volatile versions of this dynamic, immediately following the sexual "conquest," the male lover hates and despises both himself *and* his partner, often represented as an evil seductress. In effect, the woman is blamed for the lack or failure of male satisfaction. The man desires, conquers, then at once becomes the victim of female chicanery – a 1590s version of "Fatal Attraction."

The supreme irony of this anger, of course, is that it follows from a masculine economy of desire that depends on the fetishization of female chastity, or virginity – what Montaigne calls above "rare and difficult vertues" – in the first place. Perhaps even more insidiously, since the male subject is culturally inscribed as a subject in and by this economy, it appears very difficult to imagine an alternative way of being and desiring. As I shall discuss below, this partly explains the haunting sense of inevitability that pervades *Othello*, or the husband's expectation of his own cuckoldry often expressed in marriage treatises. Sexuality as conquest, jealousy and violence, it would seem, are not aberrations of male heterosexual love, they are its very conditions. Following this "logic," sonnet 129 represents male desire as an inescapable, circular sequence of desire, frustration, anger and ultimately, I think, the kind of violence exhibited by Othello.

In this chapter, I wish to apply my understanding of Montaigne's observation to a much more benign version of the economy that underlies *Othello*, that of *Love's Labor's Lost*, toward the purpose of showing that even such a lighthearted and playful comedy nonetheless participates in the economy of masculine desire that may also result in violence. As Keith Thomas reminds us, "when we laugh we betray our innermost assumptions. Moreover, laughter has a social dimension. Jokes are a pointer to joking situations, areas of structural ambiguity in society itself; and their subject-matter can be a revealing guide to past tensions and anxieties."[9] Perhaps this is also why so many critics of the play (mostly male) find themselves uneasy toward its gender dynamic, or why many critics turn to an almost moralistic reading in which Shakespeare is telling us the proper requirements for romantic love between men and women, or even why it has been so summarily dismissed as a bad play.[10]

I am especially interested in the ending of *Love's Labor's Lost* – unique among Shakespeare's comedies for its refusal to promise the typical comic closure of marriage. Up to that point, the play has already deferred, confused, even ridiculed the men's desires for their idealized women; now, in a conclusion often termed dramatically incomplete, or abrupt, the play ends (in a way Thrasonides would endorse) with an extended deferral of male desire and an increased exaltation of the women.[11] But for the moment I wish to defer my discussion of the play once more in order to discuss the Petrarchan tradition that informs *Love's Labor's Lost*. The play offers more than just comic exaggeration of this popular literary convention: Petrarchism underwrites the economy of masculine desire that structures the play and informs its action.

In general, the Petrarchan lyric supplies an influential socio-literary code through which the Renaissance could explore its fictions of masculine selfhood and desire in relation to an idealized concept of the feminine. As Nancy Vickers has written, Petrarch's "role in the history of interpretation and the internalization of woman's 'image' by both men and women can scarcely be overemphasized." The consequences of those attitudes inscribed by the Petrarchan lyric are all too familiar even today in advertising and film, if no longer in literature: quoting Vickers again, "bodies fetishized by a poetic voice logically do not have a voice of their own; the world of making words, of making texts, is not theirs."[12] Placed in the context of its popularity in the 1590s, we can surmise that Petrarchism provided a discourse available to poets and to the culture in general during historical moments of uncertainty and agitation toward the prevailing sex/gender system. As such, we may understand Petrarchism as an enabling discourse of masculine heterosexual desire and as a socio-literary convention that provides a compensatory form of masculine empowerment in response to the perception of psychic and emotional vulnerability. But at the same time, the very premise of Petrarchism is that its discursive control should fail: like Montaigne's model of desire, "writing" is impelled by the inaccessible or "hidden" qualities of its object. Petrarchism thus rests upon and exploits a "necessary" contradiction: the frustration of desire impels desire itself just as the inability to fully "capture" one's subject in writing engenders more and more writing.

In describing and anatomizing his beloved, the Petrarchan poet/lover occupies a subject position of specular and discursive control over the idealized, inaccessible figure he constructs. As Vickers has also shown, the persona of the poet/lover is *emotionally* scattered, while the beloved is represented as *corporally* scattered. This distinction suggests the ways in which Petrarchism may have functioned for individual poets and in the collective male imagination as a literary strategy of compensation: if romantic love is understood as an irrational loss of control, supposedly caused by the beloved, then writing about the experience of love and about the beloved provides at least a sense of authorial control. In other words, the lover responds to and compensates for his emotional distress by seizing the means of representation; by writing the female body, he reproduces his own desire and implicitly disavows hers.

From this model, it becomes possible to understand Petrarchism as a representation of woman-as-Other that seeks a form of "knowledge" about her that always/already remains elusive, a dynamic similar to the masculine *epistemophilia* I will discuss in the final chapter. The Petrarchan beloved is apprehended in language at the same time as she is represented as unattainable. For Petrarch, as Guisseppe Mazzotta argues, "language is the allegory of desire, a veil, not because it hides a moral meaning but because it always says something else."[13] Indeed, Petrarchan writing derives from the impossibility of *physical* satisfaction in an economy of writing in which there can never be complete *representational* satisfaction. Consequently, the limitation of language's signifying authority shapes and sustains the structure of masculine desire.

Thus we may say that the failure of language to correspond to the object of its representation, or the instances where language is in excess of what it purports to represent, *underscores* rather than obfuscates the condition of the desiring, masculine subject in patriarchy. If we apply such an insight to *Love's Labor's Lost*, the often remarked upon split between the male character's words and meanings[14] is not so much a case of true identity gone astray, but rather the very condition of masculine identity, inasmuch as it is defined in relation to woman as inaccessible other. To pursue this point a little further, it will be remembered that the play's comic eroticism is enacted on two levels: first, by an unbreached split between the male characters' thoughts and words, their signifiers and signifieds; and second, by a continual frustration of their semantic expectations. In effect, signs offered by the male characters do not reach their intended objects, nor do they achieve their desired effects. This "split" and "frustration" *produces* masculine desire instead of merely *representing* some wayward, extra-linguistic desire.

The politics of desire may thus be found through an analysis of the discursive and social forms of which *Love's Labor's Lost* is but a single example. And yet, the play reaches inevitably beyond its own literary boundaries: one might say that it is both written by Shakespeare and *underwritten* by representations of desire drawn from the contemporary fashion for Petrarchan sonnet writing, the age's abiding concern with female sexuality and the threat of cuckoldry, the politics of courtship and marriage, and at least indirectly from the presence of a virgin Queen who presided at the apex of this otherwise thoroughly patriarchal culture. And each of these elements are themselves nodes in the discursive network that constructs individual men as desiring subjects. As such, Shakespeare's own unique discernment of language and desire should not be subsumed by a ubiquitous concept of structure any more than we can claim for him or his play a status transcendent of those structures of desire and representation available in the late sixteenth century.

As I have suggested, interpretations of *Love's Labor's Lost* tend to discover counter-patriarchal moments within the play when the women expose and ridicule the men's romantic advances. Accordingly, the failure of the play to end in marriage sustains the empowered position of the women and underscores once again the inadequacies of the men.[15] This reading is supported by an understanding of the Petrarchan lover as "effeminized" in that he is disempowered by the excess and irrationality of his love – yet another example of love usurping (male) reason. Furthermore, as Patricia Parker has pointed out, rhetoric itself was often connected to or expressed in terms of the "feminine": it represented garrulity, deception and a lack of control. Dudley Fenner, for example, defines metaphor as "a figure whose movements must be carefully monitored."[16] This association means that the Petrarchan sonneteer in effect utilizes a "feminized" language to represent and express desire for his beloved. To this we may add Linda Woodbridge's observation that the Petrarchan lover of the 1590s was viewed more as a "wily-tongued seducer," once again associating him with supposedly feminine quality of linguistic unreliability or misprision.[17] But this way of understanding Petrarchism as "effeminizing" men, of course, is hardly a case for female empowerment since it relies upon the most traditional idealizations of women in the first place.

On the other hand, we can follow Vickers' argument in order to understand Petrarchism as a form of male empowerment: the Petrarchan sonnet represents the beloved as a "dispersed" (and in a sense, dismembered) Other against which the male poet can measure and retain his own "coherent," unified identity.[18] Petrarchan poetry becomes the textualized form of the male gaze: it specularizes "woman" by way of anatomical hyperbole and, as such, creates only an idealization of women. Perhaps most importantly, the basis for understanding Petrarchism as a literary form that perpetuates the empowerment of men at the expense of women is quite simply that it constructs and confirms men as looking and writing subjects. Petrarchism sustains male poets in control of the medium of representation, thus denying women any public means of representing their own subjectivity. Within this view of Petrarchism, the play's refusal of linguistic and erotic consummation upholds a masculine structure of desire because deferral is the basis of the traditionally gendered subject/object economy in the first place. In other words, deferral and "frustration" sustain men in the active position of pursuit, of doing the representing, and women in the static position of being represented.

In the opening scene of the play, the King and his lords position their mutual desire for "fame" and "honor" as dependent upon a renunciation of women and sexuality – the "grosser manner of the world's delights" (I.i.29), according to Dumaine. Masculine identity is established in the play when the men sign their names to a pact that unites the men in opposition to the *idea* of women as linked to debased corporality; in effect, the men purge themselves of their own corporality and mortality by projecting it onto a particular construction of the women. From the outset, then, the play sets up a functional concept of "woman" as that which needs to be transcended or renounced in order to purify masculinity and to establish bonds among men. This is a particularly fascinating version of the triangular model of homosocial bonding developed by Eve Sedgwick.[19] As I have discussed above, Sedgwick points out that one of the significant structures of patriarchal power is relationships of rivalry and identification between men that function through and in relation to a repudiation or idealization of women. Since masculine desire is so deeply entrenched in the idea of conquest, homosociality and heterosexuality are often cooperative, but they can quickly become antagonistic when "woman" is the source of competition among men, as in the case of Tarquin and Collatine. The cooperative model is displayed in *Henry V*, for example, where Henry rhetorically sexualizes the "penetration" of Harfleur castle to rally the English soldiers around the ideal of English unity and purity; in his "conquest" of Katharine at the end of the play, similarly, he has become a royal synecdoche for the consanguineous bonds among his "band of brothers."

In *Love's Labor's Lost* the King expresses this initial renunciation of physical desire in a metaphor drawn from military conquest:

> Therefore, brave conquerors – for so you are,
> That war against your own affections
> And the huge army of the world's desires –
> Our late edict shall strongly stand in force: (I.i.8–11)

In effect, the men are unified around the construction of a shared enemy that must be conquered. That which they must renounce in themselves (their "own affections") is projected onto a particular construction of woman as desire embodied. In this way, the beginning of the play establishes that the identities of the men and the bonds between them depend upon their ability to sustain this fictive conception of woman. Initially, then, the renunciation of women and sexuality requires the conquest of masculine desire.

A parallel way of understanding the triangle of love and power that the play sets up is in terms of masculine knowledge. Here once again we see the way in which the women function as a third term that unifies the men with each other. Abstract, pure, disembodied, philosophical knowledge – the privileged and decidedly masculine term – can only be obtained by the repudiation of what might be called carnal knowledge, or what the play understands as the knowledge of women. In effect, the men at the outset privilege a desire for disembodied forms of knowledge ("living in philosophy") over and against "the world's [physical] desires." But Berowne quickly and cleverly begins to question whether or not these two forms of knowledge are discrete, and in so doing he suggests that desire for books or desire for "some mistress fine" are in fact interchangeable objects of desire. "What is the end of study, let me know," he asks the King, who replies, "to know which else we should not know." "Things hid and barr'd, you mean, from common sense?," The Lord rejoins (I.i.55–56). The original opposition between abstract knowledge and corporal knowledge has been dissolved by Berowne's simple point that both are forms of desire for something unknown – both are generated by the deferral of their objects of knowledge: "Things hid and barr'd."

This is a pivotal moment in the opening scene because it turns the play's concerns to sexuality and courtship through an equation of written and carnal knowledge. Desire for the idea of woman as the basis of all knowledge will soon supplant desire for the fame and honor of the *vita contemplativa* that formerly relied on the repudiation of women and sexuality. But the important point is that the play depends on the same masculine structure of desire for both. It suggests, too, that masculine identity is shaped and understood by the act of desiring a form of knowledge either set in opposition to "woman" or gained *through* them. As Berowne will offer later in the play, "women's eyes" are "the books, the arts, the academes, / That show, contain, and nourish all the world" (IV.iii.348–349). Men write and study books and men "write" and study women – it is as if Shakespeare read Virginia Woolf's account of her trip to the British Museum.

Although the King and his Lords remain at least publicly faithful to the oath of renunciation until the fourth act, for Don Armado (and for the audience as well) sexual desire is let loose in the play immediately following Berowne's reluctant signing of the Oath. The King receives a letter from Armado, already noted for his fustian indulgence, that describes Armado's discovery of Costard and Jaquenetta behaving "contrary to thy established proclaimed edict" (I.i.252–253). As we learn in the next scene, Armado's own prurient interests have been aroused as a result of having spied upon Jaquenetta. It is significant that sexual desire is introduced in the play in this fashion. The audience, who finds itself in a similarly voyeuristic position, hears of the sexual transgression through the mediation of Armado's letter and the King's voice.[20] The taboo against displaying sex on stage is roughly parallel to the oath of renunciation; when the latter is transgressed by Armado's voyeuristic report of Jaquenetta and Costard, masculine desire is released into the world of the play. It is thus generated rather than curbed by taboo, renunciation and mediation.

Immediately following the edict, then, the play introduces masculine desire in a textualized and specularized form, and it follows that Armado's desire is very soon manifested in his bombastic sonnet-writing. In this sense, looking at and writing about "woman" are represented as interchangeable forms of knowledge, both directed from a safe and unthreatened male position, that is to say, a position of specular and discursive control. Once again, the Petrarchan model is informative: as Vickers points out, the lover's "description, at one remove from his experience, safely permits and perpetuates his fascination."[21] Indeed, the play's numerous references to "seeing" women are perhaps only exceeded by the men's "literary" attempts to apprehend them in letters and sonnets. Having "turn[ed] sonnet," Armado is exhorted by Moth to "learn her by heart" (III.i.34).

Once this sexual energy is released from (and simultaneously produced by) its initial restraint, the second act proceeds in a series of bawdy dialogues, first among the Princess and her court, and then in the course of the initial meeting between the prospective lovers. These scenes exemplify Stephen Greenblatt's observation that "for Shakespeare [erotic] friction is especially associated with verbal wit; indeed, at moments the plays seem to imply that erotic friction *originates* in the wantonness of language and thus that the body itself is a tissue of metaphors or, conversely, that language is perfectly embodied."[22] Greenblatt's homology between the indirect route of linguistic signification exemplified by metaphor (in which verbal chafing is the result of the friction between literal and metaphorical senses), and various social obstacles (blocking fathers or mistaken class difference, for example) that temporarily defer the lovers' union, is decidedly a masculine model of desire because it is impelled by deferral and obstacle – what Greenblatt describes in his discussion of *Twelfth Night* as "swerving." In *Love's Labor's Lost*, the verbal banter introduces a similar deferral of erotic satisfaction to that expressed both through the play's use of Petrarchan conceits and in the mediation of Armado's voyeurism through writing.

But if the theater is so resolutely masculine in its structuration of desire, as Greenblatt argues, then it remains to consider why this is so. What is it, in other words, that this structure must exclude or set itself against? As a beginning, let us turn to the initial encounter between the ladies and lords, where the lords' erotic desire is first incited. Although there is a good deal of the kind of bawdy wordplay Greenblatt notes in *Twelfth Night*, this scene requires us to look more closely at how this wordplay is distributed and at how power is enacted among those who engage in verbal sparring. The scene does not offer an equal display of verbal "chafing" on the part of both men and women; instead, the women are represented as deliberately thwarting every effort by the men to utilize language as a purposeful, expressive medium. This is accomplished by a kind of mimicry in which the women repeat all or part of what the men say in order to dissolve or transform the context of the original utterance:

KING: Fair Princess, welcome to the court of Navarre.
PRINCESS: "Fair" I give you back again, and "welcome" I have not yet. The
  roof of this court is too high to be yours, and welcome to the wide fields too
  base to be mine. (II.i.90–94)

And later, between Berowne and Rosaline:

BER. Did not I dance with you in Brabant once?
ROS. Did not I dance with you in Brabant once?
BER. I know you did.
ROS. How needless was it then
  To ask the question? (II.i.114–118)

The women refuse to play at the same "language game" as the men, and they thus "throw the rider in the mire," as Rosaline remarks, reversing a commonplace metaphor for male authority. The fact that the ladies are probably masked additionally offers a specular analogy to this linguistic model of female resistance. The women have thwarted the male gaze by inverting it: they can recognize the men without being recognized by them. As I suggested above, the play first introduced masculine desire in the form of Don Armado's scopic and linguistic apprehension of Jaquenetta; now, the male position as looking, speaking subject is "mired" (and mirrored) by women who thwart the economy of desire and representation that situates them as objects. Thus it would seem that the structure of desire so "identifiably male" in the comedies is overturned. But does this moment provide us with just a temporary inversion of the "normative," or does it offer the possibility of a sustained critique of the normative?

I would argue that the women's resistance to operations of this economy actually *impels* masculine desire, given that masculine desire is produced by deferral and resistance in the first place. In the play the clever Boyet remarks, after the lords have left, that "Navarre is infected ... With that which we lovers entitle 'affected'" (II.i.230, 232). In explaining his reasons for this observation to the Princess, Boyet describes the King as follows: "His face's own margent did quote such amazes / That all eyes saw his eyes enchanted with gazes" (246–247). The King's desires appear to have been spurred by having looked at the

Princess and having been frustrated by her wordplay; at the same time, his Lords have fallen in love as a result of their introduction to disguised women by whom they have been linguistically tripped up. And all of the men, it will be remembered, have fallen in love while still under the oath renouncing women and physical desire. In effect, the initial renunciation of sexuality as well as the women's resistance seems to have been the condition of their desire as well as the basis of its continuation, not at all unlike the "impediments" that incite Tarquin's lust for Lucrece.

The ridicule of Don Armado's bombastic letter anticipates the later revelation that the King and his Lords have each committed to print their own amorous desires: writing both informs their desire and openly proves their perjury of the oath. Or, in terms of the play's frequently used double entendre, the men's "will" (desire *and* volition) exposes their lack of "will." This double sense of "will" is perhaps the guiding trope of the play's treatment of masculine desire. Early in the play, "will" represents male renunciation of women and sexuality; as such, it marks the women as unattainable and distant. By adding to this the second connotation – "will" as masculine sexual desire – we recognize the mutual dependence between denial and desire, between not having and wanting, within the masculine economy figured by the play.

In succession, the King's poem and the sonnets of Longaville and Dumaine are read out loud and then derided by Berowne, whose own letter until now remains undiscovered. Indeed, Berowne resolutely maintains his innocence while indicting the men for breaking the bonds between them originally constituted by their mutual renunciation of women and sexuality.

> I am betrayed by keeping company
> With men like you, men of inconstancy.
> When shall you see me write a thing in rhyme?
> Or groan for love? Or spend a minute's time
> In pruning me? When shall you hear that I
> Will praise a hand, a foot, a face, an eye,
> A gait, a state, a brow, a breast, a waist,
> A leg, a limb?   (IV.iii.175–182)

The answer to Berowne's question is provided instantly when his own love letter to Rosaline is brought forth by Jaquenetta and Costard. In the above passage, Berowne perceives the articulation of love in the form of Petrarchan conceits as a sign of "inconstancy" and as a betrayal of the relations between the men. The comic irony is that Berowne delivers his claim to have upheld the oath of renunciation in the very terms of Petrarchan anatomization that encode and produce male desire in the first place. But when he is also discovered, the bonds once forged by a repudiation of sexuality are re-formed through the men's shared status as lovers. A second ceremony establishing male bonds is effected when the men read their love letters to *each other* – their collective renunciation of love at the beginning is now replaced by a collective pact formalizing their new status as lovers.

In other words, what was formerly conceived as masculine debasement is now celebrated: woman-as-Other has easily been transformed from debased corporality to the source of idealized love. "Who sees the heavenly Rosaline," Berowne offers,

> That, like a rude and savage man of Ind,
> At the first op'ning of the gorgeous east,
> Bows not his vassal head and, blind, strucken
> Kisses the base ground with obedient breast?
> What peremptory eagle-sighted eye
> Dares look upon the heaven of her brow,
> That is not blinded by her majesty?   (216–224)

In effect, the loss of power understood as the condition of heterosexual love for men is retained, but in this passage it is glorified rather than renounced: the lover is figured as a "vassal" who is willfully "obedient" to "her majesty." The functional idea of woman has been transformed from the "grosser manner of the world's delights" to a heavenly, majestic and regal figure, perhaps serving as an oblation to Elizabeth herself. Indeed, the "savage man" metamorphosed by the sheer presence of the Virgin Queen remained a popular motif in courtly entertainment.[23]

In order to justify this transformation, Berowne is called upon to "re-write" the contract in order to accommodate the men's newly confessed love: "now prove our loving lawful," the King demands, "and our faith not torn" (IV.iii.280–81). Despite having chastised the others for engaging in "pure idolatry" (1.71) and "painted rhetoric" (1.235), Berowne is no less soaring in his praise of the new feminine ideal that justifies renouncing the oath:

> From women's eyes this doctrine I derive:
> They sparkle still the right Promethean fire;
> They are the books, the arts, the academes,
> That show, contain, and nourish all the world;
> Else none at all in aught proves excellent.   (IV.iii.354–358)

In an earlier version of the same speech (which Bevington prints in his Textual Notes) "ground" is substituted for "arts," thus making clear the sense that woman is figured as the foundation of all male endeavors, a kind of "first cause" for all the world's activities. If in the initial oath the men elevated their pursuit of "fame," "honor" and abstract knowledge by debasing a corporal, material world that included women and sexuality, in this second agreement women and male desire for them become the *condition* of all knowledge; in other words, an ideal of woman now functions as the transcendent principle that "guarantees" the masculine pursuit of fame and honor, indeed, of their very existence. Berowne reproduces a formula all too familiar in western patriarchy: desire for idealized woman is either embedded in the very material world that needs to be transcended or, conversely, "woman" is wisdom itself, the idealized object of desire that functions, in Philippa Berry's phrase, as a "mediatrix between heaven and earth" for men.[24]

The love of knowledge and the knowledge of love: this chiasmus serves well to describe the way in which Berowne's speech figures masculine identity in relation to idealized woman:

> For wisdom's sake, a word that all men love,
> Or for love's sake, a word that loves all men,
> Or for men's sake, the authors of these women,
> Or for women's sake, by whom we men are men,
> Let us once lose our oaths to find ourselves,
> Our else we lose ourselves to keep our oaths.   (IV.iii.353–358)

As a kind of anatomy of masculinity in miniature, this rather dense passage deserves a moment of close attention. In the first two lines, Berowne recapitulates his earlier argument that the men will gain both wisdom *and* love by renouncing the oath; this belief employs the figure of wisdom as Sophia, or Sapientia, the chaste, idealized conduit of truth for men. The third and fourth lines appear to acknowledge that men ("the authors") indeed discursively construct women as the basis or "ground" of their own identities.

It will be recalled that in the original oath, a version of masculine identity was forged by swearing allegiance to a renunciation of love, sexuality and women – as the King proclaims, "Your oaths are pass'd; and now subscribe your / names" (I.i.19–20). The signing of names is conspicuously repeated as the men each in turn agree to uphold the bonds between them. In the subsequent pact, the love letters and sonnets provide another signatory bond: writing functions in both cases to legitimate homosociality construed in relation to "woman." Furthermore, the second, less formal agreement also results in a call to arms: "Saint Cupid, then!," cries the King, "And, soldiers to the field!" (IV.iii.340). The military metaphor is echoed by Boyet in his warning to the Princess and ladies upon the arrival of the men: "Prepare, madam, prepare! / Arm, wenches, arm! Encounters mounted are / Against your peace" (V.i.81–3). In the opening scene of the play, the men declared war against "the huge army of the world's desires" (I.i.10); by the fourth act, the object of conquest has become the women's affections rather than the men's own. If renouncing a debased notion of woman was supposed to have led the men to "find [them]selves" in the first instance, now the same objective depends on conquering an idealized, transcendent notion. Here we might recall Montaigne's observation, that by *enhancing the price of the place, we raise the price and endear the desire for the conquest.*

Disguised in Russian costume, the men lay siege to the women's camp, but once again masculine desire is confounded. The Princess and her ladies don masks and trade love tokens such that the men direct their attentions to the wrong women: male specular positions of authority are again thwarted. Earlier, the excessively Petrarchan love letters and sonnets were not received by their intended readers; in this scene the disguise of the object of male desire misdirects the men's gaze and serves to expose and ridicule them for relying on the signs rather than the substance of love. One could argue once again that the women disrupt the structure of male desire by calling attention to the medium in which it is expressed. "Following the signs," the men "woo'd but the sign," Berowne later remarks (V.ii.470). But, as I argued earlier, deterring and deferring the satisfaction of male desire can either be read as a parody of the way that desire is enacted or as the basis of producing desire within a masculine economy. Indeed, "following the signs" in the Petrarchan tradition engenders and constitutes the desiring/writing masculine subject.

Consequently, although this scene undoubtedly leaves the balance of power on the side the women – as the Princess claims, "[t]he effect of my intent is to cross theirs" – it is also possible to read the women's actions, and thus the play up to this point, as complicit in the very structure of male desire they seem to have foiled. The following exchange occurs between the Princess and the shrewd Boyet just after the men, ridiculed and exposed (at least to the audience) have departed:

> PRIN.: Will they return?
> BOYET: They will, they will, God knows,
>   And leap for joy, though they are lame with blows.
>   Therefore change favors; and, when they repair,
>   Blow like sweet roses in this summer air.
> PRIN.: How "blow"? How "blow"? Speak to be understood.
> BOYET: Fair ladies masked are roses in their bud;
>   Dismask'd, their damask sweet commixture shown,
>   Are angels vailing clouds, or roses blown.
> PRIN.: Avaunt, perplexity! – What shall we do,
>   If they return in their own shapes to woo?   (V.ii.290–300)

As Boyet seems to suggest, by masking themselves the women have fueled rather than foiled the men's desires; "fair ladies masked" increases among the men anticipation of when the women will be "dismask'd," just like "roses in their bud" promise to become "roses blown" [e.g. full-blown]. The metaphor additionally suggests that the inaccessibility of the women wearing masks resembles their as yet "unconquered" virginity: once "dismask'd," their "damask sweet commixture" represents a mingling of white (purity) and red (defloration) that suggests anticipation of sexual "conquest." According to the military metaphor already in place in the play, the more difficult the conquest, the greater the desire. If female virginity and chastity are indeed a source of power for women, as Elizabeth's own sexual politics demonstrate, such a form of power simultaneously foils *and* exercises masculine desire within a culture that fetishizes female sexuality in the first place.[25] Similarly, although the women are represented as empowered and in control of the various forms of courtship, *Love's Labor's Lost* appears only to imagine the play of desire within a distinctly masculine structure.

And yet, as I have suggested, a number of moments in the play leave the reader (and perhaps an audience) uneasy with such an interpretation. As much as the Princess plays the game of deferral and denial, she is additionally represented as challenging the rules of the game in the first place: she may be said to expose the Petrarchan idealization of woman as a masculine construct. In a dialogue at the beginning of the fourth act, she argues in favor of praise that is earned ("merit") against mere flattery based on appearance: "Nay, never paint me now; / Where fair is not, praise cannot mend the brow" (IV.i.16–17). And a few lines later:

> Glory grows guilty of detested crimes,
> When, for fame's sake, for praise, an outward part,
> We bend to that the working of the heart . . .   (IV.i.31–33)

In this passage the Princess seeks praise for her ability to shoot a bow, rejecting the "outward," Petrarchan flattery which the play so thoroughly satirizes. Boyet immediately turns her skill at archery into a metaphor for the power struggle between husbands and wives:

> Do not curst wives hold that self-sovereignty,
> Only for praise' sake, when they strive to be
> Lords o'er their lords?   (IV.i.36–38).

To which the Princess replies, "Only for praise; and praise we may afford / To any lady that subdues a lord" (IV.i.39–40). In this passage the Princess is represented in the figure of Diana, the chaste huntress illicitly spied bathing by Actaeon. This reference recalls the original scene of desire in the play when Armado voyeuristically watches Jaquenetta and

Costard and then immediately "turns sonnet." But it also underscores the threat to masculinity that informs the need for a specular and discursive apprehension of idealized woman. "Petrarch's Actaeon," according to Vickers, "realizes what will ensue: his response to the threat of imminent dismemberment is the neutralization, through descriptive dismemberment, of the threat."[26] While the Princess may thus expose the falseness of Petrarchan flattery, the play nonetheless represents her authority by invoking a literary tradition that fetishizes woman as an idealized, virginal figure who simultaneously confers and disturbs masculine identity. The Princess occupies the place of Diana and Elizabeth: she is uniquely empowered among women as an inaccessible object of male desire who consequently both serves and disrupts patriarchal authority.

The ending of the play allows for similar interpretive possibilities. We may read it as offering distinctly powerful, independent women (without the usual comedic excuse of male attire) who successfully disrupt the traditionally patriarchal structure of masculine desire; or, instead, we may see it as playing out an elaborately crafted set of courtship games that retains that structure. The argument for the former position would be built on the fact that the female characters seize the means of representation – the forms and phrases of courtship – and expose them as mere representations that operate without regard to the particular situations or people involved. The specular and discursive economy of masculine desire introduced in the play, according to this reading, is exposed and parodied at the expense of the men. This very appealing interpretation is enhanced by the closing sincerity of the men; Berowne, for example, confesses that their love was "Form'd by the eye and therefore, like the eye, / Full of straying shapes, of habits and of forms, / Varying in subjects as the eye doth roll / To every varied object in his glance" (V.ii.758–761). But the most compelling aspect of the play in support of this reading is provided by its unusual (by comedic standards) ending. If other of Shakespeare's comedies are at best ambiguous toward the final closure and reintegration provided by marriage, *Love's Labor's Lost* is unequivocal: "Our wooing doth not end like an old play; / Jack hath not Jill. These ladies' courtesy / Might well have made our sport a comedy" (V.ii.870–872).

The female characters retain a stature of independence and authority that is compromised among their counterparts in other comedies by marriage; furthermore, they dictate the terms of any imagined future marriage by imposing a series of year-long penances on the men. However explainable by Elizabeth's possible presence in the audience or by the need to cut short a play performed at court, this lack of traditional comic closure leaves the women as the arbiters of their own romantic involvements; they remain in what was often considered in the Renaissance the dangerous position of the marriageable maiden unattended, a fact underscored by the death of the Princess' father.

This interpretation is complicated, however, by the fact that the end of the play looks conspicuously like its beginning. The male characters each in turn pledge themselves to yet another renunciation of love and sexuality for a designated period of time; once again, sexual desire is spurred by deferral and by a failure to find even offstage the promised consummation suggested by comedies that end in marriage. It would thus seem that the structure of desire introduced at the outset of the play and sustained throughout its playful representations of courtship is sustained rather than challenged by the play's lack of closure. This structure, as I have suggested, positions men as desiring subjects and women as the inaccessible objects of desire; desire itself is generated by the forms in which it is mediated, by the obstacles it confronts, and by the fact that it can only glimpse rather than reach its end. But however difficult it might be for a male playwright in the Renaissance to envision an alternative economy of romantic love, *Love's Labor's Lost* is at least self-conscious about the way patriarchy constructs and reproduces masculine desire. And no matter how familiarly the ending of the play might appear to duplicate the structure of desire that impelled the lovers at the outset, it is significant that the women are represented in a position of awareness and control of the forms and phrases of masculine desire they have so thoroughly exposed.

The logic behind ending *Love's Labor's Lost* with the "cuckoo's song," if any exists, has eluded most critical treatments of the play.[27] But in many ways the association of cuckoldry and marriage provides an apt coda, for it suggests once again the way in which romantic love is construed by patriarchal thinking in terms of loss and fear. And more specifically, the reference to cuckoldry promises a continuation rather than a resolution of the power struggles that have occupied the play thus far, once more suggesting the limitations and contradictions of romantic love that are figured in terms of an idealization of woman. As I have argued, although the ability for wives to cuckold their husbands is often represented as a source of power for women, such a form of empowerment is certainly circumscribed by the fact that it depends on the fetishization of female chastity. Like Petrarchan idealizations of chaste women as powerful and unattainable, male cuckoldry anxiety employs the opposite yet complementary representation of women as dangerously powerful due to their supposedly unbridled sexuality. Indeed, the tradition of placing horns on the head of the cuckolded husband duplicates the same displacement of male fears of dismemberment through the use

of a phallic symbol of male potency.[28] The play's final reference to the
threat of cuckoldry to men thus appears to remind us of its initial
structure of male desire rather than to promise some sort of future
reconciliation between the sexes.

The play's longest treatment of the threat of cuckoldry in love and
marriage is offered by Berowne in Act Three:

> What? I love, I sue, I seek a wife?
> A woman, that is like a German clock,
> Still a-repairing, ever out of frame,
> And never going aright, being a watch,
> But being watch'd that it might still go right?
> Nay, to be perjur'd, which is worst of all,
> A whitely wanton with a velvet brow,
> With two pitch-balls stuck in her face for eyes;
> Ay, and, by heaven, one that will do the deed
> Though Argus were her eunuch and her guard.   (III.i.187–196)

Berowne understands cuckoldry as outside even the panoptical gaze of
Argus, the hundred-eyed giant of mythology. In this passage, the
cuckolded husband is "perjur'd" by his wife, the very same term used to
describe the men's failure to abide by their own oath of sexual continence
in the first act. Here the play exemplifies my discussion of jealousy below,
especially in terms of the panoptical control exercised by suspicious
husbands. As suggested in the reference to Argus and in so many
Renaissance treatments of jealousy and cuckoldry, the prevention of a
wife's infidelity depends on the specular vigilance of the husband; he is
entreated to watch her constantly and to interpret her for any signs of
wandering. As such, the threat of cuckoldry demands on the part of men
an interpretive "knowledge" that serves as a form of regulation and
control over female sexuality. But the perception that this vigilance is
never fully successful perhaps explains the need to *write* about cuckoldry
and female sexuality: the failure of specular constraint is turned into an
attempt at discursive control.

Understood in this way, male cuckoldry anxiety bears a number of
resemblances to Petrarchism: in both cases, men are lead by their fear of
emasculation in love to construct women as the objects of their specularization; the female body is either "scattered" in Petrarchism or scrutinized by the jealous husband; the wife or the beloved's sexuality is
fetishized, although in different ways; and finally, women are represented
as holding a certain power over men, but only within a way of thinking
that remains patriarchal. Indeed, the independence displayed by the
women would seem to make them more likely, in the men's imagination,
to cuckold future husbands. This connection seems to be drawn by the

play when, during the ridicule of Armado's love letter, Boyet suggests that if Rosaline marries, "horns" would soon appear on her husband's head (IV.i.111–113).

It thus seems not at all fortuitous that cuckoldry should be the theme of the closing of the play: more than just an example of male disempowerment or inadequacy, the reference functions within masculine structures of desire and representation that have been comically treated throughout. But most importantly, cuckoldry anxiety – the threatened loss of masculine honor and control – calls attention to the issue which the play has so nervously explored: the prospects of romantic love in a structure of masculine desire in which the conquest of women is dialectically bound to their idealization as chaste or virginal. If the men successfully "conquer" the women they have come to idealize in some anticipated moment beyond the end of the play, the promise is hardly one of "shared experience" between the sexes.[29]

What, then, is *Love's Labor's Lost*'s answer to Montaigne's question, would "wee not be lesse Cuckolds if we lesse feared to be so?" I think it is possible to interpret the play in such a way as to provide an affirmative answer – indeed, I hope my reading has done so. But the play itself is far more equivocal. Shakespeare anatomizes masculine desire by reproducing *and* parodying its effects; as such, the play provides an anatomy that exposes the very same limitations and contradictions it cannot fully escape.

According to Montaigne:

One must survay his [own] faults and study them, ere he be able to repeat them. Those which hide them from others, commonly conceale them also from themselves; and esteme them not sufficiently hidden, if themselves see them. They withdraw and disguise them from their owne consciences. . . . *Why doth no man confesse his faults? Because hee is yet in them.*[30]

Surely this "survay" is the first step toward dismantling the patriarchal "logic" I have discussed throughout this book, in which men project the cause of their own frustration and anger on to women. It is a "logic" marked by a profound irony: the very system that enables masculine identity and desire in the first place simultaneously restricts, agitates, even tortures, its masculine subjects. Like Montaigne, I think that the preliminary step toward reaching a place outside this vicious circle is to recognize our own complicity. Toward that end, Shakespeare and Montaigne have left behind texts that encourage us, on levels even the authors did not envision, to see "our own faults and study them."

5 Inscriptions of difference: cross-dressing, androgyny and the anatomical imperative

> I often hard, but never read till now,
> That women-kinde the codpeeces did weare;
> But in those Iles, the men to women bow,
> Which do their names of male, and female beare.
>
> William Gamage, "On the Feminine Supremacie"[1]

This lighthearted epigram printed in 1613 is part of an often fervid set of writings provoked by the London fashion of women wearing masculine attire. Addressed with considerable passion and vitriol in poems, pamphlets, plays and sermons especially (but not exclusively) during the second decade of James' reign, the controversy appears well in excess of the actual threat those few women who cross-dressed might have posed. Such a discrepancy between writing and event suggests at once that cross-dressing women are not specifically the source of the controversy as much as catalytic signs of a set of prior fears and anxieties. A relatively stable sex/gender system would hardly have been disturbed by such an infrequent and obviously theatrical play with gender identification; by contrast, the frequent virulence expressed in the cross-dressing controversy underscores and exposes the instability and agitation of sex and gender-based identity in the early modern period. The central argument of this chapter will be that what lies at the heart of this controversy is an anxiety about ambivalence itself – the perceived confusion of those gender and status boundaries by which individual and collective identities are forged and guaranteed. Similar to Bacon's response to the porosity of status delineations, the prospect that gendered identities are not clearly defined could provoke a variety of compensatory, defensive tactics. Bacon employs the figure of purity; those who attack cross-dressing women evoke natural, God-given or anatomical difference. What complicates matters considerably is that the most anxious response to androgyny or to any confusion in the semiotics of identity belies not only a fear of sameness, but also a fear of one's desire for the very figure so resolutely condemned. Thus the excoriations against androgynous women appear to protect gender difference as well as to protect against

150

(perhaps even repress) the disturbing power of transgressive desire. In other words, distinct gendered identities require distinct forms of erotic desire: androgyny confuses and confounds both.

It is necessary to historicize the cross-dressing controversy at the outset by recognizing the importance placed on outward anatomy as the basis of gender differentiation. As Thomas Laqueur argues, in the Renaissance, "sex, or the body, must be understood as the epiphenomenon, while gender, what we would take to be a cultural category, was primary or 'real.'"[2] This observation is underscored by Gamage's epigram, where the fashion of women wearing "codpieces" aligns possession of a symbol of anatomy with a real reversal of power: "men to women bow." The presence of the codpiece in men's fashion (by this period a theatrical or ceremonial rather than everyday accessory) calls attention to an insecurity toward its anatomical signified, a fear that the penis is less "guaranteed" than its symbol. In Marjorie Garber's broad study of cross-dressing, the codpiece is "a sign of gender undecidability, since it is the quintessential gender mark of 'seeming,' Lacan's third term interposed between 'having' and 'being' . . . [it] confounds the question of gender, since it can signify yes or no, full or empty, lack or lack of lack."[3] By appropriating this symbol as part of their cross-dressing, women underscore the referential ambiguity that exists when men wear codpieces; in effect, they reveal the symbol as merely symbolic rather than as an anatomically secured or naturally given. Broadly speaking, the cultural capital accorded to the phallus becomes not necessarily the property of those possessing a penis. Gamage represents this deconstruction of phallic authority somewhat blithely as a "women-on-top" reversal, while those more threatened invoke the category of female monstrosity. Both are responses to the abrogation of supposedly natural sex differences. The confusion of such differences stirred even greater anxiety precisely because, as Laqueur has shown, male and female genitalia were still understood as structurally equivalent – the male genitals having dropped from the body due to their greater heat.[4] With this merely caloric explanation in mind, male anatomical superiority must surely have been experienced as tenuous (and potentially reversible), thus encouraging the symbolic importance of the codpiece as an outward sign of something in actuality less secure. In Garber's pithy phrase, the "anxiety of male artificiality is summed up, as it were, in a nutshell."[5]

Without what would later become a biologically essentialist basis for gender identity, the early modern period requires a rhetoric of differentiation that continuously needs to assert the naturalness and immutability of its categories from other sources. Paradoxically, apparel and language

– both mutable and manipulable semiotic systems – are often the media in which "natural" differences are supposed to find accurate representation. This paradox results in an insistence on the accuracy or transparency of apparel and language as signifying media, but at the same time, its produces an anxiety over the unavoidable instances of misrepresentation, such as cross-dressing. Indeed, this parallel between apparel and language appears taken for granted in the Renaissance. As we have seen in a number of texts, highly rhetorical language is often compared to gaudy apparel, and figurative language is linked to the "feminine" for its capacity to mislead and misrepresent. The effeminate courtier, for example, was doubly guilty of gender ambiguity for wearing French fashions and for his smooth, honey-tongued phrases. Like apparel, language offers a code for self-representation in which "correct" self-identification sustains and guarantees gender differentiation. But the capacity for using the code to confuse this differentiation is an intrinsic part of the code itself – if apparel names identity it can also misname it. The Puritan moralist Philip Stubbes, whose polemics so often seem to belie his culture's masculine anxieties, all but equates apparel and identity in a passage from the *Anatomy of Abuses*. Having described in detail the men's fashions adopted by women, he writes: "& though this be a kinde of attire appropriate onely to man, yet they blush not to wear it; and if they could as wel chaunge their sex, & put on the kinde of man, as they can weare apparel assigned onely to man, I think they could as verely become men indeed."[6]

What is rarely acknowledged in the period is that both sign systems, given the absence of a biological, essentialist basis for identity, are critically important media in which gender and status identity are constituted as much as represented. In a culture in which identity is not, in theory, supposed to be mutable, there is a paradoxical reliance upon outward signs to ensure stable identification. The idea that "performance" is involved in gender identity, to use Judith Butler's recent formulation, could not be articulated precisely because it openly names what figures like Stubbes anxiously imagine might be the case – hence Stubbes' attacks on the theater as dangerous for its affective power.[7] The problem is even more acute in a culture where performance and theatricality are built into everyday life. Historicizing the cross-dressing controversy thus requires us to recognize that identity in the early modern period was achieved in part through an interpretive practice – the interpretation of cultural signifiers whose relation to their signifieds was, at the least, a source of potential uncertainty. "I have met with some of these tulles in London so disguised," William Harrison writes in his memoirs, "that it passed my skill to *discerne* whether they were men or women."[8]

That identity might depend upon discernible signs explains the Renais-sance need to articulate a rhetoric of difference by appealing, most often, to the legitimating authority of God or nature, and especially to the belief in God's unequal creation of men and women, an argument often disputed by women pamphleteers such as Esther Sowernam.[9] Daniel Rogers writes in 1642 that God "might have done otherwise, that is, yeelded to the woman coequall beginning, samenesse of generation, or relation of usefulness" in his argument for wives' subjection.[10] In this passage, any form of similarity between men and women is in direct conflict with God's design, but the very mention of what God "might have done" once again brings into dialectical play the fear of sameness that motivates Rogers' claim. In John Williams' sermon of 1619, gender similarity (in the form of the androgyne) is linked to the devil: God "divided male and female, but the devil hath joined them, that *mulier formosa*, is now become *mulier monstrosa superne*, half man half woman."[11] Williams echoes the frequent charge that women in masculine attire were "monstrous" perversions of the natural order. In a similar example from before the controversy erupted, Averell writes:

though they be in sexe Women, yet in attire they appeare to *be* men, and are like *Androgini*, who counterfayting the shape of either kind, are in deede neither, so while they are in condition women, and would seeme in apparel men, they are neither men nor women, but plaine Monsters.[12]

This passage is notable for its definition of the androgyne as possessing not both men and women's attributes, but neither. Once again the excessiveness of the terms used to depict this so-called transgression – especially monstrosity – focuses our attention on the collective masculine identity that perceived itself as threatened. What aspects of Renaissance masculinity could be so deeply unsettled by the idea of women in masculine attire?

The author of the often misogynistic "Hic Mulier" (1620) tract decrying women who wear masculine apparel repeatedly insists upon natural and God-given differences between women and men. The greatest transgression represented by those "monstrous" women who cross-dress, he argues in various ways, is their effacement of these fundamental differences. From this perspective, "Hic Mulier" is representative of many male-authored, early modern texts about gender and sexuality that produce and inscribe gender difference as if they were only identifying it. We may take a step further to say that the primary fear to which these texts respond is the intolerable possibility of sameness between women and men, a possibility that would render meaningless both the gender/ status system (and) the individual subjectivities within it. In the following remarks, I shall pursue some of the specific forms of this general observation by addressing some of the ways in which masculine subjectivity must continually produce and sustain itself by articulating its own identity and desire as distinctive. More specifically, my argument is that masculine identity and authority depend upon articulating a discourse that marks itself, and can only know itself, through its differentiation from what it *constructs* as "woman" and female desire. The necessary form of expression for this discourse is to produce and legitimate an idea of women as both objects of male desire and as objects of masculine knowledge. As we shall see, the instability of such a model of identity is evident at every turn.

What interests me most about the production of "languages of differences," to borrow Jean Howard's phrase, is their excessive and declamatory rhetoric.[13] If it were simply a question of stating agreed upon differences, surely we would not find the passion or virulence exhibited in the "Hic Mulier" tract or in Joseph Swetnam's angry "Arraignment of Lewd, idle, froward, and inconstant women" (1615), a title that speaks for itself. Nor would we find James I ordering preachers to condemn cross-dressing women from the pulpits. The greater the misogyny of this rhetoric, the more it reveals the impermanence and constructedness of the differences it claims, and the more it exhibits the anxiety of the masculinity it seeks to defend. Indeed, the men truly do protest too much. This point is not at all lost on some of the women who write in response to these misogynistic tracts, particularly Jane Anger, whose "Protection for Women" (1589) rests on her belief that misogynistic writing reveals more about its authors than its subjects. "I would," she writes, "that ancient writers would as well have busied their heads about deciphering the deceits of their own sex as they have about setting down our follies," which is in fact what her text subtly suggests they have done anyway.[14] Esther Sowernam makes a similar point in her response to Swetnam entitled "Esther hath hang'd Haman" (1617): "When men complain of beauty and say that 'wantonness and baits allure men', it is a direct means to know of what disposition they are."[15] Following Anger and Sowernam's lead, another way of posing the question I have raised is to ask: what forms of threatening sameness did these "languages of differences" seek to discredit and dispel?

Towards answering this question, I want to look at several texts written by men that display an anxiety toward the dissolution of differences between men and women, but also to attend to the writing of women, such as Anger, who find themselves in the position of arguing against particular versions of gender difference, or at least of turning the rhetoric of difference against its male authors in order to expose it as a masculine construction. Although many aspects of the "querelle des femmes" texts written by women depend upon traditional, stereotypical defenses, other moments offer useful anatomies of masculine desire and subjectivity that begin from the premise, noted above by Anger, that attacks against women are largely projections of an anxious masculinity whose rhetoric of difference-as-hierarchy was perceived as threatened.

My first example departs significantly from some of the more virulent texts I have introduced, but it displays a rhetoric of difference useful as a comparative introduction. Shakespeare's sonnet 20 achieves the marking of difference through an appeal to anatomy that seems, at first glance, more consistent with Freudian anatomy – in which male and female are characterized by presence and absence – than with the Renaissance anatomical beliefs discussed by Laqueur, Ian McLean and others.[16] But the sonnet also makes clear that anatomical difference is by no means the primary, definitive characteristic in the production of masculine desire; instead, desire is produced from the co-presence of androgynous beauty *and* specifically gendered characteristics. It thus exemplifies, as Laqueur argues, the fluidity between gender and biology in Renaissance thinking rather than the priority of biology that would characterize later anatomical science. Instead of providing an essential, irrevocable truth, the genital "facts" of the male body in the sonnet are secondary characteristics, and their mutability is by no means a source of anxiety. In this sonnet, Shakespeare articulates the other side of the declamatory rhetoric against androgyny we have seen above by writing the androgyne as an object of desire. In other words, he exposes what haunts and disturbs writers like Swetnam, Averell and the author of "Hic Mulier": the erotic appeal of the figure of ambivalence.

For a variety of reasons unique to the triangular model of desire set up in the sonnets to the young man, the speaker in sonnet 20 is not at all anxious about the ambiguity of sexual differences, which is in part created by the Renaissance belief in the structural sameness among male and female reproductive organs. In fact, the poet's desire appears occasioned by the young man's as yet undifferentiated, androgynous gender status. Here is the sonnet in full:

> A woman's face with Nature's own hand painted
> Hast thou, the master-mistress of my passion;
> A woman's gentle heart, but not acquainted
> With shifting change, as is false women's fashion;
> An eye more bright than theirs, less false in rolling,
> Gilding the object whereupon it gazeth;
> A man in hue, all hues in his controlling,

Which steals men's eyes and women's souls amazeth.
And for a woman wert thou first created,
Till Nature, as she wrought thee, fell a-doting,
And by addition me of thee defeated,
By adding one thing to my purpose nothing.
But since she prick'd thee out for women's pleasure.
Mine be thy love and thy love's use their treasure.[17]

The "master-mistress" of the poet's "passion" is initially described as both androgynous *and* distinctly male. Or, in other terms, he exhibits only the characteristics the poet finds desirable in women ("a woman's face" and "gentle heart") but not their stereotypically negative features, here represented in terms of mutability and falseness (3–5). The young man is a "man in hue, all hues in his controlling" (7), but he is still anatomically (or to be more specific, genitally) not male, at least through the first eight lines. The octave thus depicts the poet's desire as originally incited by an androgynous figure at the same time as he marks hierarchical differences between characteristics of men and women. But importantly, gender difference in this sonnet is not threatened by androgyny because the sonnet "takes place" entirely within a male, homosocial context.

It is tempting to argue that the sonnet depicts a transformation from female to male that would be consistent with the Renaissance anatomical theory of inverted male and female genitalia, the former gradually descending, given sufficient heat, in order to produce a male. But this reading is not supported by the fact that Nature adds "one thing" to "nothing" – a binary opposition rather than a structural equivalence toward anatomical difference appears to inform the poem. Thus, the sonnet is more in line with the Renaissance depiction of female genitalia as an absence. But the evocation of "nothing" in this sonnet does not carry the dark, threatening connotations associated with desire in the dark lady sonnets, where the female body is represented in terms of evil, corruption and hell (sonnet 44), and where "Desire is death" (sonnet 147). This anxiety of returning to an engulfing "nothing" haunts the Renaissance masculine imagination, often producing the misogyny of a figure like Lear. Sonnet 20, on the other hand, employs an almost playful tone in describing the all-important addition of a penis to what was formerly "nothing": radical anatomical difference does not threaten without the direct presence of women.[18]

In passing, it is worth noting that the same homosexual context may have also secured the mostly benign acceptance of the theatrical convention of boys playing female roles, despite the vociferous denunciations of Puritan anti-theatricalists. The poet's young man in sonnet 20 is very close to impersonating or "playing" a woman, at least in the octave: he is a male in form ("hue") but displays a "woman's face."[19] As in the examples of Viola in *Twelfth Night* and Rosalind in *As You Like It*, even though this impersonation is left ambiguous, it is not a source of anxiety or even discomfort in the sonnet or in the comedies. Shakespeare appears interested in exploring the erotics of androgyny in both, and the theater affords the same homosocial comfort he creates in the sonnet. A theater in which women were actually present on stage might well have discouraged this sort of exploration in its consequent need to accentuate rather than explore gender difference.

As I suggested above, the poet's desire is in place before the anatomical gender differentiation, before nature "prick'd thee out for women's pleasure" (13). In the final couplet, the addition of a penis in the young man's creation robs the poet of an erotic relationship, leaving his "love" platonic, while the young man's love will become the "treasure" of women (14). This final image specifically suggests ejaculation, as in Emilia's speech in *Othello* about sexual jealousy: "Say that they slack their duties, / And pour our treasures into foreign laps" (IV.iii.91–92). But although anatomical difference may be required for consummation, it is not the source of desire in the sonnet; indeed, the addition of "one thing" frustrates the poet's already present desire: he writes, "And by addition me of thee defeated" (11). The comparison with *Othello* is useful as a way of underscoring the difference in attitudes between the sonnet's speaker and Shakespeare's tortured protagonist. Any prospect of Desdemona's own desire profoundly threatens Othello; spurred by Iago, the precariousness of his own identity is exacerbated by her expression of desire (he believes) for someone else ("And when I love thee not, / Chaos is come again": III.iii.93–94). But the poet in sonnet 20 blithely acknowledges women's pleasures as in no way threatening to the co-existence of his own love.

It is thus difficult to argue, as Joseph Pequigney does, that the poet's initial desire for the young man is homoerotic, since he praises his "master-mistress" for possessing both male and female qualities.[20] Indeed, the young man's appeal derives from the combination of his sameness and difference in relation to the poet. According to Linda Woodbridge, the androgynous or hermaphroditic figure could either engender masculine anxiety, on the one hand, or provide an ideal of shared male and female attributes, on the other.[21] In the first case, the hermaphrodite, associated with effeminacy and impotence, represents a dissolution of masculine difference from women and thus threatens the basis of masculine identity. As I shall discuss in the next section, this is very much the attitude of Philip Stubbes' anti-theatrical attacks, as well as the source of the anxiety shown in the "Hic Mulier" pamphlet, where cross-dressing women are perceived as hermaphrodites. Hermaphroditism threatens masculinity because its possession of both male and female characteristics presents a case of non-differentiation. This may have activated a deeper fear, as Laura Levine suggests, that there really was nothing at the core of male identity.[22] In what is surely an unconscious response to this fear, masculinity projects "nothing" onto women, then anxiously defends this projection by insisting upon supposedly natural differences between men and women. Women must first be "nothing" before men can become something, or "one thing," as the sonnet has it. But such an attitude must wait until the introduction of the dark lady in Shakespeare's sonnets and until the period of his tragedies on stage.

A final note on the sonnet concerns the interaction of desire and the written inscription of difference. There are really two authors in the sonnet; besides the poet, there is Nature, who "fell a-doting" (10) over her own androgynous creation. Inasmuch as the young man is "painted" (1) by Nature and inscribed in the sonnets by the poet, an implicit parallel exists between the two authors that is played out in their contest for the young man: Nature's paint brush is the poet's pen. Since Nature has the ability to create the "proper" genital differentiation necessary for the consummation of her own (and women's) desires, the poet is left, somewhat disconsolately, with only his ability to write and inscribe his desire in the form of the sonnets to the young man. His writing is produced out of the frustration of his erotic desire or, to use a near equivalence familiar in the Renaissance, his pen is activated precisely because his penis is not.

When the poet inscribes his desire in the first five lines of the sonnet, he is careful to praise the androgynous figure's constancy over and against the "shifting change" and falseness he associates with "women's fashion" (4). This contrast places his own constant, masculine desire in opposition to women's "rolling" (roving) desire, implying that women's identities are as variable as the fashions to which they are subject, while men possess an essential and self-willed identity – the young man is a "man in hue, all hues in his controlling" (7). The sonnet inscribes a difference in subjectivity and desire between women and men that becomes the centerpiece of the cross-dressing controversy a number of years later. Women whose apparel does not match their gender and station lack sufficient self-definition to maintain constancy in their desires; as a result, they are often depicted by men as having powerful, unbridled sexual appetites. The irony of this masculinist attitude, of course, is that it constructs, then assumes, the absence of a constant, self-controlling subjectivity in women and proceeds to discover this inconstancy as the source of consuming female desire which is threatening to men.

In Shakespeare's sonnet, this attitude is played out in the sequence before the young man is given a differentiated anatomical identity. The sonnet carefully marks the differences between women and men, between masculine and feminine desire, prior to the "addition" that will anatomically secure difference. It is thus reasonable to argue that the need to mark gender differences (constancy/inconstancy, subject/subject to) arises in response to anatomical non-differentiation. Although Shakespeare's poet somewhat wistfully admits the absolute differentiation and resolution brought on by the addition of a penis ("one thing"/"nothing"), this is no resolution to his desire: the unavailability of corporal consummation finds its outlet in a body of sonnets that continuously inscribe the poet's desire for the young man in writing.

In sonnet 20, the poet's desire is provoked by a figure who displays both male and female characteristics; in this way, we may say that desire arises from a lack of differentiation that in no way appears threatening. But at the same time, the sonnet delineates a specific set of differences between men and women that rely upon the commonplace construction of women as inconstant and false. In other words, the poet's desire for the young man may be said to operate within a space of ambiguity and contradiction that arises from the tension produced in his alternatively (or simultaneously) homoerotic and homosocial bond with the young man. By contrast, "Hic Mulier" is primarily motivated by the perceived threat to male/female difference brought on by women who cross-dress. As is well known, this controversy began as a result of a few, mostly aristocratic, women who appeared in London wearing men's fashions.[23] Significantly, the "Hic Mulier" pamphlet and surrounding controversy thus respond to a threat posed by actual women, albeit very few. According to the pamphlet, such women are "manlike not only from the head to the waist, but to the very foot and in every condition: man in body by attire, man in behavior by rude complement . . ." and so on (269–270). The primary threat to gender differentiation invoked in the pamphlet is made against, as Howard has written, "a normative social order based upon strict principles of hierarchy and subordination, of which women's subordination to man was a chief instance . . ."[24] Howard's understanding depends upon the important realization that any threat to gender difference is always a threat to status difference: women who dressed as men embodied both *examples* of disobedience to authority and *analogies* for other forms of status confusion.

In my discussion of the "Hic Mulier" pamphlet, I want to suggest that what is most threatening, most potentially subversive, about the dissolution of gender difference brought on by cross-dressing women is their confusion and confutation of male desire. This claim is based on the inseparability of desire and identity: to know clearly what and who one wants is to know who one is. The anxious response to the confusing of this model by the cross-dressing woman or androgyne is to invoke the category of monstrosity in order to avoid acknowledging one's own (ambiguous) desire. Additionally, the "manly woman" challenges a masculine economy of knowledge and interpretation by confusing the very act of interpretation – a distinctly masculine prerogative in this patriarchal culture. The angry condemnation of cross-dressing thus expresses a masculine fear of non-differentiation such that what is thrown into confusion is not just identity and status differences but also a desiring male subjectivity whose definition depends upon a clearly discernible object of desire. Since subjectivity is always marked both by the status it claims and the forms of desire it takes, these two realms are always coexistent.

It is important to remember that depictions of cross-dressing women at this time emphasize both their appropriation of masculine attire and their hermaphroditic status. They dress like men, thus upholding (while inverting) a male/female binarism, but they also dissolve this binarism in their characterization as (supposedly) hermaphrodites.[25] In the "logic" of the male imagination a reversal of gender could only be categorized as confusion. Most portraits indeed show outward traits of both men and women: bobbed hair, doublets unbuttoned to reveal the breasts, broad-brimmed hats, and very often, swords, dagger or pistols. The author of "Hic Mulier" suggests that the weaponry is a sign of their aggressive behavior, and protests that there is no reason women should carry weapons. It is quite consistent with an early modern sensibility to read this addition to the cross-dresser's attire as a phallic appropriation, something like Gamage's "women-kinde the codeppeces did weare." Here the appropriation involves a symbol of the male anatomy – they've "added one thing" to their "nothing" and in so doing collapsed a key element of anatomical differentiation. Another version of this sort of appropriation will be found in the phallic power of the pen, itself a sign of the material importance of writing, when women are charged with acting as men simply because they write for public audiences.

A useful way to introduce the uneasy play of masculine desire in "Hic Mulier" is to consider briefly some aspects of Renaissance anti-theatricalism. Levine's indispensable essay on Stephen Gosson's *The School of Abuse* (1579) and on Philip Stubbes' *Anatomie of Abuses*

(1583), (which also covers several other treatises on theatricality) persuasively argues that the opposition to boy actors playing female roles is motivated by an "anxiety that there is no such thing as a stable identity."[26] Gosson's belief that the theater "effeminated" the mind, and Stubbes' suspicion that boy actors in women's clothes "adulterate" the male gender, reveal a fundamental instability in the male subjectivities of the theater's spectatorship. This suspicion is provoked by a belief in the power of the theater to provoke desire and pleasure such that the "primacy of the will" may be overthrown. In Gosson's phrase, playwrights create "effeminate gesture to ravish the sence, and wanton speache to whette desire to inordinate lust."[27] Such overwhelming desire effeminizes men because it makes them like women; that is, unable to exercise the self-control and reason that constitutes the male subject and differentiates him from women. Stubbes is even more explicit about the threat to "natural" differences raised by cross-dressing women: "Our Aparell was given us as a signe distinctive to discern betwixt sex and sex, & therfore one to weare the Apparel of another sex is *to participate with the same*, and to adulterate the veritie of his owne kinde."[28] Stubbes requires a transparent sign system ("Apparel") in order to "discern betwixt sex and sex" so as to preserve his ability to know gender difference and to maintain segregation between men and women, without which his sense of masculine purity is undermined. Once again the threat is to the security of masculine discernment; Stubbes' anxiety is very much an interpretive crisis that challenges his ability to mark the difference between men and women. But this crisis can only be motivated by an unrecognized fear that these differences are not as essential as moralists like Stubbes want to believe. In part, Stubbes' thinking enacts the contradiction unique to this period between a social imperative to mark absolute gender difference and a set of anatomical "facts" that recognizes homologies and resemblances.

The fear that men and women are not essentially different, since men always possess the potential to "revert" to women, is also underscored in William Prynne's *Historio-mastix*. Here the author suggests that men in women's clothing risk becoming women: "Doth not that valiant, that man of courage who is admirable in his armes, and formidable to his enemies degenerate into a woman with his veiled face?"[29] Prynne's point is that a "veiled" man places himself in the position of women; he becomes a disguised entity who requires interpretation. In other words, within a masculine economy, he takes the feminine position of interpreted object rather than the masculine position of interpreting subject.

Thus we find in the anti-theatrical discourse at least two constructions of masculinity that are perceived as threatened by the cross-dressing convention of the English theater and the ways desire circulated within it. On the one hand, masculinity requires the governance of one's desire rather than enslavement to it; on the other, it demands a congruence between outward appearance and inner selfhood such that no interpretive anxiety arises. Stubbes tries to guarantee an interpretive security, or transparency, for apparel by suggesting that it is a "signe" "given us" (by God?) rather than a merely arbitrary code. Self-control over desire and interpretive knowledge interact to form the basis of a very tenuous masculine subjectivity. Both of these models respond to the deeper anxiety that men have the capacity to "degenerate" into women, to take the place of women. By attacking theatricality in this way, the anti-theatrical prejudice functions to produce those differences deemed necessary to masculinity at the same time as it belies a fear of sameness between men and women, a sameness always understood as regression or debasement on the part of men. As we return to "Hic Mulier," in which the attack is against women who cross-dress, not boy actors, it will become clear that the same fear of non-differentiation generates a similarly anxious masculinity.

One of the pervasive anxieties in "Hic Mulier" is that women who cross-dress reveal "that which should be hidden" (271). Perhaps the most passionately argued moment in the pamphlet includes the following admonition to women, worth quoting at length:

Imitate nature, and, as she hath placed on the surface and superficies of the earth all things needful for man's sustenance and necessary use (as Herbs, Plants, Fruits, Corn and suchlike) but locked up close in the hidden caverns of the earth all things which pertain to his delight and pleasure (as gold, silver, rich minerals, and precious Stones), so do you discover unto men all things that are fit for them to understand from you (as bashfulness in your cheek, chastity in your eyes, wisdom in your words, sweetness in your conversation, and severe modesty in the whole structure or frame of your universal composition). But for those things which belong to this wanton and lascivious delight and pleasure (as eyes wandering, lips billing, tongue enticing, bared breasts seducing, and naked arms embracing), oh hide them, for shame hide them in the closest prisons of your strictest government! Shield them with modest and comely garments, such as are warm and wholesome, having every window closed with a strong Casement and every Loophole furnished with such strong Ordinance that no unchaste eye may come near to assail them, no lascivious tongue woo a forbidden passage, nor no profane hand touches relics so pure and religious (271–272).

This passage draws a rather curious analogy because the availability of the necessities of man's "sustenance" in nature and those things "fit for [men] to understand" in women – chastity, modesty and so on. Women should "[i]mitate nature" by displaying only those qualities men need for their "necessary use." But the passage reaches near hysteric proportions (and metaphorical vertigo) in its dire warning against any display of "things which pertain to [men's] delight and pleasure": these should be "locked up close," hidden "in the closest prisons," and "closed with a strong Casement." Why does the author of "Hic Mulier" so fearfully insist that women's erotic allurements should be kept "behind impregnable walls," as the passage adds later? And why is it that women dressed as men too seductively reveal that which should remain hidden?

The easy answer is that the author is merely calling for chastity and modesty in women, a point supported by the pamphlet's frequent linkage of female cross-dressing to "lascivious" female desire, and by the author's supposed concern that women who cross-dress might tarnish their own reputations. But this answer does not really explain why women in men's apparel are perceived as "wanton" in the first place, nor does it explain why this is so threatening to men that it must be railed against in such excessive terms. Clearly, what the author more desperately fears about the overt seductiveness of women is the ensuing seduction of himself and those of his own gender. As the passage's plea to women to keep "every window closed with a strong Casement" rises to an almost frenzied pitch, the anxiety is thus not so much the loss of women's modesty (why would this otherwise evoke such passion in a man?) but more specifically the danger women's immodesty poses to male desire. In short, masculine identity (and desire) is enabled by insisting upon women's "severe modesty" just as it is threatened by their readily apparent and available "lascivious delight." Similar to the antitheatrical treatises, the real danger to men is that their reason and self-control will be overthrown by their own desire – desire specifically generated in this case by a hermaphroditic figure.

Furthermore, the "Hic Mulier" passage states that women are allowed to "discover unto men all things that are fit for them to understand from you" – these are things "on the surface." But the dangerous moment is when the hidden sources of women's "wanton and lascivious delight" are brought from their hidden depths to the surface. One of the fears behind this horrific prospect is that the exposure of what should remain hidden would dissolve the masculine economy of interpretation by making "necessarily" inscrutable texts transparent, thus overthrowing the security of masculine interpretive authority. Once again, the principle behind this anxiety is the masculine fear of gender sameness. Women who do not present themselves as demure, chaste and bashful – who do not disguise their seductions – foil a masculine economy of interpretation and desire by taking the part of men. The author of "Hic Mulier" makes the point even more dramatically in the line directly following the long passage quoted above. Women who do *not* hide the sources of male "delight and pleasure" threaten to "enchant the weak passenger to shipwreck and destruction" (272). To paraphrase this commonplace metaphor, men are lost at sea – they don't know themselves – if they are unable to navigate by way of familiar, discernible signs. Thus women who cross-dress have, in a sense, rewritten and confused the map of masculine knowledge, desire and identity so as to make it unreadable by men.

Part of this interpretive anxiety is that interpretation is itself a model of desire if women and women's bodies are constructed as texts. In other words, if the source of men's "delight and pleasure" is immediately available, there is no mediation, no deferral, no "lets" to enflame that desire. Interpretive confusion is disorienting, but so is the lack of the need to interpret. Here the masculine logic seems to be that if there is no resistance to fulfilling desire, there is no desire. Paradoxically, then, the passage displays a fear of overwhelming desire and, at the same time, a fear that the basis for that desire might be lost. The author displays what might be called the erotic logic of the forbidden: he must insist on the impenetrability of the "pure and religious" in order to excite his "profane" desire to transgress it. This paradox is contained in the writing itself, as the author almost pornographically lists women's physical allurements at the same time as he condemns their visibility.

It still remains curious that the situation of women dressed *as men* brings out the "Hic Mulier" author's anxiety about women not hiding their bodies; one could just as easily imagine male attire as a form of enhanced modesty. Why is dressing as a man so immodest an act that it propels the author to such virulent censure of women? On one level the author is surely protecting against his own desire for the cross-dressed woman: there is something intrinsically erotic about the transgression itself, either boys dressed as women or women as men. Indeed, the author of "Hic Mulier" so closely resembles Philip Stubbes in his fear of the arousal of an audience by boys playing women that it would not seem to matter which way the cross-dressing goes. But of course the transgression is greater for the women since they are, in effect, "dressing up" in status when they apparel themselves as men. If women dress like men they presumably might act like men (wantonly and lasciviously, the passage suggests) which would also mean to desire as men do. Thus one of the operative anxieties is men's attraction not to the Other but to a mirror image of himself: a terror at the dissolution of difference that is also a source of erotic appeal. Or, the frightening prospect arises that women may in fact have desires similar to men's. It might also be possible that the figure of the hermaphrodite is a figure of desire because he/she occupies an interstitial space, an in-between, that threatens normative boundaries but at the same time secures them. This way of thinking about masculine desire would accommodate both the latent homoeroticism of the theater and the apparently heteroerotic desire in the "Hic Mulier" passage.

Indeed, as I suggested in my discussion of homoeroticism in Burton's *Anatomy*, representations of desire for men or for women are not distinct erotic economies in the early modern period. In Orgel's formulation, "[w]omen are dangerous to men because sexual passion for women renders men effeminate: this is an age in which sexuality itself is misogynistic, as the love of women threatens the integrity of the perilously achieved male identity."[30] Orgel argues that the theater avoids this potential danger by frequently disguising female characters as men during courtship, and also by the convention of boy actors, both of which produce the same homosocial security I discussed in sonnet 20. But it is also true that the Renaissance views homoerotic desire as dangerous for the same reason; it could also overthrow reason and self-governance, thus effeminizing the lover. Once again, Shakespeare's Achilles in *Troilus and Cressida* provides a useful example. Exhorting Achilles to battle, Patroclus says to his lover, "A woman impudent and mannish grown / Is not more loath'd than an effeminate man / In time of action" (III.iii.217–219). In this passage Achilles is compared to a cross-dressing woman; he outwardly appears as a man but his inward self-control and volition are gone. The play is concerned with Achilles' homoerotic relationship to Patroclus only inasmuch as it has sapped his will to act and thus cast him in the role of a woman, not because of any intrinsic opposition to homoeroticism. His transgression is that he has dissolved critical differences between men and women, abrogating the masculine privilege of self-control, volition and reason. In other words, Achilles threatens the inherent quality of status difference (outwardly marked by specific characteristics) by adopting a subordinate role. His behavior is as unnatural and foolish as that of a king who abdicates his throne.[31]

Clearly, if status differences between men and women were as secure and inherent as early modern social theory argues, we would not find such a ubiquitous masculine concern over the fear of effeminacy – very much the operative anxiety in *Antony and Cleopatra*, where the same images of shipwreck, drowning and the overflowing Nile are associated with Cleopatra's seductive power to effeminize Antony.[32] In another example, the overt misogyny of Joseph Swetnam's "Arraignment of . . . women" is clearly a response to the same fear of emasculation. He writes: "For women have a thousand ways to entice thee and ten thousand ways to deceive thee and all such fools as are suitors unto them . . . They lay out the folds of their hair to entangle men into their love; betwixt their breasts is the vale of destruction; and in their beds there is hell, sorrow, and repentance."[33] Because male desire is "insatiable," Swetnam continues, it is a very difficult task to avoid being "ensnared." Anthony Munday expresses the same anxiety in his anti-theatrical "A Second and Third Blast" where he argues that the dangers of theatrical seduction are magnified since masculine desire is "alwaies eating and never satisfied."[34]

I think the most revealing move made in all these examples is quite simply the projection onto women of what men fear most in themselves. The desperate threat posed by the emasculating potential of their own desire is represented as the fault of the seductive, siren-like woman. Thus, the demand for women to be "chaste, silent and obedient" so frequently echoed in the period is very much a self-protective strategy, a way for men to insure their ability to maintain that tenuous control over their own desire that is such a crucial constituent of masculine identity – this is exactly what cross-dressing women undermine. But this reasoning exposes a rather overwhelming contradiction that several of the treatises I have discussed seem at least partially aware of. If masculine identity is largely constructed as a desiring subject, a subject in pursuit, then the very condition of the masculinity is also the source of its potential destruction. Or, in other terms, desire is the basis of masculinity *and* emasculation, the form of differentiating a masculine subjectivity *and* the potential source of its dissolution into nothing.

Like the author of "Hic Mulier," Swetnam insists that woman is "nothing else but a contrary to man" (205). In Shakespeare's sonnet, it will be recalled, the initially undifferentiated figure of desire was transformed into the young man by the addition of "one thing" to "nothing." The paradox of this binary model of gendered identification is that it first constructs a model of difference between positive (male) and negative (female) terms, but then articulates an economy of desire that threatens to dissolve difference into nothing. At this point we can suggest that the only way for the masculine subject to exercise control over what is always/already a potentially self-destructive model of identity is to maintain control over the means of its representation. In other words, because of the endemic contradiction that lies at the core of masculinity, the only strategy left available is to articulate the contradiction itself – the fears it entails, the anxiety it raises – in writing and speech. Such articulation may thus be said to have an enabling function – enabling, that is, the perpetuation of a contradictory, volatile identity. For Shakespeare, this is a matter of representing his beloved as a "man in hue, all hues in his controlling," as well as to represent the dangerously seductive power of the dark lady. Less subtly, Swetnam and the author of "Hic Mulier" afford themselves some degree of control over the contradiction that forms the basis of their subjectivity by writing, over and over again, passionately and sometimes angrily, about the virtues of chastity in women, the perils of erotic seduction, the overthrow of male reason, and so on. We can thus understand that even the most anxiety-ridden treatises about the dangers of desire enable their male authors to maintain the power and volition that appears so threatened in the content of the treatises they write. Once again, the pen is activated because the penis is imperiled.

This masculine need to articulate a knowledge of women in writing as a way of maintaining control over their own potentially self-destructive desire explains, as I have suggested the interpretive anxiety so pervasive in texts such as "Hic Mulier." Indeed, one of the profound threats raised by cross-dressing women is that they confound a semiotic code whose interpretive authority must, in theory, reside with men. "Hic Mulier" extols the virtues of women "in the fullness of perfection" because they are "signs deceitless, plain ways fail-less, true guides dangerless" (265–266). The author reproduces a legal basis for Stubbes' insistence that apparel should be a transparent sign system: he turns to the "powerful Statute of apparel" to legitimate his argument that "everyone [should] be *known* by the true badge of their blood or Fortune" (274, my emphasis). The issue raised by cross-dressing women is certainly their confusion of status and gender difference but also the resultant confusion of inter-pretive knowledge, especially threatening to masculine identity con-structed in relation to "woman"-as-Other, or "contrast," to use Swetnam's word. The hermaphrodite status assigned to women who cross-dress thus produces an unknowability in the gendered economy in which a male construction of woman-as-Other defines and legitimates masculine identity. To rail against this "monstrous" "unnatural" self-representation among women is, in effect, to confess to the anxiety inherent in such a dependent relationship. It is to rail against a cultural logic that defines men in relation to women and, at the same time, to insist upon male independence from and superiority over women.

Women who cross-dress clearly manipulate this cultural logic by appropriating, or at least challenging, its means of representation. By representing themselves in a way that confounds the masculine economy based on desire and knowledge, cross-dressing exacerbates the contra-dictions and anxiety already present in that economy. My earlier discus-sion of *Love's Labor's Lost* offers a useful dramatic parallel to the concerns of "Hic Mulier." The play underscores in comical and parodic fashion the male characters' dependence on women through their bombastic sonnet and letter writing – their "painted rhetoric." As Berowne declares, women are "the ground, the books, the academe / From whence doth spring this Promethean fire" (IV.iii.299–300). But the women's disguises confute and confuse the men's objects of desire and thus expose this construction of women precisely as a hollow, masculine construction.

Cross-dressing as an empowering form of self-representation by women is defended in "Haec-Vir; or, The Womanish Man," a treatise written in response to "Hic Mulier" the same year. The female speaker of this pamphlet states that the arguments of "Hic Mulier" depend upon establishing "a distinct and special difference between Man and Woman, both in their habit and behaviors."[35] But her own argument is that many of these differences derive merely from "custom," which she attacks as little more than male fantasy: "And will you have us to marry ourselves to these Mimic and most fantastic customs?," she demands (283). The pamphlet also argues vehemently against the idealized image of women constructed by the author of "Hic Mulier": "And will you have poor woman such a fixed Star that she shall not so much as move or twinkle in her own Sphere?" (281). Instead, the speaker of "Haec Vir" argues, very radically by Renaissance standards, for women's self-determination: "I was created free, born free, and live free; what lets [hinders] me then so to spin out my time that I may die free?" (282). Clearly, the speaker in "Haec Vir" is addressing exactly what lies at the heart of the masculine anxiety of "Hic Mulier": that woman who cross-dress at least symbolically appropriate the traditionally male prerogative of self-representation and self-determination by, quite literally, fashioning themselves.

By dressing as men, women take on the appearance of men. But as I have been arguing, what is most threatening about this act is that it suggests that women can also be *like* men in the act of self-fashioning. Sameness in appearance thus registers a far more profound threat: the possibility of sameness in volition, self-control and desire, precisely, as we have seen, the constituents of masculine identity. Virtually all of the conduct books, marriage guides and treatises about chastity, jealousy and the dangers of desire written in this period share an interest in fashioning an identity for women that, in turn, supports a construction of masculine identity. The strategy of this discourse is to inscribe a language of gender difference as if it were natural. The female speaker of "Haec Vir" radically challenges this strategy by first distinguishing between nature and custom (placing gender difference in the latter category), and then by arguing that women have the God-given right to self-determination. Her claim for equal treatment, against the double standard she sees operating in "Hic Mulier," is thus to argue for the essential similarities between men and women: "We are as freeborn as Men," she writes, "have as free election and as free spirits; we are compounded of like parts and may with like liberty make benefit of our Creations" (284).

The close of "Haec Vir" partially compromises the radical nature of these claims by embracing many aspects of the traditional, male construction of woman. But like the capitulation of Kate in the final scenes of *The Taming of the Shrew*, this final moment of closure does not efface the powerful claims made in the body of the text. Like Kate, the female author of "Haec Vir" appropriates masculine forms of self-governance and independence, yet both texts also close with admissions of the "natural" obedience women owe to men. But I think we can read the end of "Haec Vir" in the same way that many critics and directors have understood the end of *Shrew*: as a mimetic parody of patriarchal conventions that serves not as a capitulation but rather to produce an almost contrived closure. In any case, the fact that "Haec Vir" locates and then celebrates the very anxieties beneath the passionate misogyny of "Hic Mulier" is not altered by either interpretation of its conclusion. It remains an insightful and sometimes radical critique of the shaky foundation upon which male identity uneasily rests.

That critique hinges on the articulation of essential similarities between women and men in the "Haec Vir" pamphlet that respond to the claim in "Hic Mulier" that women are "guilty of lust or imitation" (276). For it is precisely the prospect that women's desires may in fact be similar to men's that makes their imitation of male apparel so deeply troubling. As I will explore in the next chapter, this prospect haunts Othello's psyche throughout the play; his jealousy can in part be understood as the result of Iago's clever manipulation of his own fear that Desdemona may have desires of her own. This is exactly Emilia's point when she says:

> Let husbands know
> Their wives have sense like them. They see, and smell,
> And have palates both for sweet and sour,
> As husbands have. What is it that they do
> When they change us for others? Is it sport?
> I think it is. And doth affection breed it?
> I think it doth. Is't frailty that thus errs?
> It is so too. And have not we affections,
> Desires for sport, and frailty, as men have?   (IV.iii.96–104)

Emilia's plea for the recognition of sameness is intolerable to Othello and to the cultural logic by which masculine identity is constructed through the inscription of difference. Her observation is so antithetical to the masculine world of Venice that it almost seems delivered as if in a vacuum. Desdemona's crime, if it can be called that, is acting independently enough to activate the always present male suspicion that women may, in fact, have the same volition and desires as men, however discouraged by the prevailing belief system. Against her own "clime, complexion, and degree' (III.iii.237), Desdemona chooses Othello; she exercises her own subjectivity as desire/volition in a way disturbing to Othello and to her father because it imitates the conditions and contours of their subjectivities. This "logic" partly explains the power of Brabantio's taunting statement: "She has deceiv'd her father, and may thee" (I.iii.296). In Othello's imagination, Desdemona is "guilty of lust or imitation"; she acts as if she were a cross-dressing woman.

Part of the anxiety toward cross-dressing women expressed in "Hic Mulier" is not surprisingly based on the association between this "monstrous deformity" (266) and a "lascivious tongue," (271) capable of "vile and horrible profanations" (268–269). Women dressed as men may dangerously speak as men, thus violating the interdiction to remain "chaste, silent and obedient." Here we might recall again Peter Stallybrass' observation that the "surveillance of women concentrated upon three specific areas: the mouth, chastity, the threshold of the house. The connection between speaking and wantonness was common to legal discourse and conduct books." If, Stallybrass adds, "the closed mouth . . . is made a sign of chastity," women's tongues may be seen as signs of their own desire, hence the charge of "lascivious tongues."[36] The threat represented by female tongues is also figured as an appropriation of masculine speech – the primary means of representing oneself. Indeed, a good deal of Constantia Munda's counter-attack to misogynistic writing in "The Worming of a mad Dogge" (1617) dwells on men's control of the pen and their insatiable need to write about women: "yet woman, the greatest part of the lesser world, is generally become the subject of every pedantical goose-quill. Every fantastic poetaster, which thinks he hath licked the vomit of his Coryphaeus and can but patch a hobbling verse together . . ." Munda consistently draws the analogy between speaking and writing, the tongue and the pen, sometimes implicitly suggesting the phallic nature of both: "the [male] tongue, being a very little member, should never go out of that same ivory gate in which . . . divine wisdom and nature together hath enclosed it."[37] Masculine identity depends on the prerogative to speak its desires, to express its volition, but also the power to deny the privileges of the same medium to women. This is carried out in part by speaking *for* women, by articulating and enforcing their chastity, silence and obedience. Since masculine speech conditions and exercises male subjectivities, the act of speaking is perhaps more important than what is said. From this observation it follows, returning once more to Jane Anger's point, that men who speak and write about women reveal as much, or more, about themselves as they do about their supposed subjects. With this in mind it is appropriate to turn, finally, to Jane Anger's *Her Protection for Women* (1589), written some years earlier than the texts I have discussed but very much relevant to their disclosures of male anxieties.

Anger's "Protection" is written in response to a text that unfortunately does not survive. "Book: his Surfeit in Love" was registered at the Stationer's Company in 1588 by the same printer who brought forth Anger's own pamphlet. Simon Shepherd suggests that "Book: his Surfeit" may have borrowed from Lyly's "Euphues the Anatomy of Wit."[38] Whatever its origins, Anger's pamphlet is the earliest of the "querelles des femmes" writings penned by a woman and, according to the text itself, written primarily for a female readership. Not surprisingly, one of its most compelling arguments concerns the preponderance of male writing about women, the consequences of masculine control of the pen. As I quoted above, Anger wishes that "ancient writers would as well have busied their heads about deciphering the deceits of their own sex as they have about setting down our follies" (38). In order to warn and to educate women, Anger's "Protection" provides the anatomy of masculinity left unwritten by her male predecessors.

Anger opens her text with the following statement: "The desire of every man to show his true vein in writing is unspeakable, and their minds are so carried away with the manner as no care at all is had of the matter" (32). In this sentence, Anger elucidates the basis of much of what will follow. Men "show" their own "true vein" through their writing about women, but this "desire" is so "carried away" that their own rhetoric becomes more important than what they are supposedly writing about. Or, in other terms, the act of writing exercises male desire rather than the "matter" about which they write. It is clear that Anger recognizes both the power and seductiveness of representation. This passage further suggests that for men, at least implicitly, retaining a position of knowledge (through writing) is more important that imparting a specific knowledge. Masculine writing is in excess of its deliberate referent such that it becomes self-referential, and it is men whom Anger proceeds to anatomize in her own writing. What form of desire/knowledge does masculine writing reveal?

Specifically, Anger argues that masculine desire is always in "surfeit" of whatever persona women maintain. The author of "Book: his Surfeit" believes that "love" is "grounded on women," Anger reports. But no matter what "ground" women occupy, men rail against women as the cause of their own surfeit in love: "They have been so daintily fed with our good natures that like jades . . . they surfeit of our kindness . . . Yet if we bear with their rudeness and be somewhat modestly familiar with them, they will straight make matter of nothing, blazing abroad that they have surfeited with love; and then their wits must be shown in telling the manner how" (33). Men "surfeit in love" because their desire is always in excess of the female "ground" that is supposed to provide satisfaction. Since we are dealing with male constructions of women (as full of "kindness," or "familiar") the profound irony revealed by Anger is that masculine desire is always in excess of the very "ground" they have insisted upon in the first place. In other words (once again), the premise of the masculine, desiring subject is to perpetuate a gendered economy in which satisfaction remains elusive. As Anger observes, men "taste but twice of one dish, they straight surfeit and needs must a new diet be provided for them" (36). Men must continue to desire beyond surfeit because satisfaction marks the death of a subjectivity that knows itself as desire. Writing (and railing) about women becomes the supplement to the lack of satisfaction.

This explains Anger's remark that the "lion rageth when he is hungry, but man raileth when he is glutted" (36). Here the author articulates the difference between the natural need to fulfill desire in order to provide satisfaction, and the "unreasonable" need among men to continue desiring after satiety. She also speaks of a man who "was driven into a mad mood through a surfeit" (37). The anger against women that follows surfeit is a result of men projecting their own dissatisfaction onto women, the fault they register among women for the impossibility of their own contentment within a sex/gender system that constructs male subjectivity as continually desiring. Anger's probably ironic advice to women is to prevent men from reaching a point of surfeit in order to avoid their resultant "railing": "But if we do desire to have them good, we must always tie them to the manger and diet their greedy paunches, otherwise they will surfeit" (37). Paradoxically, men are "good" only when they are maintained in a state of perpetual desiring.

Another part of Anger's text reveals the double bind in which this gendered economy of desire places women. She writes, "for we woo them with our virtues and they wed us with vanities; and men, being of wit sufficient to consider of the virtues which are in us women, are ravished with the delight of those dainties, which allure and draw the senses of them to serve us – whereby they become ravenous hawks, who do not only seize upon us but devour us. Our good toward them is the destruction of ourselves; we being well formed are by them foully deformed" (35). In effect, women's virtues (insisted upon by men in conduct books and marriage manuals) produce the very same masculine desire that leads to "surfeit" as well as, inevitably, to male anger and the "destruction" of those very same qualities originally prized.

Swetnam, writing about thirty years later, describes a similar economy of male desire and surfeit: "For the pleasure of the fairest woman in the world lasteth but a honeymoon; that is, while a man hath glutted his affections and reaped the first fruit, his pleasure being past, sorrow and repentance remaineth still with him" (208). Swetnam's version of post-coital sadness turns into anger when the source of this "sorrow" is placed upon women. Indeed, Swetnam's entire harangue displays the very "railing" Anger sees as the result of men's inability to find contentment in "surfeit." The "desire for a woman," he declaims, "is both insatiable and ruinous" (202); and elsewhere, "Lust causeth you to do such foul deeds which makes your foreheads forever afterwards seem spotted with black shame and everlasting infamy" (204). Swetnam identifies the same male anger as Anger does in the "Protection" but blames it entirely on women – on their supposed failure to live up to male standards of womanhood. But Anger's point is that any standards women abide by produce the same frustration in men since male desire is by definition as unavoidable as it is insatiable.

In the opening sentence of "The Arraignment," Swetnam admits to the anger behind his writing about women: "I being in great choler against some women (I mean more than one); and so in the rough of my fury, tak[e] my pen in hand . . ." (190). Anger suggests as much throughout the "Protection": "If they have stretched their invention so hard on a last as it is at a stand, [Shepherd notes that "last" is a model of a foot used by cobblers; "stand" is the shape of the stretched leather] there remains but one help, which is, to write of us women" (32). Here Anger's metaphor from cobbling perhaps contains a bawdy allusion to the pen as an erect penis (to "stand"), thus further emphasizing her association between male desire and their writing about women. The excess that results from the impossibility of satisfaction among men, their insistent desire even after "surfeit," drives them to write. It could be said that writing and speech (Anger offers no distinction between them) serve as compensatory media for the discrepancy between male expectations for what "woman" should provide and what women actually do provide. The lack that is inherent in a gendered economy in which women are the "ground" of male identity is projected onto women, resulting in misogynistic "railing" against women.

Finally, as I have pointed out, Anger's "Protection" shows that male writing about women is, in fact, a way of writing about themselves. "[I]f you listen," she states, "the Surfeiter his pen with my hand shall forthwith show you" (44; again the sexual innuendo seems possible). What Anger tells us by turning male writing back on itself is that misogyny is a response to male lack, to the profound threat of an emptiness that cannot be filled. If men are not surfeited even after their "conquests" of women, surely that is because the conquest cannot produce the satisfaction to masculine identity which it is supposed to provide. "Man raileth when he is glutted" because the very conditions of his identity are inherently unsatisfiable. And yet, male writing about women reproduces the system that constructs such an anxious masculinity by continually inscribing differences, by writing "woman" as Other. At the bottom of Anger's "Protection" is her implicit recognition of this vicious circularity.

6   Ocular proof: sexual jealousy and the anxiety of interpretation

Who dotes, yet doubts, suspects, yet strongly loves!

Othello III.iii.174

In all the discussions so far, men have shown a tenacious preoccupation with female chastity. It thus seems appropriate to conclude this study by addressing that singularly most dreadful exhibition of anxious masculinity in the early modern period: sexual jealousy. Burton is not at all unusual in his depiction of jealousy as the most prominent and devastating of the melancholy tempers: "it ought to be treated as a Species apart," he writes, "being of so great and eminent note, so furious a passion, and almost of as great extent as Love itself" (821). Burton's humoural psychology finds in jealousy perhaps the most severe example of the body's perturbed and imbalanced fluidity, the most complete overthrow of the rule of reason. But he also suggests throughout *The Anatomy*, mostly in his citations of numerous other writers on the subject, that male sexual jealousy is an unavoidable consequence of love and desire and, as such, a constituent part of masculinity. This is true for Burton because all men share the same material basis for jealousy as a result of their volatile fluidity; indeed, jealousy and melancholy are so inextricable that Burton wonders which is the cause and which the effect. In the following discussion, I suspend the humoural explanation that this period took for granted in order to pursue jealousy as an anxiety and a potential source of violence engendered in men by an economy that constructs masculine identity as dependent on the coercive and symbolic regulation of women's sexuality. As we shall see, this gendered economy is largely driven by the impossibility of sustaining the knowledge and interpretive authority men require, if only because the "objects" of that interpretation are necessarily outside or beyond this masculine panopticon. My initial premise is that sexual jealousy is both constitutive and symptomatic of the normative operations of early modern patriarchy rather than an aberration – it is, as Burton states for different reasons, the very condition of romantic love. Furthermore, I will read male

175

jealousy and cuckoldry anxiety as instances of masculine *excess* – representations of masculine dominion that are over-staged so as to reveal the contradictions and anxieties inherent in the patriarchal system that simultaneously enables and constrains its members. Burton might call the self-consuming frustration of the jealous man a physiological compulsion; I will call it an unavoidable response to the contradictions of the very same patriarchal system that has engendered his identity in the first place.

Among the early modern literary and non-literary texts I have studied, Shakespeare's *Othello* remains the most complex and insightful treatment of jealousy as an inevitable constituent of masculine identity. Coleridge's understanding of Iago as a character impelled purely by evil – "motive-less malignancy" is his phrase – leads me to read that character not as without motive but rather as articulating and activating the cultural anxieties that produce jealousy as a condition of romantic love, indeed, of male subjectivity itself. If for a moment we deliberately assign the fallacy of consciousness to a character, Iago appears aware of much of the critique of masculinity I employ in this chapter, and is cunningly able to deploy that knowledge to expose and destroy the fragilely constructed identity of his prey. Although Othello's racial difference contributes in important ways to his insecurity in Venice, providing a component to his identity unique among the men of the play's audience, my reading of other plays and of non-literary texts convinces me that he nonetheless embodies some of the most exemplary anxieties of early modern masculinity. As the play's initial preoccupation with Othello's racial difference gives way to his own festering jealousy, the Other is ironically brought into the center in his role as the everyman of masculine sexual anxiety. Iago's piercing remark, "I never found man that knew how to love himself" (I.iii.316–317) hints at the villain's deep knowledge of the profoundly destabilizing contradictions that lie beneath the surface of Othello's placid exterior at the beginning of the play, but this division at the core of the play's protagonist does not, as the play proceeds, result from racial difference so much as from a set of assumptions about gender and sexuality quite typical in this period. The meaning of Iago's ominous observation and the reasons for its tragic accuracy are the focus of this chapter.

If Iago speaks and activates the inherent and unavoidable instability of masculine subjectivity, it is Emilia who suggests a way out of the spiral toward violence that the play enacts. Thus the most poignant aspect of the play's tragic outcome is that the knowledge she introduces is not explored, nor really even engaged, by any other characters. Her observation that jealousy is "a monster / Begot upon itself, born on itself"

(III.iv.162–163) is the initial truth necessary to prevent the projection of masculine anxiety onto woman, a projection that ironically reproduces the very construction of woman that engenders such anxiety in the first place. Emilia is the Cassandra of *Othello*; her recognition of the self-produced and self-destructive quality of male jealousy is the prophecy that cannot be faced by Othello nor, for the most part, by those whose subjectivities are so fundamentally shaped and guaranteed by early modern constructions of woman. In an important way, then, Iago and Emilia share the same knowledge about masculinity, the critical difference being that Iago's knowledge is played out to its "logical" consummation while Emilia's evaporates into thin air. If we move outside the imaginary world of Shakespeare's play, a similar but not complete silence surrounds the writings by women that in many cases reveals the same awareness of male jealousy briefly spoken by Emilia. One of the objectives of this chapter is to listen to these voices in a way the play does not, to explore the cultural conditions of Iago's knowledge of anxious masculinity from within, but also from the perspective of those who suffered from its seemingly inexplicable frustration and misdirected violence.

One of the central ideas developed in many of the previous discussions is that anxious masculinity is so often figured as an interpretive crisis, specifically a crisis in interpretive knowledge about women and their sexuality. As such, jealousy (and its more severe cousin, paranoia) is a paradigm for interpretation in general, especially but perhaps not exclusively as it is practiced by men. Burton's description of the jealous melancholic reads almost like an account of the vigilant literary critic, perhaps furiously trying to find something original to write as the deadline for his tenure file looms close ahead: "he hunts after every word he hears, every whisper, and amplifies it to himself . . . he pries into every corner, follows close, observes to an hair" (84)). In the context of jealousy, this leads to an interpretive tyranny over women, or a panoptical regulation of their bodies and behavior. Nicholas Breton's "Pasquil's Mistresse" (1600), for example, portrays jealousy as an urgent, anxiety-producing interpretive crisis:

> It workes, and watches, pries, and peeres about,
> Takes counsell, staies; yet goes on with intent,
> Bringes in one humour, puts another out,
> And findes out nothing but all discontent,
> And keepes the spirit still so passion-rent,
> That in the world, if there be a hell,
> Aske, but in love, what jelousie can tell.[1]

Breton describes a very uneasy relationship between speculation (*specere*:

to look at) and certainty, between appearance and knowledge – an interpretive dilemma poignantly explored in *Othello*. Since the only resolution to this frustration is empirical, visible proof, the jealous man reads and over-reads those signs available to him.

Cast in these terms, male sexual jealousy in the Renaissance is largely a problem in reading and interpretation of female "texts"; as such, it necessarily calls into question the critical practices of those male critics who undertake to read and interpret jealousy from a later historical moment. To ignore this metacritical question often results in an implicit duplication in one's criticism of the interpretive economy under inter-pretation – indeed, such a criticism has been levied against Freud, Lacan, and several scholars who historicize Renaissance sexuality.[2] Instead, if we undertake our critical project from the perspective that knowledge produced *about* the early modern period is dialectically poised in relation to knowledge produced *by* that period, the object of investigation becomes as much our own contemporary critical paradigms – the politics of criticism itself – as it does Renaissance constructions of gender and sexuality. Consequently, this chapter raises some of the consequences and implications of "gendered ways of knowing" in both Renaissance texts and in some of the contemporary theoretical paradigms through which we analyze those texts. On both of these levels, I want to interrogate the ways in which a masculine subject position is enabled and "guaranteed" by participation in a heterosexual economy of knowledge and interpretation anxiously sustained by constructing women and female sexuality as objects of knowledge.[3] As I have suggested, such an anxious masculinity is poignantly revealed by instances of male sexual jealousy that necessarily confront the fundamental discrepancy between patriarchal *figurations* of woman and the *realities* of women's material and sexual lives. Once again, if Iago exploits this discrepancy, it is Emilia who exposes it: "And have not we affections, / Desires for sport, and frailty, as men have?" (IV.iii.103–104).

In *Disowning Knowledge in Six Plays of Shakespeare*, Stanley Cavell addresses the problem of distinctly gendered forms of knowledge. A "masculine/feminine contest over the nature of knowing," Cavell writes in the introduction, "is not to be missed here, however difficult it will be to develop usefully."[4] In the readings that follow, Cavell historicizes Shakespeare's tragedies in terms of Descartes' early seventeenth-century philosophical skepticism which, he argues, links "masculine knowing" to "exclusive possession, call it private property."[5] Elsewhere, Cavell sug-gests that such an economy of knowledge may be linked to paternity anxiety, and furthermore, that an entirely different economy operates for women, although he does not pursue the considerable implications of this problem, either historically or theoretically. Often, it seems as if philosophical knowledge/skepticism has a kind of objectivity outside of historically specific constructions of gender; or at least, philosophy is prior to its "sexualization." When Cavell writes that "what philosophy knows as doubt, Othello's violence allegorizes (or recognizes) as some form of jealousy," he implies that sexuality is the allegorical and thus secondary term.[6] The parenthetical "or recognizes" suggests some uncertainty as to the exact nature of the relationship between philosophical knowledge and jealousy, but as an allegory, however, philosophical doubt becomes jealousy only when it is acted out violently on the body of Desdemona. By positioning philosophical knowledge in a pure, abstract realm apart from and prior to its sexualized enactment, Cavell relies upon and perpetuates a theory of philosophical knowledge which is assumed to be male. Furthermore, since "philosophical skepticism" is central to those humanistic models of interpretation originating in the Renaissance, Cavell is trapped in a kind of historical circularity in which his own interpretive method is guaranteed by the historical period under scrutiny. As I discussed above in Bacon's development of the new science, to imagine knowledge and sexuality in a reciprocal rather than hierarchical relationship – in which neither term is prior or causal – allows for the realization that forms of knowledge exist in a dialectical relationship to the ways the early modern period constructs gender identity and difference.

Even if readings like Cavell's importantly address this problem, the failure to historicize knowledge in terms of specific deployments of sexuality and gender often reproduces the assumption that knowledge and its forms are universal rather than culturally determined. Such has been the basis of many important objections to Lacan's interpretive paradigm for theorizing sexuality and identity. Despite Lacan's insistence on the *symbolic* function of the phallus, he nonetheless perpetuates an exclusion of women from psychoanalytic theory by failing to theorize – even acknowledge – female subjectivity: "man" remains in the position of subject while "woman" is dematerialized in order to function as his constituting Other. While this interpretive paradigm is useful, especially in exposing the contours of masculine subjectivity and authority, it must be accompanied by attention to the specificity of different cultural and material scenes of writing – including the critic's – in order to avoid Lacan's apparent claims to universality.

Although Lacan does not pursue such an analysis, neither does he foreclose it: the critical task becomes to historicize the construction of sexual identities within a specific linguistic and gendered economy. Such an approach requires the critic to acknowledge and work within a dialectical relationship between the historical period under investigation and the theoretical paradigms through which he or she undertakes that investigation. In this way, critical self-consciousness does not by any means dismiss the ideological implications of appropriating, for example, Lacanian analytical tools, but it does prevent a kind of methodological "colonization" that erases historical and material specificity. As such, Lacan may promote scholarship that contributes to feminism and at the same time offers male critics especially the basis for a much needed critique of masculine subjectivity – to begin to respond to Alice Jardine's challenge (quoting Cixous): "men still have everything to say about [our] own sexuality."[7]

Lacan's critique of the masculine subject offers an enabling (if not unavoidable) discourse through which our own feminist era can "read" the anxious imperatives of Renaissance patriarchy. It is not so much that Lacan can be used to describe the symbolics of Renaissance patriarchy (as if they were immutable) but rather that he provides an effective heuristic strategy for historicizing it. The specularization of women in literary forms such as Petrarchism, for example, has been remarked upon by Jacqueline Rose as particularly susceptible to Lacanian analysis: "Lacan sees courtly love as the elevation of the woman into the place where her absence or inaccessibility stands in for male lack."[8] This is not to say that Petrarchism is identical to, for example, the specularization of women that feminist film critics have critiqued; rather, it suggests that the gender politics of Petrarchism can be "recognized" only through the "defamiliarized" lens of our own historical and ideological difference.

For Lacan, any "talking about" sexuality is always in the realm of the signifier and thus functions as a substitute or compensation for something finally unknowable. Talking about sexuality is part of the process by which the individual (masculine) "I" is constituted in language, but always, according to Lacan, as a way of repressing the experience of not-being, or the possibility of not knowing. This is a version of the economy in which the masculine subject is installed through the simultaneous construction and denial of the other as lack or absence. The symbolic realm in which this operates is legitimated by the phallus, which in Lacan's system is associated with a visual or specular form of knowledge. (Lacan's insistence on the interplay between seeing and speaking has interesting suggestions for the iconicity of language in the Renaissance.) Following his legacy from Freud, Lacan constructs the vagina as absence or "not-knowledge" and as the "barred place of the male subject's origin," a separation that functions similarly – perhaps analogously – to the bar between signifier and signified. To understand this model in gendered terms, "woman" is constructed to perform the double function of origin and absence, everything and nothing, in order to enable the tenuous placing of male subjectivity.[9] This apparent contradiction is the enabling condition of masculinity in the symbolic; the double construction of woman is so quickly and seemingly inexplicably reversible because both simultaneously require expression for man to position himself. Thus Desdemona's "reversibility" from "divine" early in the play to "Des*demon*" by the end seems to have happened without sufficient cause, unless, that is, we listen to Emilia and recognize the cause as already within Othello: "They are not ever jealous for the cause, / But jealous for they're jealous" (III.iv.161). That Othello is unable to recognize this is made poignantly clear when he echoes Emilia's words upon entering Desdemona's bedchamber, having not heard them before, moments before he smothers her; looking down at her, he says, "It is the cause, it is the cause, my soul" (V.ii.1). But in this ambiguous line the play also offers the possibility that not Desdemona's but Othello's "soul" is the cause – a word for his very essence in the early modern symbolic economy.

If we read male subjectivity and desire as produced in the symbolic order, according to the Lacanian economy, the identities of men are tenuously upheld by the construction of woman as Other, thus producing a gendered subject/object relationship in which female desire and sexuality is simultaneously (in a mutually validating way) construed as either nonexistent or excessive, both versions of what Lacan called "supplementary" in the Encore seminar. In effect, men must presume a kind of knowledge about women and female sexuality which, in Jacqueline Rose's terms, "is simply a way of closing off the division or uncertainty which also underpins conviction as such."[10] Masculine anxiety results when this closure is – inevitably – not possible. We might say that Hermione in *The Winter's Tale* and Hero in *Much Ado About Nothing* among Shakespeare's characters are examples of this construction of women; the suddenness with which Leontes and Claudio establish "certainty" about their infidelity is altogether incommensurate with the evidence. Thus, the tyrannical need to establish closure and to legitimate one's over-reading as if it were objectively true (as Leontes does by appealing to the oracle) is always in response to the impossibility of closure: the discourse of masculine sexual anxiety is paradoxically necessary with or without any basis in reality. What is it about the "logic" of Renaissance patriarchy that produces jealous reactions so much in excess of the so-called evidence?

Most simply, jealousy is a form of paranoia that is always in place in an economy in which women are constructed by men as Other. In other words, the self-consuming frustration, anxiety and violence of the jealous man is a "logical" response to the inequalities of the same patriarchal economy that has engendered his very identity in the first place. This begins to explain why male characters and texts written by men in the Renaissance so often anticipate being cuckolded, as if it were an unavoidable aspect of marriage. A circularity of patriarchal logic in which women necessarily enact and thus substantiate the way they have already been constructed, insidiously – often violently – governs each of Shakespeare's three jealousy plays: *Much Ado About Nothing*, *Othello* and *The Winter's Tale*. In these examples, Shakespeare stages cases of unjustified jealous rage in order to foreground male jealousy as a discursive energy that does not require a referent. Because the audience *knows* that each of the three women is innocent in these plays, our analysis is directed away from weighing their culpability; instead, we must turn to the individual and collective male psyche engendered in a patriarchal culture: "They are not jealous for the cause," Emilia states, "[b]ut jealous for they're jealous" (III.iv.160–161).

In such a culture, there is always something left over and outside the patriarchal economy which it cannot contain or explain, something which maintains it in a state of anxiety. In linguistic terms, this may be understood as the signifying chain endlessly unconsummated by its signifieds; in gendered terms, this "elsewhere" is the fact of female subjectivity and sexual pleasure which always generates attempts at containment and yet subverts them at the same time. This tension is often played out through language itself. Drawing from the work of Patricia Parker once again, Renaissance treatises on rhetoric frequently underscore their sense of a linguistic crisis in representation through "the linking of women with the deceit, doubleness, or movable nature of tropes, and the social as well as sexual implications of such transportability."[11] One might say that the perceived instability of the linguistic sign both indicates and produces an instability in the sex/gender system of the Renaissance – the linguistically slippery Iago embodies and articulates this cultural tension. On the most obvious level, he relies on the mutable and manipulable nature of linguistic and visual signs in order to persuade Othello of Desdemona's infidelity. But he also embodies the now famous definition of a linguistic sign as that which can lie: "I am not what I am," a line Iago might have borrowed from Lacan (I.i.66). In the play, Iago becomes the anarchic demystifier of the necessary illusions that define the symbolic; he seems not only to understand but also to figure in the play the symbolic (and thus vulnerable) nature of the phallus as well as the chimerical quality of self-Other relationships: "love . . . is indeed but sign" (I.i.158–159).

That the symbolic is by definition illusory and built upon contradiction explains the most obvious paradox (so it would seem) of male sexual jealousy and cuckoldry in the Renaissance: an experience represented by men as so horrific is nonetheless pervasively – even obsessively – represented over and over again. A book entitled *The Court of Good Counsell* (1607), for example, states that there is "no greater plague, torment" than an "untoward, wicked and dishonest wife."[12] The "solution" to the contradictions of living in the symbolic is to obtain a degree of mastery in the act of representation itself. In other words, the fact that jealousy and cuckoldry anxiety – the dread of women disrupting one of the central facts and symbols of patriarchy – is so pervasively written about, nervously laughed at, ritualized, theatricalized and, we must presume, discussed, by those who considered it the worst earthly suffering imaginable, exposes the fundamental paradox at the core of masculine subjectivity. If we realize that the *discourse* of cuckoldry and male sexual jealousy is not necessarily congruent with the actual occurrences of adultery or sexual promiscuity, the preponderance of false accusations in literary and non-literary texts suggests that merely charging women with infidelity must have itself provided an *enabling* function for men. A husband's accusation functions to pre-empt and thus compensate for the impotence and dishonor he seems to have regularly feared as a result of anticipating his own cuckoldry; in short, he exercises discursive power in advance of the disempowerment he anticipates.

Indeed, masculine anxiety toward women's sexuality is both prior to and considerably in excess of any "referent" such that it seems to be the very condition of romantic love rather than an unfortunate effect. The texts and practices that enact male sexual jealousy function as a discourse produced largely by men, the referent of which – female sexual desire and sexual practices – is inevitably and necessarily elusive, rarely providing, as Othello demands, "ocular proof." The inevitable failure to attain closure or "proof" feeds and perpetuates the interpretive anxiety: "not knowing is threatening," Hélène Cixous writes, "while at the same time . . . it reinforces the desire to know." Cixous continues: "so in the end woman, in man's desire, stands in place of not knowing, the place of mystery."[13] It is precisely this construction of woman that feeds the masculine desire to know but also produces epistemological anxiety. In this way the very *copia* of representations of cuckoldry and jealousy can be read as a response to the impossibility of certainty about the matter – the necessity to interpret and to represent so excessively, implicitly acknowledges the elusiveness and "elsewhere" of its object and the impossibility of mastering it. This is something like what Freud called "epistemophilia" – the need to know – which he understood as a form of

paranoia. Or, to return to Lacan's model, we can explain this epistemological anxiety as an excess of signifiers – signs requiring an interpretive
consummation that is continually frustrated. As we shall see, early
modern treatises on jealousy, marriage and the "proper" conduct of
wives often function as interpretive manuals aimed at enabling men to
correctly "read" the signs of women's sexual behavior. Perhaps the
supreme irony of these texts is that they function as interpretive guides
intended to alleviate an anxiety that is itself derived from a prior
construction of women.

Among the wide field of non-literary texts in this period which in one
way or another discuss male jealousy, cuckoldry and sexuality, I have
selected the following examples from popular pamphlets because they
seem to me most representative of the interpretive and specular economy
with which I have identified male sexual jealousy. By reading these texts
alongside Shakespeare's *Othello*, we may understand the play as a
complex register of a broad set of cultural anxieties activated and
embodied, as I have suggested, through the character of Iago. These texts
are also useful for the ways in which they suggest that masculine
subjectivity is tenuously constructed not just in relation to female
sexuality but more specifically in the act of reading and interpreting the
signs of female chastity or adultery. Perhaps Catherine Belsey's theory of
subjectivity is most useful here. "To be a subject," writes Belsey, "is to
have access to a signifying practice – to identify with the 'I' of utterance
and the 'I' who speaks. The subject is held in place in a specific discourse,
a specific knowledge, by the meanings available there."[14] Cuckoldry and
sexual jealousy operate as such a "discourse" and "knowledge" and as
the pivotal term for other discursive and material aspects of patriarchy.

Let us first consider an account of jealousy that addresses its more
material or economic aspects in the early modern period, specifically in
terms of property and ownership. Benedetto Varchi's "The blazon of
jealousie," translated by Robert Tofte in 1615, describes the suffering of
the jealous man in typically dire terms: "all those disdainfull Disgraces,
but now spoken of, all those burning Martyrings, all those unspeakable
bloudy Passions in love . . . are nothing, or rather, passing pleasing and
sweet, in respect of that one damned Feare, or hellish suspect, or rather
uncurable Plague, and deadly Poyson, cleped Jealousie."[15] Here it is
worth noting that jealousy in men is "uncurable," as if it were an
unavoidable constituent of masculine identity indissoluble from love
itself. Varchi's treatise is also notable for its emphasis on women as
property and on the consequent fear of adultery as a kind of communal
possession: "Jealousie springeth from the Propertie or Right that wee

have, when we (enjoying our Lady or Mistresse) would have her soly and wholy unto our selves, without being able (by any meanes) to suffer or endure, that another man should have any part or interest in her, any way, or at any time."[16] Natural right is evoked to legitimize women as the private property of men. This often expressed sentiment in both texts additionally suggests that if jealousy exposes the insecurity of masculine identity as it is constructed in relation to woman, this process takes place in front of other men; in other words, masculine honor is constructed through women but conferred by men – exactly the situation, as we have seen, that opens "The Rape of Lucrece." In Varchi's treatise, Tofte adds the following marginal note: "Honor is the Reputation and Credit, or the good name and Fame, of a Man . . . before hee will have the same eclipst, he will loose all his wealth, yea, and his dearest life to . . ."[17] A later discussion underscores this rivalry between men by adding that jealousy is most "vexing" when the other man is "well-descended, learned, commendable for his qualities, and withall, potent, and mighty in Friends and Alliances . . ."[18] Thus we see once again that bonds of rivalry *and* antagonism between men obtain from their shared anxiety toward women's sexuality.

One final passage from "The blazon" introduces two important ideas which particularly resonate in *Othello*. Varchi observes that "it is wonderfull, and almost incredible to believe, that men should be such deadly enemies unto themselves (as many times they are) through these strange and foolish humours."[19] Here the author hints at what Iago understands as the fundamental split in masculine subjectivity, a division which jealousy activates by turning the husband against himself through his suspicion of his wife's infidelity. If Varchi finds "incredible" that men become "deadly enemies unto themselves," Iago appears to realize that self-loathing is at least latent in every man. Thus he does not construct Othello's jealousy but rather exacerbates pre-existent anxieties inherent in the construction of masculinity – once again, Iago's remark, "I never found man that knew how to love himself" lies at the heart of masculinity.

Varchi continues his discussion by noting that "for one word onely, or for a signe, a becke, or a glance cast upon one, without as much as a thought of any ill; nay, more, that they will (despight of their owne selves) imagine and conceit that which doth much afflict, gaule, and torment them incessantly . . ."[20] This passage introduces the interpretive overdetermination that Shakespeare plays out in *Othello*. If woman is already constructed as an opaque, unreliable body of signs requiring interpretive regulation, if she is by the same construction already "known" as adulterous, the "torment" Varchi describes is an inescapable component of being in love in the first place. Othello unwittingly articulates this in his response to Iago's supposed dream of Cassio and Desdemona kissing: after crying "O monstrous! Monstrous!" he adds, "[b]ut this denoted a foregone conclusion" (III.iii.430, 432).

Many of these attitudes provide the material of "Tell-Trothes New-Yeares Gift," published anonymously in 1593. The following passage is from the section entitled "Robin Good-fellowe his Invective against Jelosy":

> For if Jelosy be loves brother, it is by corruption of nature brought foorth unlawfully, which may thus be manifested. After the eye hath chosen an object which brings so sweet contentment to the hart . . . the eye receivinge kinde glaunces for amorous glotinges, and lovinge harte-breakinges for affectionate hart sighings. the eie beeing pleased with an eye, and the hart contented with a hart, they frolique both in glory as long as they rest in constancie; but wandring from forth that santuary, the eie either spies another eie that better pleaseth it, and the harte likes of another harte that better contentes it, or else the eie lookes curishly into his owne harte, and spies some fault in himselfe, which, displeasing, begetteth Jelosy: whereby the eie may be said to be originall and father of both.[21]

The passage suggests openly what *Othello* implies: that jealousy and love may be two sides of the same emotional attachment; as imagined above, they are half-brothers, the illegitimate one having been "by corruption of nature brought foorth unlawfully." The author appears to be distinguishing his own argument from those who have only "entertained the superficies of love, never harboring him in their hartes" and who consequently "affirme that [love] and Jelosy are brothers, and that the one cannot bee without the other."[22] Instead, jealousy is figured as the illegitimate son, corruptive of patrilineal order, while some version of authentic love is represented as the legitimate son. The absent figure in this domestic analogy is the mother, whose chastity (the pamphlet will pursue this later) will in effect beget either love or jealousy.

And yet, the passage is also striking for its understanding of the (male) "eie" as the "originall and father of both" love and jealousy. Following the Renaissance belief that desire derived from the eye, sexual desire is figured in scopophilial terms the eye finds its "chosen object" in a specular economy which produces initial attraction as well as subsequent wandering – if the "eie spies another eie that better pleaseth it." Recent formulations of the "male gaze" as a form of power in cinema and advertising, for example, describe an economy of male heterosexual desire which may be applied in a textualized (and historically specific) form to Petrarchism, "englished" in the 1590s rage for sonnet writing, in which the anatomized woman is an inaccessible object of desire.[23] Idealized and unavailable, yet objectified through the inscription of being looked at and written about, "woman" is constructed in this economy as both "knowable" (anatomized and described) and "unknowable" at once. Philippa Berry's recent understanding of the Petrarchan tradition, as I explored earlier, suggests the fear that this construction of the beloved seeks to obviate: Renaissance discourses of love have an "anxiety that the beloved's passive power might suddenly seek active expression, in an assertion of her own feelings and desires which threatened to escape the rhetorical or imaginative control of the male lover."[24] Desdemona has already at least partly activated this anxiety in her defiance of her father and her resolutely articulated affection for Othello.

On the stage, a version of this economy is reproduced for male members of an audience when suspicion of female adultery is enacted. Men would find themselves in an analogous position to the male characters who "read" through gesture and speech the suspected female character. *The Court of Good Counsell* articulates those aspects of women as "texts" which men need to read: "a woman should take heede, that she give not men occasion to thinke hardly of her, either by her Deedes, Wordes, Lookes or Apparell."[25] These four semiotic fields correspond exactly to the media of the theater: action, speech, expression and costume. The very act of viewing and hearing a play about male jealousy requires an audience (at least the men in it) to take part in the same interpretive anxiety as its protagonist. But in *Othello*, of course, we read these signs knowing full well that they are false: the gap between interpreting along with Othello and our position as complicit with Iago defines our tragic experience of the play.

Indeed, cuckoldry anxiety can only be produced when there is both a need to know and a need to see combined with the inability to do either with certainty. Such an argument has been recently made in Katharine Maus' fascinating discussion of the "voyeuristic satisfaction" experienced by an audience who knows more than the cuckold and who, in effect, interprets the actions of the suspected wife. Her argument corroborates my sense that a certain mastery over a threatening and helpless situation may have been provided by the very representations of cuckoldry – although I am not convinced that the theater is exclusive in providing this satisfaction, since the many pamphlets on the subject offer a textual correlative.[26]

As Maus further points out, on the public stage interpretive certainty is not available because "ocular proof" can never be enacted. Iago repeatedly demands of Othello, "How satisfied, my lord?" and "Where's satisfaction?" (III.iii). "The door of truth" would give Othello satisfaction, but it would also require the horror of visual certainty.

"Satisfaction," in this sense, is synonymous with the full and absolute knowledge of Desdemona – her thoughts and specifically her sexuality. According to the patriarchal "logic" of Othello, this satisfaction can be achieved only in two ways: either Desdemona is chaste and Othello is the only man who "knows" her; or, the knowledge of her infidelity will come when he "behold[s] her topp'd." In either case, he is trapped in an identity engendered by the patriarchal economy that produced it, and he is tortured by the impossibility of imagining or enacting any other form of being. As Stephen Greenblatt points out, Othello's desire for "fulfillment is characteristically poised between an anxious sense of self-dissolution and a craving for decisive closure."[27] As the basis of Othello's identity, Desdemona is by definition everything and nothing, origin and absence; she cannot be one without the other. Thus the only two responses he can entertain for himself are mastery or its opposite – "self-dissolution." Indeed, as Othello says, "when I love thee not, / Chaos is come again" (III.iii.93–94).

Edward Snow has argued that "Iago's repetition of 'satisfied' and 'satisfaction' implies a displacement of sexual desire onto the act of looking and knowing – where it becomes intrinsically unsatisfiable."[28] If Cavell's training in philosophy led him to understand sexual jealousy as an "allegory" of knowing, in this case Snow's psychoanalytic reading leads him to reverse the direction such that sexuality is primary and epistemology attendant. Taken together, these intellectual allegiances produce a third position that sees sexuality and knowledge in a reciprocal dynamic of mutual power and legitimation for men. The play's tragic denouement suggests almost an interchangeability between carnal and interpretive knowledge.

"Tell-Trothes New-yeares Gift" represents jealousy as the unnatural, illegitimate brother of love in its refutation of the belief that "one cannot bee without the other." Conversely, Othello would seem to play out at least initially the possibility that love and jealousy are indeed inseparable. The conditions of "natural" love appear to be the very same conditions, once fueled by Iago, which produce the Moor's unnatural jealous rage. Derived from an already gendered and sexualized economy in which male power and knowledge are dependent upon the construction of women as objects of knowledge, the "natural" and "unnatural" are hardly discrete categories.

Besides a wandering eye, jealousy is also born when "the eie looks curishly into his owne hart, and spies some fault in himselfe, which [is] displeasing." This perception is an interesting version of Freud's own understanding of jealousy as occurring in those who "project outwards what they do not wish to recognize in themselves."[29] An unacceptable self-realization is assigned to an Other and then responded to as if it were objective reality – exactly the dynamic of paranoia. In "Tell-Trothes," the "father" of male sexual jealousy is either the I/"eye" who strays to another object of desire, or it is a psychological construction produced by an unacceptable glimpse into one's own (male) inadequacy. Men are either *actually* cuckolded or else their projection constructs a scenario in which they *believe* they are cuckolded; jealousy either has a referent, or it is a floating signifier propelled by paranoia. In effect, male subjectivity is dis/covered (simultaneously found and uncovered) in the act of inter-preting – along the chain of signifiers or "clues" – rather than in the answer itself. The staging of false accusations, as *Othello* demonstrates, prolongs and intensifies the interpretive suspicion such that the tenuous basis of Othello's subjectivity is foregrounded and laid bare.

According to *Fancies Ague-fittes, or Beauties Nettle-bed*, an anony-mously written treatise from 1599, the reason why "jealosie is much more hurtfull in a man, then woman" is because "he feeles withall a shame and infamie, with such a blemish and dishonour, as in no way or at any tyme, repayreable agayne." On the next page, the author adds that "Jealosie . . . is as irksome to beare in a man as a woman, and so much more in a man, because therby he looseth his honour."[30] Honor and reputation are important to both genders, yet clearly it is women who confirm male honor and not the reverse, at least according to the author of this treatise, more than likely male. This explains the frequency with which female chastity is represented by men as supremely important to women. In Robert Cawdry's treatise, *A Godlye Form of Householde Government* (1598), for "a maid, the honesty and chastity is instead of all . . . the which thing only if a woman remember, it will cause her to take great heed unto, and be more a wary and careful keeper of her honesty, which alone being lost . . . [she] should think there is nothing left."[31] This commonly held sentiment is clearly a case of men projecting their own valorization of female chastity onto women (who in varying degrees internalize it) in order to forestall their worst fear. In effect, women are granted the power to cuckold men by an economy that has already constructed male honor as contingent upon female chastity – certainly a circumscribed form of power for women that if anything sustains the patriarchal economy that fetishizes female chastity in the first place. It follows that one of the ironies, if not contradictions, of patriarchal logic is that men are anxious about a form of female power that is itself invented by a system premised upon the powerlessness of women.

In order to understand the discourse of sexual jealousy as constitutive of an economy that shapes and sustains such an anxious masculine subjectivity, it is important to keep in mind my earlier discussion of early modern England's residual use of honor within a shame culture, and the emergent sense that it derived from an interior relation to God. A remarkable passage in *Fancies Ague-fittes* suggests that transition: "Honour is nothing els but populare reputation, it is no parte of the conscience: but he that feares not what men may saye of him . . . is wicked and detestable."[32] The text describes the two competing sources for the construction of male subjectivity: "conscience," which suggests an ascendant Puritan notion of accountability to God rather than to society, and "populare reputation," which argues for the precedence of one's place in the social fabric. In effect, an interior model of the self legitimated by God is set against a model of otherness dependent on social approbation.

Male sexual jealousy in the late sixteenth century traverses both of these models such that the two realms may not be discrete. On the one hand, Puritanism appropriates interiority – often figured as the conscience or heart – in its severely moralistic warnings against adultery and fornication; at the same time, a man is fashioned according to "what men saye of him." "It is not enough to have innocencie of the hart," continues the author of *Fancies Ague-fittes*, "we must as well escape the giving of occasion, to men of evill reporte."[33] On the other hand, "if then a woman doe demeane her selfe, in such sorte as hath beene declared, and yet her husbande (never-the-lesse) will be sicke in the brayne, and foolish of his own conceite: it remaynes to his owne perill, for she is no iote dishonoured thereby, but himselfe, that without any cause became distrustfull of her."[34] Male honor and reputation apparently depend just as much on the regulation and control of women's sexual lives as on the interpretation of the signs of their chastity. Texts such as *Fancies Ague-fittes* are part of a large discursive field that includes Renaissance conduct books in which women are exhorted to represent themselves in such a way as to be "correctly" interpreted by men. Cawdrey's translation of Vives offers a violent example of this point: a wife should "labor with all her power" to remain chaste lest the "fantasy" of uxoricide "come upon her husband."[35] Once more, Shakespeare is notable for his relentless pursuit of the masculine fears that underscore their obsession with female chastity. Othello has been craftily misled by Iago to misread Desdemona such that he actualizes on stage the "fantasy" of uxoricide. In both texts, it is implicitly revealed that such a "fantasy" is always in place as a result of the profound dependence of masculine identity on the chastity of women. While Othello himself (and to some extent, Iago) is made to bear the responsibility of Desdemona's death in Shakespeare's account, Vives utterly projects such responsibility onto women, thus denying any male complicity in the violence against women produced by jealousy.

Virtually all the texts on sexual jealousy acknowledge the impossibility of interpreting "for certaintie" the sexual behavior of women, "by reason the act is so secret," as *Fancies Ague-fittes* claims. In one sense, as I have suggested, the discourse of sexual jealousy is a way for men to speak and to write about female sexuality and in so doing compensate for their fundamental exclusion from what is constructed as threatening. The following passage from *Tell-Trothes New-yeares Gift* implies some of the anxiety produced by the fact that female sexuality is inevitably outside the specular and interpretive economy that "needs to know":

If she meanes to deceive thee, her invention is hard to be prevented, for, watch her never so narrowly, she will finde a time to perform her knavery. The siliest creatures are sildome catcht in order trappes: and can women want wit to frustrate a common stale? If it were possible to know their thoughts, it were likely their practices might be hindered; but as long as *secreta mihi* reignes, the rains of their liberty are at their own pleasures.[36]

The passage points out the inadequacy of scopic regulation because the thoughts of women are unfortunately unknowable. In the margin another version of the same idea is written (translated from the Latin): "You cannot watch over her mind; though you lock up everything and shut out everyone, the adulterer will be within . . . Argus had a hundred eyes on his face, a hundred on his neck, and a single love often deceived them."[37] Since female adultery is as hidden and inaccessible to men as women's minds, a panopticon of physical and mental surveillance is required but nonetheless inadequate. Moreover, it seems as if the very obstacles to interpretive mastery of women's sexuality sustain and advance the need to interpret. Female sexual pleasure is set at liberty "as long as *secreta mihi* reignes," and it is placed in the realm of that which men cannot reach.

Two metaphors in the passage have specific resonance for this historical moment: first, one sense of "rains" links the preservation of women's secrets and the unknowability of female desire to an unbridled, uncontrollable horse – a familiar metaphor in the early modern period which often suggests sexual domination as well. The physical counterpart to this metaphor is the actual "bridles" which women could be forced to wear.[38] A second metaphor, or double entendre, figures the impenetrable "secreta mihi" of women as a female monarch whose own erotic pleasures are at liberty and thus outside the regulation of men. This is probably not a deliberate or veiled reference to Elizabeth; instead, I think it is better to understand a more generalized sexual and political dynamic in which a virgin queen is figured as an object of desire whose own erotic desires are constructed as the material of a collective male fantasy. The "secreta mihi" of Elizabeth's virginity appears to have been irresistible in generating countless rumors of an active erotic life – particularly with Leicester and the supposedly concealed births of their illegitimate children.[39] Such a collective fantasy about England's monarch may be understood as a compensatory form of knowledge-as-power articulated by Elizabeth's male subjects in the face of their complete political dependence on her. From this perspective, Elizabeth is not so much an aberration but rather a figure who pivotally activates the patriarchal economy of knowledge and interpretation in which her male subjects dis/cover themselves.

To return to *Tell-Trothes New-yeares Gift*, what appears to be "left-over" or outside the panoptical structure of scrutiny and interpretation is understood as female erotic desire – "their own pleasures" as the passage reads. This is the secret that inadmissably generates the discourse of cuckoldry, producing and reproducing a structure of representation and interpretation in which the demand to know and to represent act as a displacement from the inability ever to know completely. In other terms, female sexual pleasure is constructed as outside male writing and representing, and at the same time is written and represented over and over again. Such a way of thinking in many ways exemplifies Irigaray's argument in "Cosi fan tutti": "Man seeks her out," she writes, "since he has inscribed her in discourse, but as a lack, as fault, as flaw." And this because, again following Irigaray, "[if] there is such a thing – still – as feminine pleasure, then, it is because men need it in order to maintain themselves in their own existence".[40]

One obvious opposition upon which this male economy rests is between the speaking and writing man over and against the silenced woman. In another part of *Fancies Ague-fittes*, the text recommends that women avoid speaking to men at all lest their voice and words be interpreted as signs of infidelity. In the following passage, women's speech becomes a crucial sign to be interpreted precisely because "the act is so secret":

Now to know for certaintie, whether she is not to be taxed with the crime of dishonestie or no, little can be sayd therein, by reason the act is so secret: but such as have bad reporte, and have given occasion to speake sinisterly of them (albeit they may be verily innocent,) they ought to chastise their courses and behaviour by good example, that they may shunne all hard speeches, both of themselves and their husbandes, ruminating continually betweene themselves . . .[41]

Women's speech is represented as an outward and knowable set of signs to be interpreted. But because outward signs are mere signifiers for something else – in this case the "secreta mihi" that is women's sexual pleasure – an interpretive anxiety is always in place for those men whose identity depends on such interpretation, such forms of "knowledge."

Conduct books written for women, such as Thomas Salter's *The Mirrhor of Modestie* (1580), perhaps serve to assuage this interpretive anxiety by "writing" the "secreta mihi" of women; or, in other words, by transforming what is inward and thus inaccessible to men into an outward set of interpretable sign. In so doing, female interiority is made public, the result of which is to deny or "empty out" any basis for female subjectivity. Salter aspires to teach women how to "attire the inwarde mynde, and maketh it meete for vertue, and therefore is intituled a Mirrhor, meete for Matrones and Maidens."[42] This is the stated objective of his treatise, but as I have suggested, it additionally functions as a kind of interpretation manual which produces and retains men in the position of interpreters of women and which, additionally, tries to assure before the fact that women will signify only virtuous conduct.

My final example from the treatises written by men purports to be a marriage guide for men, but it often reads like an argument for the necessity of interpreting women to one's own (male) advantage. In the following passage from "How to choose a good wife from a bad," the third chapter of *A Discourse of Marriage and Wiving* (1615), Alexander Niccholes draws an elaborate metaphor based on the perils of Renaissance navigation:

This undertaking is a matter of some difficulty, for good wives are many times so like unto bad, that they are hardly discerned betwixt, they could not otherwise deceive so many as they doe, for the divell can transform himselfe into an Angell of Light, tho better to draw others into the chaines of darknesse . . . and because it is such a sea, wherin so many shipwrecke for want of better knowledge and advice, upon a rock, that tooke not better counsell in the haven, I have therefore in some sort, to prevent this danger, erected (as it were) certaine Land markes and directions in the way, to give aime to such passengers as shall hereafter expose themselves to the merry of this fury, and rather because our age is so adventurous . . .[43]

The passage announces an initial interpretive difficulty due to the outward and easily mistakable similarities between "good" and "bad" women. The devil's active interest in promoting misinterpretation further complicates the issue. In Niccholes' richly developed metaphor, women are figured as a dangerous, engulfing ocean, while men are intrepid explorers whose navigational instruments are the "knowledge and advice" provided by Niccholes' manual. The interpretive knowledge offered in the treatise would seem to be the foundation of a male subjectivity constantly defined in terms of – and yet threatened by –

women and female sexuality. The author has linked female sexuality to one of the most fearful (and in another sense, unknowable) elements of the Renaissance imagination – death and loss at sea. In addition to a number of similar allusions in Spenser's *Amoretti*, Joseph Swetnam in his *The Arraignment of Lewde, Idle, Froward, and Unconstant Women* (1615), applies the metaphor somewhat differently in his description of male, heterosexual desire as "being carried headlong into the deepe and dangerous Sea of raging affection . . . into the bottomlesse gulfe of endlesse perdition."[44] And yet, perhaps these metaphors are importantly linked: both Swetnam's identification of male desire as a "dangerous Sea" and Niccholes' linkage of marriage and "shipwrecke" depend upon an *a priori* fear of disempowerment and loss of identity that derives from two forms of male dependence – erotic and matrimonial – on women. And both are certainly more poignant from the perspective of humoural psychology, where the male body's inherent fluidity is by definition a potential source of emasculation.

The prevalence of figuring ocean travel in terms of a feminized danger of death by drowning may also be explained by the fact that the exploration and dominion of the seas was one of the most significant instances of masculine prerogative in the Renaissance. Raleigh's social status came to depend in part on Elizabeth's rewards for his discoveries and conquests, as is obsequiously evident in his *Discoverie of Guiana*. Among Shakespeare's plays, Antony's "feminization" at sea and perhaps Prospero's mastery of the sea in *The Tempest* reproduce a similar set of metaphorical identifications. These texts construct a compensatory form of mastery – in an imaginary realm – over something that cannot, finally, be mastered. But most relevant to the concerns of this chapter is the storm that nearly drowns Othello during his voyage to Cyprus. Not only does the storm metaphorically prefigure what Othello undergoes on the island, but it also suggests that his vulnerability precedes any actions taken by Iago, Cassio or Desdemona; as such, his jealousy is, once again quoting Emilia, "a monster / Begot upon itself, born on itself."

This early scene in *Othello* merits further analysis, for although it has received little critical attention, it lays out virtually all of the play's subsequent issues. Echoing Niccholes' metaphor, Cassio remarks: "O, let the heavens / Give him defense against the elements, / For I have lost him on a dangerous sea" (II.i.45–47). Asked if he is "well-shipped," Cassio responds: "His bark is stoutly timber'd, and his pilot / Of very expert and approv'd allowance" (49–50). Threatened with drowning, Othello's defense is described in terms of masculine agency with vaguely phallic suggestions. This moment would not merit attention if it were not echoed moments later in a specifically sexual exchange, one that constructs an implicit parallel between Othello's love for Desdemona and the threat of engulfment by the sea.

As the conversation on land turns to Desdemona, Cassio remarks:

> He hath achiev'd a maid
> That paragons description and wild fame,
> One that excels the quirks of blazoning pens,
> And in th' essential vesture of creation
> Does tire the ingener.   (II.i.62–66)

In this the first description of Desdemona, she is portrayed as exceeding representation, specifically that offered by the "blazoning pens" of the Petrarchan tradition. Indeed, the aspiring sonnet writer would "tire" in his effort to capture her beauty and virtues. That she is the "essential vesture of creation" reveals one of the contradictions of Petrarchism since she is both "essential" in her virtues but only in "vesture," in the apparel or outward show of the poet's language. But the most significant aspect of this representation is that Desdemona is outside the descriptive range and authority of language; she is both the ground upon which Othello's identity rests but also the "elsewhere" what disturbs the operations of language in the symbolic. Potentially lost at sea, the security of Othello's identity is already erected on very insecure land, and it is precisely the volatility inherent in the gap between Othello's construction of Desdemona and her actual behavior that will be exploited by Iago as the play unfolds.

Echoing her earlier "blazoning," Cassio then explains that the "divine Desdemona" is Othello's greatest advantage against the storm:

> Tempests themselves, high seas, and howling winds,
> The gutter'd rocks and congregated sands –
> Traitors ensteep'd to clog the guiltless keel –
> As having sense of beauty, do omit
> Their mortal natures, letting go safely by
> The divine Desdemona.   (II.i.68–73)

In other words, Desdemona in her idealization as "divine" will rescue Othello from engulfment, but in the impossibility of that idealization she will also become the source of his engulfment as Iago implodes the contradiction inherent in constructing woman as everything and nothing. To Montano's question, "[w]hat is she," Cassio responds:

> She that I spake of, our great captain's captain,
> Left in the conduct of the bold Iago,
> Whose footing here anticipates our thoughts
> As se'nnight's speed. Great Jove, Othello's guard,

> And swell his sail with thine own pow'rful breath,
> That he may bliss this bay with his tall ship,
> Make love's quick pants in Desdemona's arms,
> Give renew'd fire to our extincted spirits,
> And bring all Cyprus comfort!   (II.i.75–83)

In this extended metaphor, the anticipated consummation of the marriage between Othello and Desdemona is suggested by a prayer to Jove for Othello's sexual potency. Carnal knowledge of Desdemona is the image of Othello's safe landing just as it is the source of "comfort" for Cyprian society. But this form of knowledge will be played out against the knowledge of Desdemona herself, which has already been introduced as beyond description, outside of language. Or, to employ the play's terms, the wind with which Jove is implored to "swell" Othello's "sail" is the same wind that has "lost him on a dangerous sea." Thus the play sets up Othello's dilemma as between engulfment and sexual potency figured by the simultaneously knowable and unknowable Desdemona. That we have already heard Othello describe his sexual "appetite" as "defunct" (I.iii.265–267) further anticipates the impossibility of fulfillment for Cassio's prayer.

Returning to Niccholes' discussion, the text also provides an initial catalogue of those outward signs that indicate either an "honest woman" or, conversely, "lascivious petulancy." The "promising" candidates for marriage should "be of a sober and mild aspect, courteous behaviour, decent carriage, of a fixed eye, constant looke and unaffected gate . . . [because] . . . an honest woman dwells at the signe of an honest countenance." Conversely, "wilde lookes (for the most part) accompany wilde conditions; a rowling eye is not fixed, but would fixe upon objects it likes, it lookes for, and affected nicety is ever a signe of lascivious petulancy."[45] Even though all of this is presented by Niccholes with a slightly exaggerated humor, there is an underlying sense of urgency which is perhaps assuaged in part by committing it to print: again, registering his anxieties in writing may be understood as an attempt to "resolve" discursively that which experience cannot.

Marriage is a very perilous "adventure" that the author figures in terms of one of his own age's most abiding fears. Represented as a tempestuous ocean, "woman" becomes a potential source of emasculation. Niccholes' advice on marriage provides a way to assuage this danger just as exploration and navigation of the seas is an exclusively masculine prerogative linked to the conquest and possession of land. "A Discourse of Marriage and Wiving" thus offers a detailed index of women's behavior in order to promote "correct" interpretations of women by their prospective husbands. His text responds to the dread (and expectation) of cuckoldry among men by providing an empowering, interpretive knowledge of female sexuality. But at the same time, Niccholes envisions this form of masculine power over and against a profound fear and anxiety that unsettles whatever satisfaction his advice might promise – this undercurrent in his text rises to the surface in *Othello*. Just as the knowledge he propagates about women can only derive from a gendered economy in which "woman" is the object of masculine knowledge, so, too, does that same economy produce the perpetual masculine anxiety displayed in sexual jealousy. Masculine identity is thus simultaneously empowered and threatened by the very system that shapes and sustains it – a system foundationally unsettled by its determination to maintain a gender dynamic that requires differences to be transformed into hierarchy. In this way, we can begin to understand male sexual jealousy and the knowledge it demands as an enabling discourse that, ironically to say the least, produces and perpetuates the fact of gender difference as justification for the subordination of women. Niccholes envisions knowledge (his "Land markes and directions") as the terra firma upon which the masculine subject stands, perilously surrounded by a sea that threatens to "expose" and engulf him.

The frustration I feel in reading *Othello* derives not just from the relative unimportance attached to Emilia's keen observations concerning jealousy and women's sexual pleasures, but also from the fact that the play does not develop Desdemona's character in response to her husband's obsessive jealousy, at least not much further than as a general state of bewilderment. Yet this omission does not consign us to repeating her silenced position in our analysis of the play, nor to ignoring the perspective of Emilia as the male characters do. I therefore want to conclude this chapter by listening to Emilia through the writings of women in this period who address the issue of male jealousy and sexuality in general.

The critique of the double standard toward male and female sexuality that Emilia speaks at the end of the fourth act is a significant issue in several pamphlets written by women as part of the "querelles de femmes" debate. In "Esther hath hanged Haman," Sowernam's response to Swetnam's "The Arraignment of Lewd, idle, froward, and unconstant women," the author complains that "if a man abuse a Maid and get her with child, no matter is made of it but as a trick of youth, but it is made so heinous an offense in the maid that she is disparaged and utterly undone by it. So in all offenses, those which men committ are made light and as nothing, slighted over, but those which women do committ, those are made grievous and shameful."[46] But Sowernam appears to compromise this claim, at least from our perspective, as she argues that this discrepancy has "just cause" since God made women more pure than men and originally "put hatred betwixt the woman and the serpent." There is no question that Sowernam writes within a set of religious attitudes that shape and supports the construction of woman I have located as the cause of masculine anxieties about jealousy and cuckoldry – among the early modern writings by women her treatise is especially committed to arguing within a Christian sensibility. But if we acknowledge that framework as more or less unavoidable Christian morality and misogyny may be seen as a necessary rhetoric in which genuine anger and frustration are encoded.

At the end of "Esther hath hanged Haman," Sowernam reiterates her argument that Eve was more sinned against than sinning: "As Eve did not offend without the temptation of a Serpent, so women do seldom offend but it is by provocation of men."[47] The equation between the devil and men at least implicitly questions the masculinist ideology inherent in the creation story. It also unleashes in Sowernam one of the most virulent attacks in the entire text:

Let not your impudence, nor your consorts dishonesty charge our sex with those sins of which you yourselves were the first procurers. I have in my discourse touched you and all yours to the quick. I have taxed you with bitter speeches; you will (perhaps) say I am a railing scold. In this objection I will teach you both wit and honesty. The difference between a railing scold and an honest accuser is this: the first rageth upon passionate fury without bringing cause or proof; the other bringeth direct proof for what she allegeth. You charge women with clamorous words and bring no proof. I charge you with blasphemy, with impudence, scurrility, foolery, and the like; I show just and direct proof for what I say.[48]

This passage slips very easily from an explanation of women's fallen state based in Genesis to a bitter indictment of men for constructing an unjust system. Sowernam's anger nearly bursts through her otherwise calm prose as she repeats the first person pronoun in nearly every sentence. Retreating somewhat in the next sentence ("It is not my desire to speak so much"), she concludes the treatise by making explicit what had only been suggested before: "forbear to charge women with faults which come from the contagion of Masculine serpents."[49] Sowernam's arguments may be inscribed by the Christian, patriarchal hegemony, but they are by no means completely congruent with it.

Lady Mary Wroth's prose romance, *The Countesse of Montgomery's Urania* (1621), also confronts what Josephine A. Roberts describes as "the fundamental inequality of the double standard, in which women are expected to remain constant whereas men are not."[50] The following sonnet from Wroth's sequence "Pamphilia to Amphilanthus," printed as a coda to the 1621 edition of the prose romance, might have appropriately been spoken by Desdemona to Othello:

> Cruell suspition, O! bee thou now att rest,
> Let dayly torments bring to thee some stay;
> Alas make nott my ill thy ease-full pray,
> Nor give loose raines to rage when love's oprest.
> I ame by care sufficiently distrest,
> Noe rack can strech my hart more, nor a way
> Can I find out for least content to lay
> One happy foote of joye, one step that's blest;
> Butt to my end thou fly'st with greedy eye,
> Seeking to bring griefe by bace jealousie,
> O in how strang a cage ame I kept in?
> Noe little signe of favor can I prove
> Butt must bee way'de, and turning to wronging love,
> And with each humor must my state begin.[51]

In the introspective fashion characteristic of the sonnets as well as the romance, Pamphilia addresses Amphilanthus ("the lover of two") in regard to her lover's unfounded jealousy. It is useful to compare Wroth's depiction of the eye of the jealous man as a kind of panoptical tyrant with the same image from "Tell-Trothes." The male author of the "Tell-Trothes" acknowledges regrettably that even if women are watched "so narrowly," the inaccessibility and invisibility of their private thoughts means that "the rains of their liberty are at their own pleasures." Wroth provides the counter-perspective: the "greedy eye" of the jealous man keeps the woman prisoner in a figurative cage. The third stanza also implies that Amphilanthus on some level *wants* to find evidence to support his "[c]ruell suspition": the "greedy eye" is "seeking to bring griefe" as if it (he) needed to fulfill a pre-existent, rapacious desire. Similarly, Othello is also driven by an almost addictive need to find "satisfaction" through knowing the "truth" of Desdemona once his suspicions are activated. In the last stanza, Wroth portrays the interpretive tyranny of her jealous lover I discussed above. Any "signe" offered by the woman already signifies only what the man appears to want to find in the first place: it is "way'de, and turnd to wronging love." The woman in the poem is thus encaged not just in a spatial sense but also in her inability to represent or signify herself since no matter what signs or proof she offers, the interpretation is already determined. She is not allowed a subjectivity within this interpretive economy because she must function as the object of interpretation in order to confer an anxious male subjectivity – precisely the position Wroth contradicts by writing the sonnet in the first place.

Indeed, any assertion or agency by the woman in this economy is read necessarily as an intent to deceive – her real meaning, of course, already decided. Iago and Brabantio are able to utilize this "logic" by turning Desdemona's most powerful and willful sign of her love for Othello into a sign of her infidelity: "She did deceive her father, marrying you;" (III.iii.210), echoing Brabantio's earlier remark: "She has deceiv'd her father, and may thee" (I.iii.296). Othello's response to Brabantio reveals the tragic irony of his own inability to see that his own jealousy is "a monster / Begot upon itself, born on itself." He says: "My life upon her faith" (I.iii.297) when it is truly the impossibility of his own faith that possesses him.

The jealousy treatises I have discussed depend upon a specular and interpretive economy that situates men in the position of "reading" and interpreting women as "texts"; if this were not pernicious enough, the interpretations to these "texts" are already fixed by a prior construction of woman. This is perhaps the most significant awareness Iago deploys. "Trifles light as air," he tells Emilia, "Are to the jealous confirmations strong / As proofs of holy writ" (III.iii.327–329). For men, the difficulty of escaping from this economy is that masculine subjectivity – even in its most agitated, self-torturing state – is in part engendered by those discourses that reproduce such forms of "knowledge." The paranoia and sometimes violence that accompanies the jealous interpreter of female sexuality exposes the profound anxiety inherent in the perceived necessity of constructing masculine identity in relation to the idea of "woman" rather than to women themselves. And this, finally, is Emilia's unheeded perception.

Now almost 400 years after the first boy actor played the role of Emilia on the Jacobean stage, one would like to think that the basic truths her character articulates are indisputable. Yet women still need to fight through the vestiges of a history that too often reduced them to portraits drawn by men, one that still requires them to legitimate their voices according to discursive rules not of their own making. No doubt our culture registers in countless ways its own crisis in gender relations, but many recent books in the popular press (such as Robert Bly's *Iron John* and John Gray's *Men Are From Mars, Women Are From Venus*), as well as studies that argue for genetic or biological differences, are little more than contemporary revisions, even further mystifications, of the patriarchal ideologies this book has tried to unveil. Such texts and beliefs seem to me to confirm rather than to challenge the history we have inherited.

In the preceding pages I have tried to show that truly listening to Emilia – listening to women – involves a much more radical re-thinking of the very categories men have constructed as the basis of our identities, a far more rigorous critique of the very *idea* of binary gender difference. No such critique can be accomplished without a period of considerable difficulty and disturbance since what is at stake is not just an adjustment to whom we think we are but rather a seismic shift in the ground upon which our identities so uneasily rest. Today, this difficulty too often fosters a renewed valorization of supposedly traditional values. A far more profitable response is to understand that our history of masculine privilege has also brought with it an accumulation of anxieties, contradictions and paradoxes that, while shaping who we are have not at all been salutary – certainly not for women, but also not for men. In this way, the critical portraits of men in *Anxious Masculinity* have not been intended to show how things have always been, but rather to encourage us to recognize that it is also in *all* of our interests to regenerate the history we have inherited.

Notes

INTRODUCTION

1 E. M. W. Tillyard, *The Elizabethan World Picture* (New York: Macmillan, 1944): *passim*.

2 "The Homily on Obedience" (1559), reprinted in *Elizabethan Backgrounds: Historical Documents of the Age of Elizabeth I*, Arthur M. Kinney, ed. (Archon Books, 1975): p. 61.

3 See Louis Althusser, *Lenin and Philosophy, and Other Essays*, Ben Brewster, trans. (New York: Monthly Review Press, 1972).

4 Robert Burton, *The Anatomy of Melancholy*, Floyd Dell and Paul Jordan-Smith, eds. (New York: Tudor Publishing Company, 1927): p. 728. All references to Burton's *Anatomy* will be from this edition and will be cited in the main body of the text according to page number, partition and section. References to the preface, "Democritus to the Reader," will be cited by page number only. Dell and Jordan's translations of Burton's passages in Latin will appear in italics throughout.

5 *The Compact Edition of the Oxford English Dictionary*, vol. 1 (Oxford: Oxford University Press, 1971): p. 378.

6 Paul Smith, *Discerning the Subject* (Minneapolis: University of Minnesota Press, 1988): p. 87.

7 James Clifford, "On Ethnographic Allegory," in *Writing Cultures: The Poetics and Politics of Ethnography*, James A. Clifford and George E. Marcus, eds. (Berkeley: University of California Press, 1986), *passim*.

8 Sigmund Freud, *Beyond the Pleasure Principle*, James Strachey, ed., *The Standard Edition of the Complete Works of Sigmund Freud*, vol. XVIII (London: The Hogarth Press, 1955): pp. 12–13.

9 Gayle Rubin, "The Traffic in Women: Notes on the 'Political Economy' of Sex," in *Toward an Anthropology of Women*, Rayna Reiter, ed. (New York: Monthly Review Press, 1975): p. 168.

10 *Ibid.* p. 168.

11 Tillyard, *The Elizabethan World Picture*, p. 67.

12 Luce Irigaray, *This Sex Which is Not One*, Catherine Porter, trans. (Ithaca, NY: Cornell University Press, 1985): p. 68.

13 Jacques Derrida, "Sign, Structure and Play in the Discourse of the Human Sciences," in *Writing and Difference*, Alan Bass, trans. (Chicago: University of Chicago Press, 1978): p. 285.

14 Some of the most prominent and influential studies include: Alan Bray, *Homosexuality in Renaissance England* (London: Gay Men's Press, 1982); Jonathan Goldberg, *Sodometries: Renaissance Texts/Modern Sexualities* (Stanford: Stanford University Press, 1992); Gregory Bredbeck, *Sodomy and Interpretation: From Marlowe to Milton* (Ithaca, NY: Cornell University Press, 1991); Valerie Traub, *Desire and Anxiety: Circulations of Sexuality in Shakespearean Drama* (London and New York: Routledge Press, 1992); and Bruce Smith, *Homosexual Desire in Shakespeare's England: A Cultural Poetics* (Chicago: University of Chicago Press, 1991).

15 John Aubrey, *Aubrey's Brief Lives*, Oliver Lawson Dick, ed. (London: Secker and Warburg, 1958).

16 Louis Montrose, "The Elizabethan Subject and the Spenserian Text," in *Literary Theory/Renaissance Texts*, Patricia Parker and David Quint, eds. (Baltimore and London: The Johns Hopkins University Press, 1986): p. 306. See also the introduction to Smith, *Discerning the Subject*, p. xxx.

17 See Judith Butler, *Gender Trouble: Feminism and the Subversion of Identity* (New York: Routledge Press, 1990): p. 25.

18 *Ibid.* p. 33.

19 Stephen Greenblatt, *Renaissance Self-fashioning: From More to Shakespeare* (Chicago and London: University of Chicago Press, 1980): p. 9.

20 *Ibid.* pp. 244–245.

21 *Ibid.* p. 10.

22 Joseph Swetnam, "The Arraignment of lewde, idle, froward, and inconstant women" (1615), in *Half Humankind: Contexts and Texts of the Controversy about Women in England, 1540–1640*, Katherine Usher Henderson and Barbara F. McManus, eds. (Urbana and Chicago: University of Illinois Press, 1985): p. 205.

23 John Williams, "A Sermon of Apparell" (London: 1619): p. 7.

24 See Stephen Greenblatt, "Psychoanalysis and Renaissance Culture," in *Literary Theory/Renaissance Texts*, Patricia Parker and David Quint, eds. (Baltimore and London: The Johns Hopkins University Press, 1986): pp. 210–214, and Juliana Schiesari's brief response to Greenblatt in *The Gendering of Melancholia: Feminism, Psychoanalysis, and the Symbolics of Loss in Renaissance Literature* (Ithaca and London: Cornell University Press, 1992): pp. 22–25.

25 Greenblatt, "Psychoanalysis," pp. 222–223.

26 *Ibid.* p. 216.

27 Stephen Orgel, "Nobody's Perfect: Or, Why Did the English Stage Take Boys for Women?" *South Atlantic Quarterly* 88 (1989): p. 13.

28 *Ibid.* p. 14.

29 Coppélia Kahn, *Man's Estate: Masculine Identity in Shakespeare* (Berkeley: University of California Press, 1981): p. 12.

30 Janet Adelman, *Suffocating Mothers: Fantasies of Maternal Origins in Shakespeare's Plays, Hamlet to The Tempest* (New York and London: Routledge Press, 1992): p. 3, 4.

31 Kahn, *Man's Estate*, p. 19, *passim*.

32 Gail Kern Paster, *The Body Embarrassed: Drama and the Disciplines of*

Shame in Early Modern England (Ithaca NY: Cornell University Press, 1993): *passim*.

33 *The Oxford English Dictionary*, p. 95.

34 *Ibid.* p. 95.

35 D. E. Underdown, "The Taming of the Scold: the Enforcement of Patriarchal Authority in Early Modern England," in *Order and Disorder in Early Modern England*, Anthony Fletcher and John Stevenson, eds. (Cambridge: Cambridge University Press, 1985): p. 116.

36 William Gouge, *Of Domesticall Duties: Eight Treatises*, 3rd edn. (London, 1634): p. 17.

37 Philip Stubbes, *The Anatomie of Abuses*, 4th edn. (London: 1595): Epist. Ded.

38 John Dod and Robert Clever, *A Godly Forme of Household Government: for the ordering of private families, according to God's Word* (London: 1612): p. A8v.

39 Underdown, "The Taming of the Scold," p. 122.

40 Susan Bordo, "The Cartesian Masculinization of Thought," *Signs: Journal of Women and Culture* 11 (1986): p. 453.

41 Lawrence Stone, *The Family, Sex and Marriage in England 1500–1800* (New York: Harper & Row, Publishers, 1977): p. 519. See also: Martin Ingram, *Church Courts, Sex and Marriage in England, 1570–1640* (Cambridge: Cambridge University Press, 1987): pp. 299–304; Richard M. Wunderli, *London Church Courts and Society on the Eve of the Revolution* (Cambridge, Mass.: Medieval Academy of America, 1981); and Ralph Houlbrooke, *Church Courts and the People During the English Reformation*, 1520–1570 (Oxford: Oxford University Press, 1979): pp. 75–88.

42 Susan Dwyer Amussen, *An Ordered Society: Gender and Class in Early Modern England* (Oxford: Basil Blackwell Ltd., 1988): p. 102.

43 Ingram, *Church Courts, Sex and Marriage*, p. 152.

44 See Peter Laslett, *The World We Have Lost*, 2nd edn. (New York: Charles Scribner's Sons, 1971): pp. 132–178.

45 Statute of James (1610), cited in Alan Macfarlane, "Illegitimacy and Illegitimates in English History," in Peter Laslett, Karla Oosterveen and Richard M. Smith, *Bastardy and its Comparative History* (Cambridge, Mass.: Harvard University Press, 1980): p. 73.

46 Stone, *The Family, Sex and Marriage*, p. 501.

47 Esther Sowernam, pseud., "Esther hath hanged Haman" (1617), in Henderson and McManus, eds., *Half Humankind*, p. 103.

48 Underdown, "The Taming of the Scold," p. 119.

49 *Ibid.* p. 121.

50 Keith Thomas, *Religion and the Decline of Magic* (London: Weidenfeld and Nicolson, 1971): p. 679. See also Marianne Heste, *Lewd Women & Wicked Witches: A Study of the Dynamics of Male Domination* (London and New York: Routledge Press, 1992).

51 Swetnam, "Arraignment," in Henderson and McManus, eds., *Half Humankind*, p. 201.

52 Sowernam, "Esther," in Henderson and McManus, eds., *Half Humankind*, p. 238.

53 Cited in *Half Humankind*, p. 17.

54 Suzanne Hull, *Chaste, Silent and Obedient: English Books for Women, 1475–1640* (San Marino: Huntington Library, 1982): p. 137, *passim*. See also Linda Woodbridge, *Women and the English Renaissance: Literature and the Nature of Womankind, 1540–1620* (Urbana and Chicago: University of Illinois Press, 1986).

55 Hull, *Chaste, Silent and Obedient*, p. 135.

56 Virginia Woolf, *A Room of One's Own* (1929; San Diego, New York, London: Harcourt Brace Jovanovich, Publishers, n.d.): pp. 34–35.

57 Leonard Tennenhouse, *Power on Display: The Politics of Shakespeare's Genres* (New York and London: Methuen, 1986): p. 17.

58 Jane Anger, "Her Protection for Women" (1589), in Henderson and McManus, eds., *Half Humankind*, p. 183.

59 Underdown, "The Taming of the Scold," p. 117.

60 Amussen, *An Ordered Society*, p. 123.

61 *Ibid*. pp. 27–33.

62 *Ibid*. p. 42.

63 Gouge, "Of Domesticall Duties," pp. 3–4.

64 Amussen, *An Ordered Society*, p. 42.

65 Stone, *The Family, Sex and Marriage*, p. 499.

66 *Ibid*. p. 22.

67 Clifford, "On Ethnographic Allegory," p. 99.

68 Michael McCanles, "The Authentic Discourse of the Renaissance," *Diacritics* (Spring, 1980): p. 81.

69 Clifford, "On Ethnographic Allegory," p. 121.

70 Stephen Greenblatt, *Shakespearean Negotiations: The Circulation of Social Energy in Renaissance England* (Berkeley and Los Angeles: University of California Press, 1988): p. 5.

1 FEARFUL FLUIDITY: BURTON'S *ANATOMY OF MELANCHOLY*

1 Lawrence Babb, *Sanity in Bedlam: A Study of Robert Burton's Anatomy of Melancholy* (East Lansing: Michigan State University Press, 1959): p. 9.

2 Gail Kern Paster, *The Body Embarrassed: Drama and the Disciplines of Shame in Early Modern England* (Ithaca, NY: Cornell University Press, 1993), p. 16.

3 Lawrence Babb, *The Elizabethan Malady: A Study of Melancholia in English Literature from 1580 to 1642* (East Lansing: Michigan State University Press, 1951), pp. 21–41. Another useful, general study of melancholy is Raymond Klibansky, Erwin Panofsky, and Fritz Saxl, *Saturn and Melancholy* (New York: Basic Books, 1964).

4 Paster, *The Body Embarrassed*, p. 9.

5 *Ibid*., p. 13.

6 Juliana Schiesari, *The Gendering of Melancholia: Feminism, Psychoanalysis, and the Symbolics of Loss in Renaissance Literature* (Ithaca and London: Cornell University Press, 1992).

7 *Ibid*., p. ix.

8 *Ibid*., p. 112.

9 *Ibid.*, p. 52, Schiesari's emphasis.

10 *Ibid.*, pp. 98–101.

11 *Ibid.*, p. 21.

12 Babb, *The Elizabethan Malady*, p. 157, n. 67. Babb also discusses the vogue for melancholy in early modern England in *Sanity in Bedlam*, pp. 2–3.

13 See Schiesari's discussion of Petrarchism in *The Gendering of Melancholia*, pp. 167–168.

14 Babb, *Sanity in Bedlam*, p. 3.

15 See Michel Foucault's now familiar argument in the first chapter of *The Order of Things*, trans. of *Les mots et les choses* (New York: Vintage Books, 1973).

16 Thomas Wilson, *The Arte of Rhetorique* (1553), Thomas J. Derrick, ed. (New York and London: Garland, 1982): p. 375 (my emphases). A different conception of rhetoric begins to emerge in the latter half of Elizabeth's reign, approximately concomitant with the translation of Ramus' *Logic* in England: see Peter Ramus, *The Logike of the Moste Excellent Philosopher P. Ramus Martyr* (1574), Catherine M. Dunn, ed., Roland MacIlmaine, trans. (Northridge, California, 1969). Ramus subsumes rhetoric under the larger category of logic and thus abolishes classical memory, which relied, according to Frances Yates, on corporeal similitudes. For this discussion I have borrowed from my article, "'... the hole matter opened': Iconic Representation and Interpretation in 'The Quenes Majesties Passage'," *Criticism* 28 (1986): pp. 1–25. See especially n. 23, pp. 23–24.

17 Henry Peacham, *The Garden of Eloquence* (London: 1577), facsimile edition, R. C. Alston, ed. (Menston, England: Scolar Press, 1971), sig. B1v.

18 George Puttenham, *The Arte of English Poesie* (1588), facsimile edition, Baxter Hathaway, ed. (Kent, Ohio: Kent State University Press, 1970), p. 166.

19 Foucault, *The Order of Things*, p. 21.

20 "Homily on Obedience" (1559), reprinted in Kinney, ed., *Elizabethan Backgrounds*, pp. 44–48.

21 Devon Hodges, *Renaissance Fictions of Anatomy* (Amherst: University of Massachusetts Press, 1985): p. 113.

22 Schiesari, *The Gendering of Melancholia*, p. 247.

23 The first quotation is from Herschel Baker (1952), the second from Sir William Osler (1915). Both are cited in David Renaker, "Robert Burton and Ramist Method," *Renaissance Quarterly* 24 (1971): p. 210.

24 Ruth A. Fox, *The Tangled Chain: the Structure of Disorder in the Anatomy of Melancholy* (Berkeley: University of California Press, 1976): p. 9.

25 See Renaker, "Robert Burton and Ramist Method," p. 220. Bridget Gellert Lyons accounts for the unruly nature of the text on the basis of its broad, diverse subject matter, and as an effect of Burton's desire to present a self-portrait of the "curious and restlessness" of the melancholy man. See *Voices of Melancholy: Studies in Literary Treatments of Melancholy in Renaissance England* (New York: Barnes & Noble, Inc., 1971), pp. 113–148. Stanley Fish carefully develops (among other things) the way the disappearance of an authoritative author deprives the reader of any fixed perspective; see *Self-Consuming Artifacts: The Experience of Seventeenth-Century Literature* (Berkeley: University of California Press, 1972), esp. pp. 322–343.

26 Hodges, *Renaissance Fictions*, p. 117.
27 Michael O'Connell, *Robert Burton*, Arthur F. Kinney, ed., Twayne's English Author Series (Amherst: University of Massachusetts Press, 1986): p. 62.
28 Fox, *The Tangled Chain*, p. 128.
29 Stephen Orgel, "Nobody's Perfect," p. 14.
30 Paster, *The Body Embarrassed*, p. 90.
31 Thomas Lacqueur, *Making Sex: Body and Gender from the Greeks to Freud* (Cambridge, Mass., and London: Harvard University Press, 1990), p. 54, Lacqueur's emphasis.
32 Jacques Ferrand, *Erotomania or a Treatise ... of Love, or Erotique Melancholy*, Edmund Chilmead, trans., (Oxford, 1640), p. 261. Babb discusses this text in *The Elizabethan Malady*, esp. pp. 128–142.
33 Paster, *The Body Embarrassed*, pp. 82–84.
34 William Vaughan, *Approved Directions for Health, Both Naturall and Artificiall* (London, 1612): p. 70.
35 Stephen Greenblatt develops this logic in his superb discussion of Spenser's Bower of Bliss. He writes: "Virtually all of Spenser's representations of sexual fulfillment, including those he fully sanctions, seem close to excess and risk the breakdown of the carefully fashioned identity." See Greenblatt, *Renaissance Self-Fashioning*, p. 176.
36 The association between suicide and the melancholic personality led quickly upon Burton's death to rumors that he had killed himself. See J. B. Bamborough's introduction to Robert Burton, *The Anatomy of Melancholy*, vol. I, Thomas C. Faulkner, Nicholas K. Kiessling and Rhonda L. Blair, eds. (Oxford: Clarendon Press, 1989), p. xxxvi. Unfortunately, only the first two of three projected volumes of this much needed scholarly edition of the *Anatomy* have been published at the time of writing.
37 Especially in the chapter "Covering His Ass: The Scatological Imperatives of Comedy," Paster develops the idea that "ambiguities of gender formation become encoded and hierarchized as a question of personal bodily discipline." See *The Body Embarrassed*, p. 125.
38 Schiesari, *The Gendering of Melancholia*, p. 252.
39 *Ibid.*, p. 237.
40 Alan Bray, *Homosexuality in Renaissance England* (London: Gay Men's Press, 1988): 25.
41 Goldberg, *Sodometries*, p. 10.
42 See Bray, *Homosexuality*, pp. 19–24, and Goldberg, *Sodometries*, pp. 18–19.
43 Babb, *The Elizabethan Malady*, pp. 36–37.
44 Andre du Laurens, *A Discourse of the Preservation of the Sight: of Melancholike Diseases; of Rheumes, and of Old Age*, Richard Surphet, trans. (London, 1599). Reprinted in *Shakespeare Association Facsimiles* (1938): pp. 93–94.

2 PURITY AND THE DISSEMINATION OF KNOWLEDGE IN BACON'S NEW SCIENCE

1 Mary Douglas, *Purity and Danger: An Analysis of Concepts of Pollution and Taboo* (New York: Praeger, 1966): p. 138.

2   Jean Calvin, quoted in Keith Thomas, *Puritans and Revolutionaries: Essays in Seventeenth-Century History Presented to Christopher Hill*, Donald Pennington and Keith Thomas, eds. (Oxford: Clarendon Press, 1978): p. 262.

3   The indispensable discussion of this dynamic is Eve Kosofsky Sedgwick, *Between Men: English Literature and Male Homosocial Desire* (New York: Columbia University Press, 1985): see especially chapters one and two.

4   Alan Bray, "Homosexuality and the Signs of Male Friendship in Elizabethan England," *History Workshop: A Journal of Socialist and Feminist Historians* 29 (1990): pp. 3–4.

5   Bray, "Homosexuality and the Signs of Male Friendship," p. 7.

6   Sedgwick, *Between Men*, pp. 28–48.

7   Bray reprints Simonds D'Ewes' description of Bacon's "horrible and secret sin of sodomy . . ." See Bray, "Homosexuality and the Signs of Male Friendship," p. 14. See also Graham Hammill, "The Epistemology of Expurgation," in *Queering the Renaissance*, Jonathan Goldberg, ed. (Durham and London: Duke University Press, 1994): pp. 236–252.

8   Bray, *Homosexuality in Renaissance England*. See also Smith, *Homosexual Desire in Shakespeare's England* and Goldberg, *Sodometries*.

9   Hammill, "The Epistemology of Expurgation," p. 247.

10 David Harris Sacks, "Searching for 'Culture' in the English Renaissance," *Shakespeare Quarterly* 39 (1988): p. 476. For a more detailed account of the permeability, even confusion, of the English social hierarchy, see Keith Wrightson, *English Society, 1580–1680* (London: Hutchinson, 1982): esp. pp. 17–38. Leonard Tennenhouse shows how aristocratic women on the Jacobean stage are either "the subject of clandestine desire or else they have become an object of desire which threatens the aristocratic community's self-enclosure." See *Power on Display*, p. 116. Tennenhouse's book has influenced my own formulations in many important ways; however, following Sacks' critique of the very idea of an "aristocratic community," I have been led to see the term more as a legitimating social trope rather than as an actual social entity. Reading the female, aristocratic body as the site of either class pollution or purity is also explored in Frank Whigham's superb essay, "Sexual and Social Mobility in *The Duchess of Malfi*," *PMLA* 100 (1985): pp. 167–186.

11 Baldassare Castiglione, *The Book of the Courtier*, Thomas Hoby, trans. (London, 1561; reprint, London, 1966): p. 219.

12 Lawrence Stone, *The Crisis of the Aristocracy*, abridged ed. (London and New York: Oxford University Press, 1967): p. 22.

13 *Ibid.* p. 94.

14 *Ibid.* p. 352.

15 F. J. Furnivall, ed., *Harrison's Description of England*, New Shakespeare Society, 6th series, no. 1 (London, 1877): pt. 1, ch. 5.

16 Wrightson, *English Society*, p. 23.

17 See Joel J. Epstein, *Francis Bacon: A Political Biography* (Athens, Ohio: Ohio University Press, 1977): p. 154.

18 Francis Bacon, "An Advertisement Touching a Holy War," in *The Works of Francis Bacon*, 7 vols., ed. James J. Spedding (London, 1875): VII, pp. 33–34. Whenever possible, citations from Bacon's works are from

Spedding's edition and are incorporated in the text using the standard notation (volume: page). For quotations from "The Masculine Birth of Time" ("Temporis Partus Masculus"), "The Refutation of Philosophies" ("Redargutio Philosophiarum"), and "Thoughts and Conclusions" ("Cogitata et Visa de Interpretatione Naturae"), texts left untranslated by Spedding, I have used the translations contained in Benjamin Farrington, *The Philosophy of Francis Bacon: An Essay on its Development from 1603 to 1609 with New Translations of Fundamental Texts* (Liverpool: Liverpool University Press, 1964). These texts are cited in the notes.

19 "Homily on Obedience" (1559), Kinney, ed. *Elizabethan Backgrounds*, pp. 60–61.

20 See Louis Montrose's fascinating discussion of this topos in "*A Midsummer Night's Dream* and the Shaping Fantasies of Elizabethan Culture: Gender, Power, Form," in Margaret W. Ferguson, Maureen Quilligan and Nancy J. Vickers, eds., *Rewriting the Renaissance: The Discourse of Sexual Difference in Early Modern England* (Chicago: University of Chicago Press, 1986): pp. 65–87.

21 For a very suggestive discussion of the normal/perverse binarism, including a brief discussion of Bacon, see Jonathan Dollimore, "The Cultural Politics of Perversion: Augustine, Shakespeare, Freud, Foucault," *Textual Practice* 4 (1990): pp. 179–196.

22 Bacon, "Thoughts and Conclusions," trans. Farrington, p. 83.

23 Bacon, "The Masculine Birth of Time," trans. Farrington, p. 62.

24 Evelyn Fox Keller, *Reflections on Gender and Science* (New Haven: Yale University Press, 1985): p. 41.

25 Morris Croll, *Style, Rhetoric, and Rhythm: Essays by Morris Croll*, ed. J. Max Patrick and Robert O. Evans (Princeton: Princeton University Press, 1966). Croll describes the anti-Ciceronian style as "a bare and level prose style adopted merely to the exact portrayal of things as they are" (p. 67).

26 See Genevieve Lloyd, *The Man of Reason: 'Male' and 'Female' in Western Philosophy* (London: Methuen, 1984) and Keller, *Reflections on Gender and Science*. Keller argues that Bacon "provided the language from which subsequent generations of scientists extracted a more consistent metaphor of lawful sexual domination" (p. 34). Her most provocative argument is developed in the discussion of "The Masculine Birth of Time" (1602–1603), where she points out that there is an element of "impotence and feminization" (p. 40) in the way Bacon describes the scientist's relationship to God. According to Keller, this is a manifestation of "a prior co-optation of the female mode – a co-optation which, given the initial impulse toward denial, necessitates an ever more urgent and aggressive repudiation" (pp. 41–42). Keller's argument is that Bacon's metaphor for the dissemination of knowledge compensates for what he perceives as the "unfortunate" necessity of involving women in procreation; "purity" functions tropologically as a way of avoiding the mediation of the female – it is "a way of doing without the mother." Masculine subjectivity is thus constructed and empowered in Bacon's text by blending a fantasy of male parthenogenesis with the "simultaneous appropriation and denial of the feminine" (p. 42). This essay

owes a general debt to Keller's important book. See also Hammill's criticism of Keller in "The Epistemology of Expurgation," pp. 246–247.

Among recent articles that address questions of gender in Bacon's work, see Sharon Achinstein, "How To be a Progressive Without Looking Like One: History and Knowledge in Bacon's *New Atlantis*," *Clio* 17 (1988): pp. 249–264, and Londa Schiebinger, "Feminine Icons: The Face of Modern Science," *Critical Inquiry* 14 (1988): pp. 661–691. For an overview of recent work on gender and science, see Lawrence Stone, "A Lab of One's Own," *The New York Review of Books* 37, no. 17 (November 8, 1990): pp. 19–23.

27 Brian Vickers, *Francis Bacon and Renaissance Prose* (Cambridge: Cambridge University Press, 1968): p. 6.

28 *Ibid.* p. 14.

29 *Ibid.* pp. 154–155.

30 See Lia Formigari, *Language and Experience in 17th-Century British Philosophy* (Amsterdam and Philadelphia: John Benjamin Publishing Co., 1988). Formigari argues that in Bacon's philosophy "Adam's language endures . . . as a sort of ideal model for human speech" and as a "symbol of wish fulfillment" (pp. 10–11).

31 Vickers, *Francis Bacon and Renaissance Prose*, p. 5, *passim*.

32 John C. Briggs, *Francis Bacon and the Rhetoric of Nature* (Cambridge, Mass.: Harvard University Press, 1989): pp. ix–x.

33 William Wimsatt, cited in Vickers, *Francis Bacon*, p. 24.

34 Bacon, "Thoughts and Conclusions," trans. Farrington, p. 13.

35 Martin Elsky, "Bacon's Hieroglyphs and the Separation of Words and Things," *Philological Quarterly* 63 (1984): p. 456.

36 Bacon, "The Refutation of Philosophies," trans. Farrington, p. 109.

37 Bacon, "The Masculine Birth of Time," trans. Farrington, p. 72.

38 I have discussed this historiographical impulse at length in my article entitled "The Flesh Made Word: Foxe's *Acts and Monuments*," *Renaissance and Reformation* 13 (Fall, 1989): pp. 381–407.

39 George Puttenham, *The Arte of English Poesie*, p. 166.

40 Dudley Fenner, *The Artes and Logicke of Rhetorike*, quoted in Patricia Parker, *Literary Fat Ladies: Rhetoric, Gender, Property* (London: Methuen, 1980): p. 108.

41 Parker, *Literary Fat Ladies*, pp. 110–111.

42 *Ibid.* p. 116.

43 Lloyd, *The Man of Reason*, p. 11.

44 Bacon, "Thoughts and Conclusions," trans. Farrington, p. 99.

45 Timothy J. Reiss, *The Discourse of Modernism* (Ithaca, NY: Cornell University Press, 1982): p. 181. Reiss demonstrates elsewhere that in Bacon's *New Atlantis*, "the new scientist *imposes* the discursive *I* upon the world"; he is an "*I* in search of knowledge that will allow him to enlarge the universe" (pp. 189–190). Much of my argument is indebted to Reiss' brilliant study.

46 Farrington, *The Philosophy of Francis Bacon*, p. 17.

47 Bacon, "The Masculine Birth of Time," trans. Farrington, p. 62.

48 *Ibid.* p. 72.

49 Ben Jonson, *Works*, vol. VIII, C. H. Hereford, P. and E. Simpson, eds., 11 vols. (Oxford: Clarendon Press): p. 620.
50 Bacon, "Thoughts and Conclusions," trans. Farrington, pp. 80–81.
51 Quoted in Epstein, *Francis Bacon*, p. 85.
52 Bacon, "The Masculine Birth of Time," trans. Farrington, p. 63.
53 Michel Foucault, *The Order of Things*, trans. of *Les mots et les choses* (New York: Vintage Books, 1973): p. 59.
54 Douglas, *Purity and Danger*, p. 192.

3 PUBLISHING CHASTITY: SHAKESPEARE'S "THE RAPE OF LUCRECE"

1 William Shakespeare, "The Rape of Lucrece," in *The Complete Works of William Shakespeare*, ed. David Bevington, 3rd edn. (Glenview, Illinois: Scott, Foresman and Company, 1980): 11, pp. 1478–1479. References to Shakespeare's plays are from this edition and will be cited in the text.
2 Charles Barber, *The Idea of Honour in the English Drama, 1591–1700* (Goteborg: Gothenburg Studies in English, 1957): pp. 47–57, *passim*.
3 Heather Dubrow points out that "throughout 'The Rape of Lucrece' . . . the characters' most private actions (or other people's ill-informed speculations about them) are continually made public through a network of surveillance and slander . . ." Dubrow further argues that this "helps to establish Lucrece's Rome as what anthropologists have termed a shame culture." See Heather Dubrow, *Captive Victors: Shakespeare's Narrative Poems and Sonnets* (Ithaca, NY: Cornell University Press, 1987): pp. 89–91.
4 Valerie Traub, *Desire and Anxiety: Circulations of Sexuality in Shakespearean Drama* (London and New York: Routledge, 1992): p. 7.
5 Friedrich Nietzsche, *Beyond Good and Evil*, Marianne Cowan, trans. (1885: Chicago: Henry Regenery Company, 1955): p. 175.
6 See Althusser, *Lenin and Philosophy*, *passim*. I am also indebted to David Wilbern's understanding of desire in the poem as "circulations of desire through the poem as independent of, and prior to, those nominal agents that conventionally articulate them." See David Wilbern, "Hyperbolic Desire: Shakespeare's 'Lucrece,'" in *Contending Kingdoms: Historical, Psychological and Feminist Approaches to the Literature of Sixteenth-Century England*, Marie-Rose Logan and Peter L. Rudnytsky, eds. (Detroit: Wayne State University Press, 1991): p. 202.
7 Peter Erickson has usefully remarked that the "study of patriarchal ideology in Shakespeare's work is chiefly a matter of identifying stress points, not of explicating fixed doctrine." See Peter Erickson, *Rewriting Shakespeare, Rewriting Ourselves* (Berkeley: University of California Press, 1991): p. 23.
8 Shakespeare, sonnet 129, in *The Complete Works*, pp. 1605–1606.
9 In Coppélia Kahn's terrific analysis of the poem, Lucrece's suicide "symbolically restores her body to its previous sexual purity by the purgation of shedding blood, thus removing the stain which would dishonor Collatine."

See Coppélia Kahn, "The Rape in Shakespeare's 'Lucrece,'" *Shakespeare Studies* 9 (1976): p. 65.

10   Several critics have commented on this point in various ways. In the context of the Lucretia story in Italian humanism, see Stephanie Jed, *Chaste Thinking: The Rape of Lucretia and the Birth of Humanism* (Bloomington: Indiana University Press, 1989): p. 44. In reference to Shakespeare's "Lucrece," see: Kahn, "The Rape," p. 56; Wilbern, "Hyperbolic Desire," p. 215; and Nancy J. Vickers, "'This Heraldry in Lucrece' Face'," *Poetics Today* 6 (1985): p. 176.

11   Rene Girard, *A Theater of Envy* (Oxford: Oxford University Press, 1991): p. 22.

12   *Ibid.*, p. 3.

13   Eve Sedgwick, *Between Men*, p. 22.

14   Robert Ashley, "Of Honour" (1596), quoted in Norman Council, *When Honour's at the Stake* (London: Allen and Unwin, 1973): p. 15.

15   Jean Calvin, *Institutes*, quoted in Council, *When Honour*, p. 26.

16   See Raymond Williams, "Base and Superstructure in Marxist Cultural Theory," reprinted in *Contemporary Literary Criticism: Literary and Cultural Studies*, 2nd edn., Robert Con Davies and Ronald Schleifer, eds. (New York and London: Longman Press, 1989): pp. 377–390.

17   Robert Ashley, "Of Honour," cited in Council, *When Honour's at the Stake*, p. 15.

18   Fulke Greville, "An Inquisition Upon Fame and Honor," in Fulke Greville, *Certaine Learned and Elegant Workes* (1633; Delmar, New York: Scolars' Facsimiles & Reprints, 1990): pp. 33–49. References to the poem will be cited in the text by stanza.

19   Barber, *Honour in the English Drama*, p. 99.

20   *Ibid.* p. 57.

21   *Ibid.* p. 268. See also Lawrence Stone, *The Crisis of the Aristocracy, 1558–1641* (Oxford: Clarendon Press, 1965), *passim.*

22   See Vickers, "'This Heraldry'," p. 176. Kahn makes a similar point: ". . . the chaste wife is seen as a precious jewel which tempts the thief . . . the husband's boasts initiate the temptation, in effect challenging his peers to take that jewel." See Kahn, "The Rape," p. 53.

23   Kahn, "The Rape," p. 49. Kahn also provides a useful discussion of Augustine's understanding of chastity, in which he argues, according to Kahn, that "the only consideration is spiritual: whether Lucrece's will remained steadfast in mental opposition to the rape, or whether she consented to it" (p. 63). Augustine's position coincides with, and indeed may be the basis for, the version of honor I have taken from Calvin.

24   Katharine Maus draws attention to the way Lucrece's suicide re-enacts Tarquin's rape by "plunging the phallic knife into the 'sheath' of her breast," noting the Latin "sheath" as the word for vagina. See Katharine Maus, "Taking Tropes Seriously: Language and Violence in Shakespeare's 'Rape of Lucrece,'" *Shakespeare Quarterly* 37 (1986): p. 72. See also Catherine Stimpson, "Shakespeare and the Soil of Rape," in Carolyn Ruth Swift-Lenz, Gayle Greene and Carol Thomas Neely, eds., *The Woman's Part: Feminist Criticism of Shakespeare* (Urbana: University of Illinois Press,

1980). Stimpson writes: "Their [Lucrece's and Lavinia's] deaths purge the lives and honor of the men whom they have ornamented . . ." (p. 59).

25 Stone, *Crisis of the Aristocracy, passim.*

26 See Frank Whigham, "Sexual and Social Mobility in *The Duchess of Malfi.*" A similar claim forms the basis of Leonard Tennenhouse's *Power on Display: The Politics of Shakespeare's Genres.*

27 Coppélia Kahn has discussed this anxiety at length in *Man's Estate.* In her discussion of "Lucrece," a similar point is made: ". . . the social order depends on the institution of marriage as the boundary line between legitimate and illegitimate procreation." See Kahn, "The Rape of Lucrece," p. 60.

28 Stimpson, "Shakespeare and the Soil of Rape," p. 58.

29 Jed, *Chaste Thinking*, pp. 6–7.

30 Peter Stallybrass, "Patriarchal Territories: The Body Enclosed," in *Rewriting the Renaissance: The Discourses of Sexual Difference in Early Modern Europe*, Margaret W. Ferguson, Maureen Quilligan, and Nancy J. Vickers, eds. (Chicago: University of Chicago Press, 1986): pp. 126, 127.

31 Jed, *Chaste Thinking*, p. 45.

32 See Erickson, *Rewriting Shakespeare*, p. 44.

33 Kahn provides a useful reading of this stanza: "The heroine becomes an image for two fields of political conquest, the expanding Roman empire and the New World (similarly, Virginia is named for a woman), and Tarquin, correspondingly, is a rival power who would snatch the newly won territory from its rightful possessor." See Kahn, "The Rape of Lucrece," p. 57.

34 Jed, *Chaste Thinking*, pp. 30, 34.

35 See Louis Montrose, "The Elizabethan Subject and the Spenserian Text," in Parker and Quint, eds., *Literary Theory/Renaissance Texts*, pp. 315–316. Erickson contextualizes the poem in terms of Elizabeth as "an aggressive counter-fantasy of male violation of a woman," similar to the Essex rebellion. See Erickson, *Rewriting the Renaissance*, p. 41.

36 John Day, "The Printer to the Reader," in Thomas Sackville and Thomas Norton, *Ferrex and Porrex, or Gorboduc*, facsimile rpt., John S. Farmer, ed. (1908; rpt. New York: AMS Press Inc., 1970). References to the play will be from this edition and cited in the text. I have discussed Day's note and the play in the context of the desire for original purity in Protestant translations of the Bible in "Reading Elizabethan Iconicity: *Gorboduc* and the Semiotics of Reform," *English Literary Renaissance* 18 (1988): pp. 194–217.

37 W. W. Greg, cited in H. S. Bennett, *English Books & Readers, 1558–1603* (Cambridge: Cambridge University Press, 1965): p. 256.

38 I. B. Cauthen, "Gorboduc, Ferrex and Porrex: the First Two Quartos," *Studies in Bibliography* 15 (1962): 231–233.

39 Jed, *Chaste Thinking*, pp. 47–48.

40 Shakespeare, sonnet 129, in *The Complete Works*, pp. 1605–1606.

41 Shakespeare, sonnet 144, in *The Complete Works*, p. 1608.

42 Traub, *Desire and Anxiety*, p. 7, her emphasis.

43 *Ibid.* p. 7.

44 Shakespeare, sonnet 129, in *The Complete Works*, pp. 1605–1606.

4 THE ANATOMY OF MASCULINE DESIRE IN *LOVE'S LABOR'S LOST*

1 *The Essayes or Morall, Politike and Millitarie Discourses of Lord Michaell de Montaigne*, trans. John Florio (London: V. Sims, 1604): pp. 505–537.
2 *Ibid.* pp. 508, 509.
3 *Ibid.* pp. 537, 512. Here and throughout the quotations from Montaigne, the italics are Florio's.
4 *Ibid.* pp. 523, 518.
5 *Ibid.* pp. 521, 516.
6 *Ibid.* p. 531. In this regard, one might also turn to Montaigne's discussion of female sexual appetite as it regulates to male impotence, and to his discussion of the dangers of exaggerating penis sizes to women (pp. 531–533). Sometimes Montaigne's understanding is distinctly male, even when he speaks in general terms; for example, love is *"an insatiate thirst of enjoying a greedily desired subject . . . a tickling delight of emptying ones seminary vessels"* (p. 526).
7 In regard to the idea that male representations of women and female sexuality are often compensations or projections of masculine anxieties, see Abbe Blum's wonderful essay on Shakespeare's monumentalization of female characters. See Abbe Blum, " 'Strike all that look upon with mar[ble]': Monumentalizing Women in Shakespeare's Plays," in *The English Woman in Print, 1500–1640*, Anne M. Haselkhorn and Betty S. Travitsky, eds. (University of Massachusetts Press, 1989): pp. 99–118.
8 Montaigne, *The Essayes*, pp. 528–529.
9 Keith Thomas, "The Place of Laughter in Tudor and Stuart England," *Times Literary Supplement*, 3906 (January 21, 1977): pp. 77–81.
10 A brief account of the play's criticism may be found in William C. Carroll's *The Great Feast of Language in Love's Labor's Lost* (Princeton, NJ: Princeton University Press, 1976): pp. 3–8. For example, Dr. Johnson found many phrases "mean, childish and vulgar" (p. 6); and H. B. Charlton thought the play "deficient in play and characterisation" (p. 7). Alexander Leggatt suggests that "the play's ultimate effect is to provide an image of insecurity." See *Shakespeare's Comedy of Love* (London: Methuen, 1974): p. 88. Most critics have worked with the two most salient features of the play: its attention to linguistic confusion/misprision and its concern with heterosexual love and courtship. An interesting study could be done on the way critics have linked these two issues. Generally, the argument is that, in Mary Beth Rose's words, the "overblown rhetoric" and "narcissistic posturing" of the men prevent a "shared experience" between the lovers. The play is thus a call for honest feelings expressed in the "plain style." See Mary Beth Rose, *The Expense of Spirit: Love and Sexuality in English Drama* (Ithaca NY: Cornell University Press, 1988): p. 36. Karen Newman's interesting reading is much more attentive to the way language additionally shapes identity in the play; still, she retains a belief that beneath its linguistic games the play offers a model of transparent communication and authentic selfhood: "Shakespeare's use of language to further

the theme of error and misunderstanding" results in characters who "delude themselves with their own language . . .": see *Shakespeare's Rhetoric of Comic Character: Dramatic Convention in Classical and Renaissance Comedy* (New York: Methuen, 1985): p. 87. The best socio-literary study of the play as "a cynosural staging of Elizabeth's court" is Louis Montrose's " 'Sport by sport o'erthrown': *Love's Labour's Lost* and the Politics of Play," *Texas Studies in Literature and Language* 18 (1977). Finally, Carolyn Asp has read the play through rather strictly defined Lacanian categories. Male subjectivity, constructed in terms of an idealization of women, is placed in the imaginary stage, while the female characters have mastered the symbolic order. See her *"Love's Labour's Lost*: Language and the Deferral of Desire," *Literature and Psychology* 35 (1989): pp. 1–21. The play has always seemed to me highly susceptible to Lacanian analysis, and my own reading is an attempt to historicize the play through the interpretive lens Lacan provides.

11   The only interpretation I have found that does *not* read the cuckoo song as integrating or harmonizing disparate elements is the fine chapter on the play by John Turner in Graham Holderness, Nick Potter and John Turner, *Shakespeare: Out of Court* (London: Macmillan, 1990): pp. 19–48.

12   Nancy J. Vickers, "Diana Described: Scattered Woman and Scattered Rhyme," *Critical Inquiry* 8 (1981): pp. 265, 274. See also Guiseppe Mazzotta, "The *Canzoniere* and the Language of the Self," *Studies in Philology* 75 (1978): pp. 271–296. Mazzotta points out that "the lyric emerges as the conventional privileged form of literary discourse because it is the representation of the will and the direct and spontaneous expression of the self . . ." (p. 274). For a superb account of the popularity of sonnet writing in the 1590s as a way of encoding political ambition, see Arthur F. Marotti, " 'Love Is Not Love': Elizabeth Sonnet Sequences and the Social Order," *ELH* 49 (1982): pp. 396–428.

13   Mazzotta, "The *Canzoniere*," p. 291.

14   For example, J. Dennis Huston has written that "Berowne's manipulation of language thus divorces words from fact and undermines the basic foundation on which human communication and community are built." See *Shakespeare's Comedies of Play* (New York: Columbia University Press, 1974): p. 44. Carroll's book-length study of the play remains one of the best accounts of rhetoric and referentiality in the Renaissance.

15   A number of readings see the play as empowering the women while ridiculing the men. According to Peter Erickson, for example, "male relations" are "made laughable" in the play. See *Patriarchal Structures in Shakespeare's Drama* (Berkeley: University of California Press, 1985). Montrose shows that sexual and moral shame is cast as masculine in the play, producing "a loss to female superiority in the game of sexual politics." See " 'Sport by sport o'erthrown'," p. 535.

16   Patricia Parker, *Literary Fat Ladies*, p. 107.

17   Linda Woodbridge, *Women and the English Renaissance*, pp. 184–185.

18   Vickers, "Diana Described," *passim*.

19   See Eve Sedgwick, *Between Men*. For a discussion of the way male bonds are effected around the exclusion of women, see also the introduction to Peter

Erickson's *Patriarchal Structures*. Karen Newman's argument linking the economic "structures of exchange" to the love relationships in *The Merchant of Venice* also provides a useful model for understanding male bonding in the Renaissance. See Karen Newman, "Portia's Ring: Unruly Women and Structures of Exchange in *the Merchant of Venice*," *Shakespeare Quarterly* 38 (1987): pp. 19–33.

20 Katharine Eisaman Maus, "Horns of Dilemma: Jealousy, Gender, and Spectatorship in English Renaissance Drama," *ELH* 54 (1987): p. 565.

21 Vickers, "Diana Described," p. 273.

22 Stephen Greenblatt, *Shakespearean Negotiations*, p. 89.

23 For example, at the entertainment at Elvetham (1591), Elizabeth "tames" Sylvanus, the god of the woods cast as a wild animal.

24 Philippa Berry, *Of Chastity and Power: Elizabethan Literature and the Unmarried Queen* (London and New York: Routledge, 1989): p. 4.

25 For an excellent analysis of this dynamic, see Louis Montrose, "Celebration and Insinuation: Sir Philip Sidney and the Motives of Elizabethan Courtship," *Renaissance Drama* 8 (1977): pp. 3–35. Montrose's discussion of the *Triumph of the Fortress of Perfect Beauty* offers a useful model for the way masculine desire is figured in relation to the Queen and to the symbolic power represented by her virginity. Indeed, there are enough parallels between *Love's Labor's Lost* and this text that, according to Glynne Wickham, Shakespeare intended the play as a direct satire on the courtly entertainment. See '*Love's Labor's Lost* and 'The Four Foster Children of Desire'," *Shakespeare Quarterly* 36 (1985): pp. 49–55.

26 Vickers, "Diana Described," p. 273.

27 Given the pervasive male anxiety toward cuckoldry, it is difficult to agree with Mary Beth Rose's observation that "*Love's Labor's Lost* concludes with a song celebrating summer and winter and suggesting the alliance among fruitful sexual love, the predictably recurring cycle of the seasons, and the ongoing life of society": see Rose, *The Expense of Spirit*, p. 36. On the contrary, the final song's choric references to cuckoldry would seem to suggest a future disruption of what Rose anticipates as "fruitful sexual love."

28 See Kahn, *Man's Estate*, p. 122.

29 Rose, *The Expense of Spirit*, p. 35.

30 Montaigne, *The Essayes*, pp. 507–508.

5 INSCRIPTIONS OF DIFFERENCE: CROSS-DRESSING, ANDROGYNY AND THE ANATOMICAL IMPERATIVE

1 William Gamage, "On the Feminine Supremacie," cited in Linda Woodbridge, *Women and the English Renaissance*, p. 142.

2 Thomas Laqueur, *Making Sex*, p. 8. Laqueur's argument that socially determined roles are natural and in theory more stable than anatomy provides the necessary historical frame for understanding why the Renaissance invested apparel with such importance, and conversely, why

cross-dressing could be so threatening to social order. Laqueur writes: "To be a man or a woman was to hold a social rank, a place in society, to assume a cultural role, not to *be* organically one or the other of two incommensurable sexes" (p. 8). Laqueur's biological and anatomical arguments lend support to David Kastan and Peter Stallybrass' remark that "[g]ender was manifestly a *production*, in which sexual difference was constructed and transformed." See the introduction to *Staging the Renaissance: Reinterpretations of Elizabethan and Jacobean Drama*, David Scott Kastan and Peter Stallybrass, eds. (New York and London: Routledge, 1991): p. 8.

3 Marjorie Garber, *Vested Interests: Cross-dressing and Cultural Anxiety* (New York: Harper Collins Publishers, 1992): p. 122.

4 Laqueur, *Making Sex*, pp. 25–62. By the same logic, it seems to me that the simultaneous orgasm theory of conception (Laqueur, pp. 43–52) may have also been felt as a potentially threatening moment of biological sameness that would contribute to the male anxiety toward female sexual pleasure – pleasure that in its "extreme" versions was also labeled monstrous.

5 Garber, *Vested Interests*, p. 125.

6 Phillip Stubbes, *The Anatomy of Abuses* (1583) cited in Simon Shepherd, *Amazons and Warrior Women: Varieties of Feminism in Seventeenth-Century Drama* (New York: St. Martin's Press, 1981): p. 67.

7 Judith Butler, *Gender Trouble, passim.*

8 William Harrison, *Harrison's Description of England*, F. J. Furnivall, ed., New Shakespeare Society, 6th series, no. 1 (London, 1988): p. 73, my emphasis.

9 For example, Esther Sowernam writes: "You are women: in Creation, noble; in redemption, gracious; in use, most blessed. Be not forgetful of yourselves nor unthankful to that Author from whom you receive all." Sowernam proceeds to argue against Joseph Swetnam's biblical basis in creation for the inferiority of women. See Esther Sowernam (pseud.), *Esther hath hang'd Haman* (London: 1617), reprinted in Simon Shepherd, ed., *The Women's Sharp Revenge: Five Women's Pamphlets from the Renaissance* (New York: St. Martin's Press, 1985): p. 88.

10 Daniel Rogers, *Matrimoniall Honour: or, The Mutuall Crowne and comfort of godly, loyall and chaste Marriage* (1642), cited in Shepherd, *Amazons and Warrior Women*, p. 54.

11 John Williams, "A Sermon of Apparell," (London: 1607): p. 7.

12 Averell, *Mervaillous Combat* (1588) cited in Shepherd, *Amazons and Warrior Women*, p. 67.

13 Jean Howard, "Crossdressing, The Theatre, and Gender Struggle in Early Modern England," *Shakespeare Quarterly* 39 (1988): p. 423.

14 Jane Anger, *Her Protection for Women* (London: 1589), Shepherd, ed., *The Women's Sharp Revenge*, p. 38. All further references will be cited in the text.

15 Esther Sowernam (pseud.), *Esther hath hang'd Haman* (London: 1617), Shepherd, ed., *The Women's Sharp Revenge*, p. 109.

16 See Laqueur, *Making Sex*, pp. 25–35, passim. Recent work on Renaissance beliefs about sexuality and reproductive anatomy include: Ian

MacLean, *The Renaissance Notion of Women* (Cambridge: Cambridge University Press, 1980); Thomas Laqueur, "Orgasm, Generation, and the Politics of Reproductive Biology," *Representations* 14 (1986): pp. 4–16; and Stephen Greenblatt, "Fiction and Friction," in *Shakespearean Negotiations*, pp. 66–93.

17 Shakespeare, Sonnet 20, in Bevington, ed., *The Complete Works*, p. 1587. Further references to this sonnet will be cited in the text.

18 About sonnet 20, Eve Sedgwick writes that the speaker is "relaxed and urbane . . . on the subject of sexual interchangeability of males and females" because of the "suasive context of heterosexual socialization" in which the sonnet takes place. See Sedgwick, *Between Men*, p. 35.

19 This parallel is suggested by Joseph Pequigney in his *Such Is My Love: A Study of Shakespeare's Sonnets* (Chicago: University of Chicago Press, 1985): p. 37.

20 *Ibid.* p. 11, *passim.*

21 Woodbridge, *Women and the English Renaissance*, p. 140.

22 See Laura Levine, "Men in Women's Clothing: Antitheatricality and Effeminization from 1579 to 1642," *Criticism* 28 (1986): pp. 130–131, *passim.*

23 "Hic Mulier; or, The Man-Woman" is reprinted in an abridged form in Henderson and McManus, eds., *Half Humankind*, pp. 264–276. References to the pamphlet are from this edition and cited in the text.

24 Howard, "Crossdressing," p. 418.

25 Woodbridge, *Women and the English Renaissance*, p. 145.

26 Levine, "Men in Women's Clothing," p. 123.

27 Stephen Gosson, *The Schoole of Abuse* (1579; facs. rpt., Amsterdam: Theatrum Orbis Terrarum Ltd., 1972), p. B7v.

28 Stubbes, *The Anatomy of Abuses*, cited in Shepherd, *Amazons and Warrior Women*, p. 67.

29 William Prynne, *Historio-mastix: The Player's Scourge or Actor's Tragedy* (New York: Garland Publishing Company, 1974): p. 197.

30 Stephen Orgel, "Nobody's Perfect," pp. 14–15.

31 See Bray, *Homosexuality in Renaissance England, passim.*

32 For a discussion of Shakespeare's use of metaphors of shipwreck and drowning at sea in terms of England's fear of foreign invasion, see Linda Woodbridge, "The Elizabethan Body Politic," *Texas Studies in Literature and Language* 33 (Fall, 1991): pp. 337–340.

33 Joseph Swetnam, "The Arraignment of Lewd, idle, froward, and unconstant women," in Henderson and McManus, eds., *Half-Humankind*, p. 201. Further references will be cited in the text.

34 Anthony Munday, "A Second and Third Blast of Retrait from Plaies and theaters" (London: 1580): p. 69.

35 "Haec Vir," reprinted in abridged form in Henderson and McManus, eds., *Half Humankind*, p. 287. Further references will be cited in the text.

36 Peter Stallybrass, "Patriarchal Territories," p. 126.

37 Constantia Munda, *The Worming of a Mad Dogge: Or, A Soppe for Cereberus the Jaylor of Hell* (1617), in Shepherd, ed., *The Women's Sharp Revenge*, p. 131.

38 Shepherd, *The Women's Sharp Revenge*, pp. 30–31.

6 OCULAR PROOF: SEXUAL JEALOUSY AND THE ANXIETY OF INTERPRETATION

1 Nicholas Breton, *Pasquils Mistresse: Or the worthie and unworthie woman. With his description and passion of that Furie, Jealousie* (London, 1600): n.p. Breton wrote several books in the "querelle des femmes" tradition, including *The Wil of Wit* (1597), printed in three editions.

2 For example, see Carol Thomas Neely, "Constructing the Subject: Feminist Practice and the New Renaissance Discourses," *English Literary Renaissance* 18 (1988), and Lynda Boose, "The Family in Shakespeare Studies; or – Studies in the Family of Shakespeareans; or – the Politics of Politics," *Renaissance Quarterly* 40 (1987). In Neely's polemic against the critical uses of Lacan and deconstruction in Shakespearean scholarship, gender "vanishes or turns into something else, something less anxiety producing, more abstract, more fun. Women, female sexuality, and gender become merely allegorical." Neely proceeds to argue that Jacqueline Rose's reading of *Hamlet* critically displaces the "problem of female sexuality" on to "the problem of meaning," the assumption of which is that Rose not only separates the realms of sexuality and meaning/knowledge but, worse yet, privileges the latter and erases the former. Neely's position, it seems to me, overlooks the important ways in which interpretation and female sexuality function dialectically in Rose's article, one product of which is an important critique of T. S. Eliot's reading of *Hamlet*. See also Jacqueline Rose, "Sexuality in the Reading of Shakespeare: *Hamlet* and *Measure for Measure*," in John Drakakis, ed., *Alternative Shakespeares* (London and New York: Methuen, 1985): pp. 95–118.

3 Certainly a different interpretive model would be required to analyze jealousy in homoerotic relationships, such as those depicted in Marlowe's *Edward II* and Shakespeare's sonnets, or between Buckingham and King James. However, as I suggested in the introduction it might be that the cultural codes in which erotic desire is expressed are likely to be based on a heterosexual model even if individual practices are not always consonant with that model; this may partly explain the seeming contradiction between a moralistic *public* condemnation of same-gender sex and a relative tolerance toward homoerotic *private* practices in the Renaissance.

4 Stanley Cavell, *Disowning Knowledge in Six Plays of Shakespeare* (Cambridge: Cambridge University Press, 1987): p. 9.

5 *Ibid.* p. 10.

6 *Ibid.* p. 7.

7 Quoted in Alice Jardine, "Men in Feminism: 'Odor di Uomo or Compagnons de Route?'" in Alice Jardine and Paul Smith, eds., *Men in Feminism* (London and New York: Methuen, 1987): p. 60.

8 Jacqueline Rose, "Introduction II," Juliet Mitchell and Jacqueline Rose, eds., *Feminine Sexuality: Jacques Lacan and the école freudienne* (New York: W. W. Norton, 1982): p. 48.

9 Jacques Lacan, quoted in Bice Benvenuto and Roger Kennedy, *The Works of Jacques Lacan* (New York: St. Martin's Press, 1986): p. 186. See also the

interesting psychoanalytic study of Shakespeare's multiple uses of "nothing" in David Wilbern, "Shakespeare's Nothing," in Murray M. Schwartz and Coppélia Kahn, eds., *Representing Shakespeare: New Psychoanalytic Essays* (Baltimore: The Johns Hopkins University Press, 1980): pp. 244–263.

10 Rose, "Introduction II," p. 51.

11 Parker, *Literary Fat Ladies*, p. 108.

12 *The Court of Good Counsell. Wherein is set downe the true rules, how a man should choose a good wife from a bad, and a woman a good husband from a bad* (London, 1607): p. B1^r.

13 Hélène Cixous, "Castration or Decapitation," Annette Kuhn, trans., *Signs: Journal of Women in Culture and Society*, vol. 7, no. 11 (1981): pp. 48–49.

14 Catherine Belsey, *The Subject of Tragedy: Identity and Difference in Renaissance Drama* (London: Methuen, 1985): p. 5.

15 Benedetto Varchi, "The blazon of jealousie," trans. R. Tofte (London: 1615): p. 5.

16 *Ibid.* p. 19.

17 *Ibid.* p. 21n.

18 *Ibid.* p. 30.

19 *Ibid.* p. 25.

20 *Ibid.* p. 25.

21 *Tell-Trothes New-yeares Gift* (1593), Frederick J. Furnivall, ed. (London: N. Trubner and Co., 1876).

22 *Ibid.* p. 28.

23 On the other hand, Linda Woodbridge argues that by the late sixteenth century, the Petrarchan lover was increasingly viewed as effeminate in part because his "wily tongue" resembled the way women use language to deceive. See Woodbridge, *Women and the English Renaissance*, pp. 184–185.

24 Philippa Berry, *Of Chastity and Power: Elizabethan Literature and the Unmarried Queen* (London and New York: Routledge, 1989): p. 4. See also Vickers, "Diana Described," pp. 265–279.

25 *The Court of Good Counsell*, p. D3.

26 Katharine Eisaman Maus, "Horns of Dilemma: Jealousy, Gender, and Spectatorship in English Renaissance Drama," *ELH* 54 (1987): p. 565, *passim*.

27 Greenblatt, *Renaissance Self-fashioning*, p. 243.

28 Edward P. Snow, "Sexual Anxiety and the Male Order of Things in *Othello*," *English Literary Renaissance* 10 (1980): p. 396.

29 Sigmund Freud, "Further Remarks on the Neuropsychology of Defence," Standard Edition, vol. 3, p. 226. Katharine Maus observes that sexual jealousy for Shakespeare and Jonson is "connected with a flaw in masculine self-knowledge or with its loss"; see Maus, "Horns of Dilemma," p. 570. The need for a masterful "knowledge" of women may be a projection away from such an admission.

30 "Of Jealosie," in *Fancies Ague-fittes, or Beauties Nettle-Bed* (London: 1599).

31 Robert Cawdry, *A Godlye Form of Householde Government* (1598), cited in Max James, *Our House is Hell: Shakespeare's Troubled Families* (New York: Greenwood Press, 1989): p. 70.

32 *Fancies Ague-fittes*, p. 16.

33 *Ibid.*, p. 17.

34 *Ibid.* p. 17.

35 Vives, *A very fruteful and pleasant booke*, cited in James, *Our House*, pp. 77–78.

36 "Tell-Trothes," p. 35.

37 My thanks to Eliot Wirshbo for this translation.

38 See Lynda E. Boose, "Scolding Brides and Bridling Scolds: Taming the Woman's Unruly Member," *Shakespeare Quarterly* 42 (1991): pp. 179–213.

39 My remarks on Elizabeth are based largely on Louis Montrose's brilliant work on the ways in which the Virgin Queen is fashioned (and fashions herself) in the Elizabethan sex/gender system. Montrose points out the "often scurrilous counter-discourse [that] carnivalized the official cult of mystical royal virginity by insisting upon the physicality of the royal body, the carnal inclinations of the queen." Later in the same essay, Montrose cites the case of Thomas Playfere, who in 1580 was tried and "convicted of rumoring that the queen had two children by the earl of Leicester." See Louis Montrose, "The Elizabethan Subject and the Spenserian Text," pp. 303–340.

40 Luce Irigaray, *This Sex Which Is Not One*, pp. 86, 97.

41 *Fancies Ague-Fittes*, p. 16.

42 Thomas Salter, *A mirrhor mete for all mothers, matrones, and maidens, intituled the mirrhor of modestie . . .* (London: 1579).

43 Alexander Niccholes, "A discourse of marriage and wiving: And the greatest mystery therein contained: How to choose a good wife from a bad . . ." (London: 1615).

44 Joseph Swetnam, *The Arraignment of Lewde, Idle, Froward and Unconstant Women* (London: 1615): n.p.

45 Niccholes, "A Discourse," pp. 8–9.

46 Sowernam, "Esther hath hanged Haman," in *Half Humankind*, Henderson and McManus, eds., p. 232.

47 *Ibid.* p. 242.

48 *Ibid.* p. 242.

49 *Ibid.* p. 242.

50 Josephine A. Roberts, ed., *The Poems of Lady Mary Wroth* (Baton Rouge: Louisiana State University Press, 1983): p. 49. Roberts points out that Wroth identifies herself as Pamphilia by signing that name as the author of the prose romance (p. 42).

51 Lady Mary Wroth, "Pamphilia to Amphilanthus," in *The Poems of Lady Mary Wroth*, Roberts, ed., p. 121.

Index